Depressed Older Adults
Education and Screening

Jacquelin Berman, PhD, MSW, has worked in the field of gerontology for more than two decades. As director of research at the New York City Department for the Aging, she oversees various research and demonstration projects related to aging, including mental health, elder abuse, and grandparenting. She has authored numerous articles on aging and has presented at national and international conferences throughout the years. Dr. Berman is also an active member of various aging advisory committees and coalitions throughout New York City. She is a graduate of the Columbia University School of Social Work.

Lisa M. Furst, LMSW, is director of Public Education for the Mental Health Association of New York City (MHA-NYC). She develops and implements public education programming that provides information about mental health and mental illnesses and their treatment to targeted audiences of professionals, paraprofessionals, and the public at large. In addition, in her role as the director of Education for the Geriatric Mental Health Alliance of New York, a project of the MHA-NYC, she creates public education and training/technical assistance programs to educate professionals and the general public about the mental health needs of older adults. She is a graduate of the Hunter College School of Social Work and is a licensed social worker in New York State.

Depressed Older Adults
Education and Screening

Jacquelin Berman, PhD, MSW
Lisa M. Furst, LMSW

SPRINGER PUBLISHING COMPANY
NEW YORK

Springer Publishing Company, LLC
11 West 42nd Street
New York, NY 10036
www.springerpub.com

Acquisitions Editor: Sheri W. Sussman
Senior Editor: Rose Mary Piscitelli
Cover design: Mimi Flow
Project Manager: Gil Rafanan
Composition: Absolute Service, Inc.

ISBN: 978-0-8261-7102-3
E-book ISBN: 978-0-8261-7103-0

10 11 12 13/ 5 4 3 2 1

The author and the publisher of this work have made every effort to use sources believed to be reliable to provide information that is accurate and compatible with the standards generally accepted at the time of publication. Because medical science is continually advancing, our knowledge base continues to expand. Therefore, as new information becomes available, changes in procedures become necessary. We recommend that the reader always consult current research and specific institutional policies before performing any clinical procedure. The author and publisher shall not be liable for any special, consequential, or exemplary damages resulting, in whole or in part, from the readers' use of, or reliance on, the information contained in this book. The publisher has no responsibility for the persistence or accuracy of URLs for external or third-party Internet Web sites referred to in this publication and does not guarantee that any content on such Web sites is, or will remain, accurate or appropriate.

Library of Congress Cataloging-in-Publication Data

Berman, Jacquelin.
  Depressed older adults : education and screening / Jacquelin Berman, Lisa M. Furst.
    p. ; cm.
  Includes bibliographical references and index.
  ISBN 978-0-8261-7102-3 — ISBN 978-0-8261-7103-0 (e-book)
  1. Depression in old age. I. Furst, Lisa M. II. Title.
  [DNLM: 1. Depression—diagnosis. 2. Aged. 3. Community Mental Health Services. WM 171]
  RC537.5.B47 2011
  618.97'68527—dc22

                          2010026047

Special discounts on bulk quantities of our books are available to corporations, professional associations, pharmaceutical companies, health care organizations, and other qualifying groups.

If you are interested in a custom book, including chapters from more than one of our titles, we can provide that service as well.

For details, please contact:
Special Sales Department, Springer Publishing Company, LLC
11 West 42nd Street, 15th Floor, New York, NY 10036-8002
Phone: 877-687-7476 or 212-431-4370; Fax: 212-941-7842
Email: sales@springerpub.com

Printed in the United States of America by Hamilton Printing Company.

This book is dedicated to the special people in our lives.

*Jason Horowitz, Dylan Horowitz, Jesse Horowitz,
Samantha Horowitz, Jeri Berman, and David Berman,*

and

*Eli Brown, Jennifer Furst, Michael Wagner, Jennifer Wagner,
Sara Murphy, Christian Burgess, and Asha Sanaker
for their ongoing encouragement and love throughout
the entire process of writing this book.*

Contents

Preface

Depression, a serious illness, prevents older adults from maintaining optimal functioning and interferes with successful aging. Older adults with undiagnosed and untreated depression often struggle with poorer health, increased disability, increased social isolation, disengagement in occupational and civic pursuits, and decreased ability to engage in the routine activities of daily living.

Increasingly, aging service professionals are aware of the importance of addressing the mental health needs of older adults. From their vantage points as providers of essential services to older people, they are witness to the challenges older adults face as they struggle with the symptoms of unaddressed depression. They also experience their own challenges as they try to serve these older adults, who may be more difficult to support and engage successfully in services.

Aging service and mental health providers, working in their own silos, may be unaware of opportunities for collaboration in addressing the needs of older adults with depression. Aging service providers often lack methods to identify depression and to connect at-risk older adults to treatment resources. Mental health professionals are not usually available, within aging service programs, to address the mental health needs of older adults. Additionally, they might not regularly reach out to aging service programs to identify older adults with mental health needs and may not know about local aging service programs to which they can refer their older adult clients for socialization and support.

Although there are evidence-based models of mental health service provision for older adults with depression, they were not initially focused on serving older adults within community-based aging services settings. Only recently have they begun to be evaluated for their viability in settings such as senior or community centers. In addition, these models have not primarily focused on supporting older adults at risk for depression to make the initial connection to mental health treatment. Might there be a way for both systems to work in partnership to address the unmet needs of older adults with depression?

Depressed Older Adults: Education and Screening describes a collaborative model of outreach and intervention for older adults at risk for depression. This two-time award-winning model, entitled *Educating About and Screening Elders for Depression*, or EASE-D, offers a practical, flexible, and culturally sensitive approach to mental health education, which can be adapted by service programs seeking to identify clinical depression among their older adult clientele. In addition, this model provides a framework for incorporating depression screening to identify older adults at risk for depression, and includes a supportive service to link them to treatment resources within the community.

Older adults who participate in EASE-D are able to (a) increase their awareness of the role of mental health in successful aging, (b) increase their knowledge about the symptoms of depression and about effective treatment options, (c) learn if they are at risk for depression, and (d) receive supportive services to help them connect to community resources for evaluation and treatment for depression.

Aging service programs implementing EASE-D are able to (a) address the stigma associated with depression among older adults; (b) incorporate depression screening, an evidence-based practice, into their complement of services; and (c) create long-standing collaborative relationships across the professional disciplines of aging, mental health, and health care services to address the mental health needs of older adults.

Acknowledgments

The authors are grateful to the Mental Health Association of New York City, the New York City Department for the Aging, and the New York City Department of Health and Mental Hygiene. Without the generous support and guidance from these agencies, this project would not have been possible. The authors would also like to thank the senior centers and the older adults who have participated in the workshops and programming over the years. Their enthusiastic participation in this program has been invaluable. Lastly, the authors would like to thank their families and friends for their unwavering support and understanding throughout this process.

1

Depression Among Older Adults

The senior center where we are having our meeting could be any other we have visited in the last several years. Like many others, it is located in a nondescript building in an urban residential neighborhood. When we speak with the senior center director, we describe our project, a special citywide program of mental health education and depression screening designed to identify older adults at risk for depression and to help them connect to treatment services. We would like to include this particular center in our project, we explain, to help address the stigma many older adults experience about mental illness, particularly depression.

We are prepared to justify our reasons for wanting to implement this program. We are ready to explain the risk factors for depression faced by many older adults; the terrible toll depression takes on their health, self-esteem, and well-being; the stigma associated with acknowledging emotional difficulties; and the challenges many older adults face when they recognize that they need help and do not know where to go. As we begin to provide all of these reasons for conducting our project, the director stops us in midconversation.

"I'm so glad you chose to come to my center," she says. "I already know which older adults here need this kind of help."

WHY FOCUS ON DEPRESSION?

In our society, we are confronted with two very distinct notions of older age. Now, more than ever before, we are exposed, through the media, to images of healthy and lively older adults—people enjoying the fruits of their labor in their retirement or continuing to have success in their careers, possessing robust health, enjoying their families, and having close and satisfying relationships with friends and intimate partners. Aging successfully—even happily—seems to be an ever-realistic and achievable goal. At the same time, we live in an ageist society that equates older age with decline in every aspect of life. Older people, according to this view, are or will become physically frail, psychologically fragile, isolated, and lonely as the inevitable consequences of reaching late life. Either picture begs the questions: Why focus on depression in older age? If successful aging is being achieved by so many, is depression really a problem? Alternatively, if emotional difficulties and loneliness are simply the natural and ordinary outcomes of having a long life, is there any point in trying to do something about them?

Most people would agree that sound physical health is a critical component of healthy aging. However, many do not realize that without good mental health, successful aging is not achievable. Clinical depression, a serious mental illness, can interfere with the capacity to live a rewarding life in older age. When depression develops, it severely affects an older adult's ability to maintain good physical health, to stay active occupationally and socially, and to maintain optimal functioning at home and in the community. Depression also negatively affects those who are close to older adults who have it. Family members and friends who may have counted on that older adult for emotional support and companionship or concrete support may find that they are no longer able to do so once depression becomes significant. Providers who work with older adults may find, too, that they are unable to serve older adults with depression as well as they would wish, because these older adults may withdraw from services, become more irritable, and have more difficulty following through with the programs and services with which they are engaged. The good news is that depression is very treatable and older adults can benefit from interventions to help them achieve a higher quality of life.

This chapter will review the symptoms, prevalence, and common risk factors for depression in older adults. The most common types of clinical treatments and other supportive interventions for depression will also be considered, as will the challenges of identifying and treating older adults with depression. Finally, this chapter will introduce a model for aging services providers to conduct their own outreach to at-risk older adults called Educating About and Screening Elders for Depression (EASE-D). This model illustrates the ways in which providers of aging services, mental health providers, and health care professionals can collaborate successfully to identify at-risk older adults and link them to evaluation and treatment for depression.

DEFINING DEPRESSION

Most of us use the word *depression* on a regular basis in ordinary speech; when we do, we are usually not referring to clinical depression. More often than not, we speak of depression in everyday language referring to feelings of sadness that come and go in response to particular life circumstances. Although sadness is a normal human emotion, which everyone experiences from time to time, clinical depression is not normal at any age, including in later life.

Clinical depression is a treatable mood disorder. Also known as affective disorders, mood disorders are mental illnesses that cause a disturbance in a person's emotional state. Mood disorders include various forms of clinical depression, as well as bipolar disorder, otherwise known as manic–depressive illness. Depression is characterized by emotional, physical, cognitive, and behavioral symptoms. The most common types of clinical depression affecting older adults include *major depressive disorder, dysthymia*, and *minor* or *subsyndromal depression*. Although these are related conditions, they differ in the number of symptoms they cause and in the severity and duration of the symptoms that older adults experience.

Major Depression

Major depression can be experienced as a single episode, a series of recurrent episodes, or a chronic problem spanning many years of someone's life. To diagnose major depression, at least five out of a total of nine symptoms must be present for a minimum of 2 weeks and must cause significant distress or impairment in daily functioning. Major depression is characterized by the presence of at least one of two primary or cardinal emotional symptoms, which are:

- Depressed mood most of the day, nearly every day
- Loss of interest or pleasure in activities one formerly enjoyed (American Psychiatric Association [APA], 2000)

It is important to note that when we think about major depression, we most commonly associate it with having a sad mood most of the time. However, it is possible to have major depression without having a persistently depressed mood. Having a prolonged lack of interest or pleasure in activities, plus four of the following symptoms described, is also considered major depression, even if depressed mood is not an identified symptom. Major depression of this type has been called "depression without sadness" and is considered more common among older adults than among other age groups (Blazer, 2009).

In addition to at least one of the primary or cardinal symptoms, a minimum of four of the following symptoms must also be present in major depression (APA, 2000):

- Diminished or increased appetite, often leading to weight loss or gain;
- Sleeping difficulties, such as insomnia or sleeping too much;
- Psychomotor agitation or psychomotor retardation (noticeable restlessness or noticeable slowness of movement stemming from mental tension or mood);
- Fatigue and/or loss of energy;
- Feelings of worthlessness or excessive or inappropriate guilt;
- Difficulty thinking, concentrating, or focusing; or
- Recurrent thoughts of death or suicide (not including fear of dying or thinking about mortality as a result of growing older).

The following vignette provides an illustration of some ways in which the symptoms of major depression might affect an older adult.

Case Vignette: Ms. A.

Ms. A., a woman in her early 70s, has plans to meet a friend for lunch at her local senior center. She did not sleep well the night before because she was troubled, as she is most nights, by intense feelings of sadness and despair, accompanied by crying spells, lasting long into the night. She spends the morning lying in bed exhausted but unable to drift off. About an hour before she is supposed to have lunch, she slowly rises to dress and make her way to the senior center. She is very slow moving and finds it difficult to muster the energy to select clothes to wear and put them on. As she starts to dress, she decides not to visit with her friend at the senior center, after all. It seems like too much effort to get to the senior center. Their usual weekly plan to have lunch together and then play bingo has not been very appealing to her in the last several weeks. She also realizes that she is not very hungry and does not feel like eating lunch. After deciding not to leave her home, she tries to distract herself by reading a book but is unable to concentrate well enough to do so. It even seems like watching television requires too much effort. She returns to her bed, where she remains for the rest of the day.

Dysthymia

Dysthymia is a form of depression in which a fewer number of depression symptoms are experienced over a relatively long period. Despite the presence of fewer symptoms than in major depression, dysthymia can be quite a distressing problem. Unlike in major depression, for which depressed mood does not have to be present, the criteria for diagnosis of dysthymia always includes having a persistently depressed mood, most of the day, nearly every day, for a period of at least 2 years. Remission of symptoms, if it arises, does not occur for more than 2 months at a time.

In addition to a continually depressed mood, at least two to four of the following symptoms must also be present for a period of at least 2 years (APA, 2000):

- Diminished appetite or overeating;
- Difficulty sleeping or oversleeping;

■ Fatigue and/or low energy;
■ Poor self-esteem;
■ Difficulty concentrating or making decisions; or
■ Hopelessness.

The following vignette provides an illustration of some of the ways in which the symptoms of dysthymia might affect an older adult.

Case Vignette: Mr. B.

Mr. B., a man in his late 60s, has been retired for 3 years. Although he initially enjoyed the first 6 months following his retirement, he finds that most of the time since then, he feels generally down in the dumps, even though nothing in his life seems particularly troubling or difficult to manage. He feels especially sad when he has thoughts about not having much to show for his life, or to accomplish, now that he is retired. As he thinks back, he finds he cannot remember the last time he was in a good mood for more than a day or two at a time. Even though he seems to be in generally good health, he has gained nearly 20 lb over the last 2 years and is usually fatigued during the day, even when he gets enough hours of sleep at night. He still manages to do volunteer work at his local senior center once a week and spends time with his family and friends, but he just does not feel like his old self.

Minor or Subsyndromal Depression

Minor depression, also known as subsyndromal depression, is thought to occur at least as often in the general population as major depression. At the time of this writing, subsyndromal depression is not a category of depression with which one can be formally diagnosed in the current edition of the *Diagnostic and Statistical Manual of Mental Disorders*, the diagnostic guide used by medical and mental health professionals. However, it is increasingly recognized in research as a subtype of depression.

Subsyndromal depression presents with at least two, but fewer than five, symptoms of depression for a minimum of 2 weeks and is generally more episodic, and less chronic, than dysthymia (APA, 2000; Kroenke, 2006; Williams et al., 2000). As in both major depression and dysthymia, subsyndromal depression usually includes either a persistently sad mood or a loss of interest or pleasure in activities. Like major depression or dysthymia, subsyndromal depression can cause significant impairment in daily functioning. Like dysthymia, this encompasses fewer distinct symptoms than in major depression. However, the duration of subsyndromal depression is generally less than in dysthymia.

Subsyndromal depression can be a precursor to major depression. Research suggests that depressive disorders occur on a continuum of less to more severe and that people who develop subsyndromal depression are more likely to also develop major depression over time if the earlier stage of the illness is not addressed (Kroenke, 2006; Lyness et al., 2006).

The following vignette demonstrates the ways in which symptoms of subsyndromal depression might affect an older adult.

Case Vignette: Ms. C.

Ms. C., an 80-year-old woman, describes her concerns about her health to her doctor for the third time this month, this time reporting having frequent headaches. She currently takes medications for high blood pressure, diabetes, and a thyroid condition. Upon examination, all of her chronic health problems appear to be well controlled and her medications do not need adjustment. When Ms. C. hears, once again, that she is fine and has nothing to worry about, she does not feel any better. She hesitantly explains to her doctor her real reasons for the visit, which are that she feels sad most of the time, has trouble sleeping at night, and is often fatigued during the day. These problems bother her tremendously, although she takes pains to hide her unhappiness and discomfort from her family, because she does not want to sound like a "complainer." She also tries her best to "put on a happy face," particularly when she is socializing with her friends during the classes and trips she takes at her local senior center. She does not understand why she feels this way, is tired of pretending that nothing is wrong, and does not really know what to do about it.

EPIDEMIOLOGY OF DEPRESSION AMONG OLDER ADULTS

As the baby boom generation ages over the next quarter century, the United States will see significant growth in the number of people 65 years old and older, from approximately 39 million in 2010 to 69 million by 2030. In addition, the percentage of older adults will increase from 13–20% of the country's total population (Bartels, Blow, Brockmann, & Van Citters, 2005; Day, 1996). As a result, projections indicate that the number of older adults with any mental illness will double from 7 million to 14 million between 2000 and 2030 (U.S. Department of Health and Human Services [DHHS], 1999; Bartels et al., 2005).

Despite the estimated growth in the number of older adults with mental illness, older people do not have clinical depression more often than younger people do. In fact, there is considerable evidence that they have a lower rate of major depression than other age groups (Chapman & Perry, 2008; Kessler et al., 2005). According to the data from the Epidemiologic Catchment Area (ECA) survey, the prevalence of all affective disorders (including depression as well as other mood disorders) among community-dwelling adults aged 65 and older is 2.5%; the highest prevalence of depression, 3%, was observed among adults 25–44 years of age (Hybels & Blazer, 2003). For major depression, older adults were found to have a lifetime prevalence rate of 2%, and a 1-year prevalence rate of 1.4%, compared to 3.7% for younger individuals (Kohn, Gum, & King-Kallimanis, 2009). In another study examining data from the National Household Survey on Drug Abuse (NHSDA), the point prevalence of depression symptoms for community-dwelling older adults was found to be only 1.9% for older women and 1% for older men (Wu & Anthony, 2000).

Other sources document the prevalence of major depression to range between 1 and 4% (Alexopolous, 2005). Despite the generally lower prevalence of diagnosable major depression, 15–20% of older adults experience clinically meaningful symptoms of depression, without necessarily warranting a diagnosis (Kohn et al., 2009). Older adults are more likely than other age groups to experience subsyndromal depressive symptoms that, although not enough to correspond to a diagnosis of major depression or dysthymia, are significant enough to cause distress and impair functioning. Prevalence studies for subsyndromal depression in late life yield an estimated range of 3–26% (Hybels & Blazer, 2003). Additional evidence for higher rates of subsyndromal depression among older adults comes from the Established Populations for Epidemiological Studies of the Elderly (EPESE). Data from this study indicates that although the prevalence of diagnosable depression among older adults is 8.4%, the prevalence of subsyndromal depression is 9.3% (Hybels, Blazer, & Pieper, 2001).

Women have been shown generally to have a higher prevalence of depression than men do across age groups, including in later life (Kessler et al., 2005). One study of older adults living in the community found that women older than age 60 are twice as likely to experience depressed mood as men in the same age demographic (Harwood, Barker, Ownby, Mullan, & Duara, 1999). This trend has been confirmed by other studies. For example, both ECA and NHSDA studies found elevated risk for depressive symptoms for older women, compared with older men. In particular, the NHSDA researchers found that older women's risk of developing depressive symptoms was 5.93 times that of older men (Wu & Anthony, 2000). Furthermore, a study conducted in 2006 among community dwelling older women indicates that women between the ages of 65 and 74 were more likely to report both current and past episodes of depression than men in the same cohort (McGuire, Strine, Vachirasudlekha, Mokdad, & Anderson, 2008).

The literature examining the role of race and ethnicity on depression has been mixed, with some studies indicating that certain ethnic minorities are less likely to have depression than Caucasians, whereas others indicate that these same ethnic minorities are more likely to have depression. Although some studies indicate that mental disorders are as prevalent among ethnic minorities as among Caucasians, others challenge this assumption. In several large community-based samples, race or ethnicity does not appear to be significantly associated with depression prevalence (Chapman & Perry, 2008; Hybels & Blazer, 2003).

Other studies find an association between race/ethnicity and depression. In a study of preretirement-age adults (aged 54–65), symptoms of major depression were found to occur more frequently among members of minority groups than among Caucasians (Dunlop, Song, Lyons, Manheim, & Chang, 2003). The implications of this study include the possibility that older adults from minority groups may be more likely to have depressive disorders in later life, because they may have past histories of depression, which could recur or become exacerbated as age-related risk factors are encountered in older age. There has been some evidence of greater frequency of depressive symptoms among individuals of Hispanic descent, notably among Mexican Americans (Hybels & Blazer, 2003; Dunlop et al.), although data from the National Comorbidity Survey Replication study indicate that the Hispanic community has a lower risk of mood disorders than Caucasians (Kessler et al., 2005). African Americans appear to have similar rates of depression as Caucasians (Blazer, Hybels, Simonsick, & Hanlon, 2000; Colemon & Ahmed, 2009), although some studies document that African American older adults experience fewer symptoms of depression, compared to Caucasian older adults (Kessler et al., 2005). Among Asian Americans, the rates of major depression appear to be lower than other ethnic groups, with a lifetime prevalence of 3.4%, compared to the general population's rate of 5.28% (Colemon & Ahmed). The 1-year prevalence rate of major depression has been documented to be approximately 5% among Asian older adults living in the community; however, as with other ethnic groups, depressive symptoms that did not warrant a diagnosis of major depression were more prevalent for Asian older adults, estimated to range between 8 and 20% (Mui, 2003).

Poor health status is associated with a higher incidence of depression. Indeed, the estimated prevalence of depression among older adults is higher in primary care settings than among older adults surveyed in the community and has been documented to range from 5–10% (Unützer et al., 2003). The prevalence of depressive symptoms is also higher among older adults who are homebound, receive health care in the home, or are being treated in hospitals, nursing homes, or other institutional settings. As much as 10–12% of older adults seen in hospital settings are estimated to have major depression (Alexopolous, 2005). Additionally, a study of the medical records of nursing home residents found a depression prevalence rate of 20.3%, and a study of older adult recipients of home health care found a depression prevalence rate of 13.5%, compared to the 1-year prevalence rate of 0.9% for community-dwelling older adults found in the ECA study (Chapman & Perry, 2008; Hybels & Blazer, 2003).

Depression does not manifest uniformly among all generations of older adults. Some experts believe that clinical depression may be a more significant problem for the baby boom generation as it ages, compared to the current cohorts of older adults. Baby boomers have been found to have a higher lifetime prevalence of depression than both people in younger age groups and the current group of adults aged 65 years and older (Hasin, Goodwin, Stinson, & Grant, 2005). There are also prevalence differences for depression among subgroups of older adults throughout later life. Most studies tend to classify older adults into a single cohort of those aged 65 years or older; however, there are significant differences within subgroups of older adults. Although research indicates that older adults are less likely than adults in midlife to have depression, the distribution of depression changes with very old age. The incidence, or development of new cases, of major depression has been shown to double in any given year for older adults aged 70–85 years (Alexopolous, 2005). Additionally, a study of German older adults yielded similar findings, because depression prevalence appeared to increase with advancing age; those who are 85 years old or older had a 70% higher risk of developing depression than those aged 74–79 (Weyerer et al., 2008).

RISK FACTORS FOR LATE-LIFE DEPRESSION

Although depression affects people across all age groups, older adults may possess an increased number of risk factors for depression, compared to people of other ages. The risk factors associated with late-life depressive disorders are numerous, and, for many older adults, depression may arise from a confluence of biologic, psychosocial, and socioeconomic factors.

Biologic Factors

Although age in and of itself does not cause depression, age-related biologic risk factors have been implicated in its onset. Common biologic risk factors include comorbid chronic illness, sensory or mobility impairment, cognitive impairment, and the presence of vascular lesions in the brain (Chapman & Perry, 2008; Hybels et al., 2001; Weyerer et al., 2008). Increased rates of depression have been found among older adults diagnosed with chronic illnesses such as cardiovascular disease, diabetes, arthritis, and other disorders that may decrease physical functioning, increase disability, and contribute to social isolation (Blazer & Hybels, 2005). Additionally, physiological changes associated with aging, such as decreased neurotransmitter activity in the brain and lowered functioning of the endocrine system, are also associated with depression (Blazer & Hybels).

The correlation between depression and medical comorbidities among older adults is complex. For reasons not yet entirely understood, the outcomes of physical illness dramatically worsen when depression is present, particularly in the case of cardiovascular disease (Alexopolous, 2005). Older adults who have histories of chronic illness, but no past histories of clinical depression, have been shown to have an increased incidence of depression over time. At the same time, older adults diagnosed with clinical depression who do not initially have comorbid medical illnesses are more likely to develop such diseases over time compared to their peers who are not depressed (Krishnan et al., 2002).

The burden of comorbid health conditions is a particularly significant predictor of depressive symptoms in older age, especially if disease impairs an older adult's ability to perform activities of daily living or connect with sources of social support (Hybels et al., 2001). For example, a study of Asian American older adults found a depression prevalence of 24.2% for those with chronic illness, compared to 13.7% for those without such medical problems (Chapman & Perry, 2008). The role of physical illness may also be particularly significant for older women with depression, who appear to incur greater risk of developing a first-time occurrence of clinical depression when suffering from poor physical health than do older men (Sneed, Kasen, & Cohen, 2007). Depressive illness has also been associated with dementia and other forms of cognitive decline; it is also associated with increased risk for the onset of Alzheimer's disease (Alexopolous, 2005).

The Role of Functional Disability

Worsening health problems may encourage the development of additional psychosocial risk factors for depression. Functional disability, or the loss of the ability to maintain activities of daily living because of illness or injury, may play as critical a role in the development of depression among older adults as medical comorbidities. This is particularly the case if the medical illness or resultant physical frailty compromises an older adult's ability to sustain social support networks.

Research suggests that poor health status may precipitate the loss of social networks and support by decreasing an older adult's ability to engage in meaningful social contact outside of the home, in addition to preventing them from performing the usual activities of daily living. In addition, an older adult's personal experience of disability may be an important factor in the development of depression. One recent study indicates that when older adults with impaired physical functioning are able to engage in what they perceive as meaningful social activity, the likelihood of depression is decreased, even if the level of disability does not improve (Yang, 2006).

Psychosocial Risk Factors

Psychosocial risk factors common to this age group include relationship loss, caused by either death of a loved one or more prolonged periods of separation as friends or family members move to other, more distant communities, loss of social role functioning, and loss of social status (e.g., after retirement), which accompanies aging in a culture that does not respect older adults (Bartels et al., 2005; Blazer & Hybels, 2005). Other significant psychosocial risk factors for older adults include past or current traumatic experiences, as well as the lack of actual or perceived emotional or social support (Bruce, 2002).

Depending on the exposure to other precipitating psychosocial factors, older adults may exhibit differing patterns of depression onset. Some older adults may have prior histories of psychological dysfunction that are associated with the development or exacerbation of depression in older age (Vink, Aarsten, & Schoevers, 2008); in fact, most older adults who experience depression have had at least one episode of depression earlier in life (Kohn et al., 2009). Others develop depression for the first time late in life, often in conjunction with the emergence of new psychosocial stressors. For example, a study of older adult women indicated that those who have depression for the first time as older adults struggled with stressors that did not exist earlier in their lives, particularly physical illness and resultant disabilities that contributed to social isolation. Those who had an early onset of depression, on the other hand, were found to have experienced psychosocial difficulties throughout their lives, including having more episodes of depression or anxiety, as well as family histories of depression (Sneed et al., 2007).

Socioeconomic Risk Factors

Having a lower income status, economic hardship relative to income, and lower overall educational attainment, most notably among those who have received fewer than 12 years of education, are all associated with an elevated risk for depression (Kim & Durden, 2007). Both planned retirement and involuntary job loss have also been identified as socioeconomic risk factors for depression, particularly when accompanied by a relative lack of financial assets and economic hardship following the change in employment status (Mojtabai & Olfson, 2004).

DEPRESSION AND SUICIDE

Depression has been shown to increase older adults' risk of mortality, particularly when symptoms are severe and protracted. Data from the ECA study indicates that the risk of death was four times greater for older adults with depression than for those without a mood disorder (Blazer, 2009). Not only does depression increase the risk of mortality among older adults who are medically ill, but it also is a major risk factor for death by suicide, particularly when medical illness and depression are comorbid (Abrams, Marzuk, Tardiff, & Leon, 2005).

Estimates suggest that the rates of suicide among older adults will double between 2000 and 2040 (Kennedy, 2000). Thoughts about suicide—otherwise known as suicidal ideation—are estimated to occur among 5–10% of the general population of older adults. Older adults with depression are more at risk of dying by suicide than either their nondepressed peers or the general population (Butler, Cohen, Lewis, Simmons-Clemmons, & Sunderland, 1997). Although they currently comprise just fewer than 13% of the total population, adults aged 65 and older complete 16% of all suicides. The national rate of suicide among older adults is five times higher among older Caucasian men, particularly among those aged 85 years old or older (Bharucha, 2009), than among other groups. Older adults who make suicide attempts are more likely to have experienced the death of a spouse, to live alone, to have poor perceptions of their health, to have sleep disturbances, to be socially isolated, and to experience stressors such as financial hardship and relationship difficulties (Blazer, 2009).

Older adults complete suicide through various means, the most common of which is by using firearms. Although older men are more likely to complete suicide using firearms, older women are increasingly at risk of using this method to complete suicide (Bharucha, 2009). Other common means older adults use to complete suicide include the lethal ingestion of drugs (Blazer, 2009), suffocation, hanging, self-injury by stabbing, jumping from a significant height (buildings, bridges), and carbon monoxide poisoning, among others (Kennedy, 2000).

Most older adults who complete suicide experience a period of depression prior to their deaths, and up to 20% of these older adults were seen by their doctors within the 24 hours prior to their suicides. A tragic statistic such as this indicates the many missed opportunities by health care providers to identify depression among older adults by health care providers, many of whom did not recognize the presence of depressive symptoms in their older patients (Kennedy, 2000). The lack of a systematic way to identify depression and other suicide risk factors remains a continuing challenge for health care and other providers who work with older adults.

TREATMENT OPTIONS FOR OLDER ADULTS

Depression can become a chronic disorder for older adults if it is not identified and treated. A study of older adults diagnosed with major depression found that without clinical treatment, 90% of older adults experienced recurrent depressive episodes, compared to recurrence rates of 20% for older adults treated with medication and psychotherapy and 43% for older adults receiving medication alone (Alexopolous, 2005).

Fortunately, both psychotherapy and psychotropic medications are effective treatments for depressive disorders among older adults. There is general agreement that the optimal treatment of major depression and dysthymia in older adults is a combination of medication and psychotherapy, whereas subsyndromal depression may be responsive to psychotherapeutic or other supportive interventions alone (Alexopolous, 2005). Antidepressant medications are effective treatments for older adults who have depression, with more than half of all older adults treated with antidepressants experiencing a minimum of a 50% reduction in symptoms (Bartels et al., 2004).

The most effective forms of psychotherapy for older adults with depression include cognitive, behavioral, and combined cognitive–behavioral therapeutic approaches (Bartels et al., 2004; Blow, Bartels, Brockmann, & Van Citters, 2005), such as problem-solving therapy (PST). Other helpful psychotherapeutic modalities include supportive psychotherapy and interpersonal psychotherapy (Alexopolous, 2005). Additional nonpharmacologic interventions, which are beneficial, include regular physical exercise, involvement in stimulating social and intellectual activities, engaging older adults about their mental health through education (Center for Mental

Health Services [CMHS], Substance Abuse and Mental Health Services Administration [SAMHSA], 2005) and early intervention, such as screening for depression.

DETECTING DEPRESSION IN OLDER ADULTS

Many older adults who receive treatment for depression do so within the context of their primary care physician's office, rather than in specialty mental health treatment programs (Wang et al., 2005). In the United States, of the 7 million older adults with mental illness, only half, or approximately 3.5 million, receive any treatment. Of those who do, just more than 1.9 million receive treatment from their primary care physicians (U.S. DHHS, 2001) rather than mental health specialists. Despite the significant prevalence of depression and medical comorbidities within the general older adult population, and in spite of the documented higher risk of suicide among older adults, depressive disorders remain inadequately diagnosed and treated by primary care physicians.

There are several challenges to identifying depression in older adults. Although there are many tools available to help screen for depression (for more information about depression screening instruments, refer to chapter 4 ["What Depression Screening Tools Exist?"]), these have not yet been universally incorporated into the health care and other sectors commonly serving older adults. As a result, most older adults with depression do not receive appropriate clinical assessment or treatment. Physicians' insufficient recognition of depressive disorders also may be influenced by attitudinal factors endemic to both doctors and patients. These include the belief among older adult patients that depression is a natural function of the aging process. For example, one study indicated that more than 50% of women aged 65 or older believe that depression is a normal part of growing older (McGuire et al., 2008) and might be unlikely to report depressive symptoms because of misconstruing them as an expected part of aging. Physicians may miss the opportunity to identify depressive disorders in their older adult patients if they, too, believe that depression is a normal part of the aging process because of expected losses coinciding with aging (e.g., bereavement or diminished physical capacities). Such attitudes among both primary care physicians and older adults may lead inadvertently to a "don't ask/don't tell" policy about depression, decreasing the likelihood of treatment.

In addition to the barriers associated with ageism and lack of awareness about depression, the diagnostic factors contributing to the challenge of recognizing late-life depression may be significant. A review study indicates older adults have a higher "threshold for reporting symptoms of depression" than middle-aged adults and might suffer for a significant period before address-ing the problem (Jeste, Blazer, & First, 2005) with a health care professional or other service provider. Moreover, there are notable differences in the clinical presentation of depressive symptoms among older adults compared to younger adults. Older adults may visit their health care providers com-plaining of specific somatic symptoms, such as frequent headaches, fatigue, difficulty sleeping, appetite or weight changes, and increased pain, none of which may initially be associated with depression, particularly if emotional symptoms are not disclosed or if persistently sad mood is not present.

Many of these somatic complaints are characteristic of subsyndromal depression, which rises in prevalence among older adults. Subsyndromal depression among older adults is often accompanied by depressed mood, lowered ability to concentrate, psychomotor retardation, lowered percep-tion of good health, and increased anxiety about health in general. Except for depressed mood, these symptoms are not seen as often in younger adults with depression and may be assessed incorrectly as functions of the natural aging process rather than as indicators of depressive illness (Jeste et al., 2005; VanItallie, 2005). The difficulty of detecting subsyndromal depres-sion is of particular significance to health care providers, because there is evidence that subsyndromal depression is a predictive risk factor for the development of major depressive illness among older adults (Lyness et al., 2006). An older adult experiencing minor depression has a much higher risk of developing a more serious form of depression over time; failure to iden-tify subsyndromal depression is another missed opportunity to prevent the exacerbation of the disorder and its attendant complications.

Even when primary care providers identify depression, treatment is not uniformly available and adequate. Some groups of older adults seem less likely to receive treatment than others. For example, a study of Medicare enrollees in primary care found that nearly one third (32.3%) of older adults diagnosed with depression did not receive any treatment. These older adults were primarily those who were 75 years old or older, had low income, lacked supplemental insurance or drug coverage, and were a race other than Caucasian (Crystal, Sambamoorthi, Walkup, & Akincigil, 2003). Similarly, in a study of 1,801 older adults with depression in primary care, those found to be most at risk of not receiving treatment were those who were Latino, African American, male, and who stated a preference for nonpharmacologi-cal treatment (Unützer et al., 2003).

Finally, another challenge to the successful identification and treat-ment of depression in older adults is the general lack of geriatric medical and mental health specialists (Bartels et al., 2005), particularly those who are bilingual and bicultural. Figure 1.1 illustrates the current lack of spe-cialty geriatric mental health providers and the widening of the gap that is

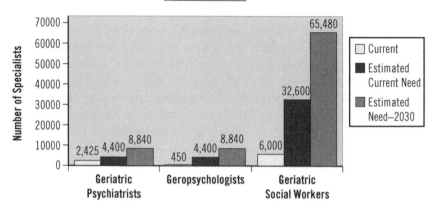

SHORTAGE OF GERIATRIC MENTAL HEALTH
PROFESSIONALS

Halpain, Maureen C. et al. (1999). Training in Geriatric Mental Health: Needs and Strategies. *Psychiatric Services*, 50:9, 1205–1208.

Jeste, Dilip V. et al. (1999). Consensus Statement on the Upcoming Crisis in Geriatric Mental Health. *Archives of General Psychiatry*, 56, 848–853.

FIGURE 1.1   Geriatric mental health providers 2000–2030. *Source:* Copyright Michael B. Friedman, 2009.

estimated to occur by 2030. The growing lack of geriatric mental health providers is particularly troubling as the demand for mental health treatment among older adults is likely to increase in the coming decades, including among older adults whose first language is not English. Increased demand will be driven by baby boomers, a group that has been shown to have less stigma about depression and may be more likely to seek mental health treatment (Bartels et al., 2005). Without adequate means of ascertaining depression in older adults seeking health care and social services, older adults who have depression will be at a disadvantage, unless alternative methods of connecting at-risk older adults are made available.

HOW CAN PROVIDERS OF AGING SERVICES HELP?

Without help, older adults who have depression symptoms are at risk for a poorer quality of life. They are less likely to connect with community resources, including aging services agencies, such as senior and community centers, as well as other programs, which support their optimal functioning and civic engagement. They are more likely to experience worsening medical outcomes, increased levels of disability, social isolation, and increased mortality. Despite the generally lowered prevalence of major depression in older adults, compared to midlife and younger adults, the prevalence of depression symptoms increases with age, particularly in the face of age-associated risk factors. Although there is some evidence for generally enhanced emotional well-being among senior center participants than among older adults who are not involved in such programming (Choi & McDougall, 2007), the demographics of senior center attendees points to the potential risk for depression among this population. For example, research indicates that many older adults who routinely attend senior centers are more likely to be female, to live alone, to have experienced the death of a spouse, and to have incomes in the middle-to-low range (Calsyn, Burger & Roades, 1996; Calsyn & Winter, 1999; Krout, Cutler & Coward, 1990; Pardasani, 2004; Turner, 2004). All of these are risk factors for depression.

In addition, senior centers and other aging services programs are increasingly focusing on health and wellness promotion as central aspects of service provision (Beisgen & Kraitchman, 2003; Pardasani, Sporre, & Thompson, 2009; Ryzin, 2005). What, then, can aging services providers do to engage older adults in a meaningful discussion about mental health as a component of overall health and well-being? How can these providers, who are often not located within medical or mental health settings, identify older adults who may be at risk for depression? In what ways can they support older adults with depression to ensure that they receive the treatment they need?

If we are to promote successful aging among older adults, their mental health needs must be addressed from multiple service sectors, including aging services programs. Professionals who work in senior centers, community centers, case management agencies, and area agencies on aging may be aware of depression's devastating effects on older adults but often do not have the internal resources to routinely identify at-risk older adults and connect them to treatment resources. Many providers also know firsthand that it can be difficult to enter into a productive conversation with the older adults they serve about mental health, partly because of the stigma associated with mental illness and partly because they are not sure what to do if an older adult acknowledges that he or she is depressed.

To provide increased opportunities to identify older adults at risk for depression, the Mental Health Association of New York City, the New York City Department for the Aging, and the New York City Department of Health and Mental Hygiene have developed a collaborative model of outreach to older adults that providers of aging services can replicate in their own communities. This model, entitled EASE-D, is an approach that emphasizes the partnership between providers of aging services, mental health agencies, and, where possible, health care practitioners to identify older adults who are at risk for depression and connect them to treatment.

EASE-D consists of three main components, including (a) mental health education, (b) screening for depression, and (c) linkage to treatment.

MENTAL HEALTH EDUCATION

The first component of the model, mental health education, provides a means of outreach to older adults who may be at risk for depression. Education is instrumental in helping older adults overcome the stigma associated with depression and other mental disorders and is a recommended strategy for engaging older adults about the role of mental health in aging successfully (CMHS, SAMHSA, 2005). Education addresses stigma by providing useful information about the signs and symptoms of depression, the benefits of treatment and self-care, and resources older adults can use to obtain treatment services.

In this book, you will learn about several approaches to engage older adults in an educational discussion about depression. In particular, chapter 3 ("Educating About Depression: Approaches for Older Adults, Their Service Providers, and Community Members") addresses ways to recruit older adults to participate in mental health education, how to create an environment conducive to learning about mental health, and how to go beyond the topic of depression to address additional mental health topics. In addition, this chapter also addresses the provision of mental health education about depression for health care practitioners and providers of aging services. This book will also provide principles for developing engaging and easy to understand educational and outreach information for older adults and for other service providers in the community. Chapter 6 ("Developing Program Materials for Outreach and Education") includes useful guidelines for creating these materials and provides a set of exercises that can help you design your own program resources.

EARLY INTERVENTION AND DEPRESSION SCREENING

Chapter 2 ("Evidence-Based Models...") will introduce you to different models of early intervention for depression with older adults, including evidence-based models in nontraditional settings, such as aging services organizations. This chapter will also review the pros and cons of using these models within community settings and explain how to use EASE-D as a complement to or in place of these models to provide early intervention for at-risk older adults.

The second component of EASE-D, screening for depression, involves creating the opportunity for older adults to voluntarily screen for depression risk. Depression screening is recognized as a useful early intervention to help identify at-risk older adults to link them to treatment. Depression screening following mental health education provides a nonstigmatizing way of engaging at-risk older adults about their personal experience of symptoms and help to initiate a discussion about seeking help. In chapter 4 ("Implementing Depression Screening"), you will learn about the advantages of incorporating depression screening as a part of a mental health education program in an aging services setting, even when implemented outside of the structure of an evidence-based program. This chapter will also present information about the different depression screening tools available for use with older adults. In addition, it will underscore the advantages of partnering with mental health and health care services to ensure that depression screening helps older adults connect with qualified treatment providers.

LINKAGE TO TREATMENT

In addition to mental health education and depression screening, EASE-D includes a method of helping at-risk older adults to connect with treatment services in their communities. Chapter 5 ("Connecting Older Adults to Treatment: Pretreatment Care Management") outlines a method of supportive intervention, called *pretreatment care management*, which providers of aging services can use to help older adults navigate successfully through the health care or mental health service system as they seek out a qualified clinical evaluation and treatment for depression.

WHO CAN USE EASE-D?

EASE-D may be conducted in various types of programs serving older adults, but is particularly applicable in community-based settings such as senior or community centers. Certain components of the model, such as depression screening and linkage to treatment, also may be conducted easily within the context of providing case management or other services to homebound adults.

Although providers in the aging services field can choose to offer the program components on their own, this model is particularly well-suited to and intended for collaborative partnerships between providers of aging services, mental health agencies, and, where possible, health care practitioners. In chapter 7 ("How to Implement EASE-D in Your Community"), you will learn more about how to build EASE-D into your community through partnerships with these other stakeholders. Additionally, chapter 8 ("The Benefits and Challenges of Program Implementation") will review the advantages of implementing this model and will address some of the more common technical challenges encountered when using EASE-D.

EASE-D can pave the way for providers of aging services to open a dialogue with older adults about their mental health, to identify those who may be at risk for depression, and to provide worthwhile information, referral, and linkage services to help the older adults in their community continue to live satisfying and meaningful lives.

REFERENCES

Abrams, R. C., Marzuk, P. M., Tardiff, K., & Leon, A. C. (2005). Preference for fall from height as a method of suicide by elderly residents of New York City. *American Journal of Public Health*, 95(6), 1000–1002.

Alexopolous, G. S. (2005). Depression in the elderly. *The Lancet*, 365(9475), 1961–1970.

American Psychiatric Association. (2000). *Diagnostic and statistical manual of mental disorders* (text revision). Washington, DC: Author.

Bartels, S. J., Blow, F. C., Brockmann, L. M., & Van Citters, A. D. (2005). *Substance abuse and mental health among older Americans: The state of the knowledge and future directions*. Rockville, MD: Older American Substance Abuse and Mental Health Technical Assistance Center, Substance Abuse and Mental Health Services Administration.

Bartels, S. J., Dums, A. R., Oxman, T. E., Schneider, L. S., Areán, P. A., Alexopolous, G. S., & Jeste, D. V. (2004). Evidence-based practices in geriatric mental health care. *Focus: The Journal of Lifelong Learning in Psychiatry*, 2(2), 268–281.

Beisgen, B., & Kraitchman, M. (2003). *Senior centers: Opportunities for successful aging*. New York: Springer Publishing Company.

Bharucha, A. J. (2009). Late-life suicide. In J. M. Ellison, H. H. Kyomen, & S. K. Verma (Eds.), *Mood disorders in later life* (2nd ed., pp. 123–132). New York, NY: Informa Healthcare USA, Inc.

Blazer, D. G. (2009). Depression in late life: Review and commentary. *Focus: The Journal of Lifelong Learning in Psychiatry*, 7(1), 118–136.

Blazer, D. G., & Hybels, C. F. (2005). Origins of depression in later life. *Psychological Medicine*, 35(9), 1241–1252.

Blazer, D. G., Hybels, C. F., Simonsick, E. M., & Hanlon, J. T. (2000). Marked differences in antidepressant use by race in an elderly community sample: 1986–1996. *American Journal of Psychiatry*, 157(7), 1089–1094.

Blow, F. C., Bartels, S. J., Brockmann, L. M., & Van Citters, A. D. (2005). *Evidence-based practices for preventing substance abuse and mental health problems in older adults*. Rockville, MD: Substance Abuse and Mental Health Services Administration. Retrieved January 26, 2010, from http://www.samhsa.gov/OlderAdultsTAC/EBPLiteratureReviewFINAL.pdf

Bruce, M. L. (2002). Psychosocial risk factors for depressive disorders in late life. *Biological Psychiatry, 52*(3), 175–184.

Butler, R. N., Cohen, G., Lewis, M. I., Simmons-Clemmons, W., & Sunderland, T. (1997). Late-life depression: How to make a difficult diagnosis. *Geriatrics, 52*(3), 37, 41–2, 47–50.

Calsyn, R., Burger, G., & Roades, L. (1996). Cross-validation of differences between users and non-users of senior centers. *Journal of Social Service Research, 21*(6), 39–56.

Calsyn, R., & Winter, J. (1999). Who attends senior centers? *Journal of Social Service Research, 26*(2), 53–69.

Center for Mental Health Services, Substance Abuse and Mental Health Services Administration. (2005). *Mentally healthy aging: A report on overcoming stigma for older Americans* (DHHS Publication No. SMA 05-3988). Rockville, MD: Author.

Chapman, D. P., & Perry, G. S. (2008). Depression as a major component of public health for older adults. *Preventing Chronic Disease, 5*(1), A22.

Choi, N., & McDougall, G. (2007). Comparison of depressive symptoms between homebound older adults and ambulatory older adults. *Aging & Mental Health, 11*(3), 310–322.

Colemon, Y., & Ahmed, I. (2009). Barriers to psychiatric treatment for the geriatric patient: Cultural issues. In J. M. Ellison, H. H. Kyomen, & S. K. Verma (Eds.), *Mood disorders in later life* (2nd ed., pp. 209–220). New York, NY: Informa Healthcare USA, Inc.

Crystal, S., Sambamoorthi, U., Walkup, J. T., & Akincigil, A. (2003). Diagnosis and treatment of depression in the elderly Medicare population: Predictors, disparities, and trends. *Journal of American Geriatrics Society, 51*(12), 1718–1728.

Day, J. C. (1996). *Population projections of the United States by age, sex, race, and Hispanic origin: 1995 to 2050*. Washington, DC: U.S. Bureau of the Census, Current Population Reports, P25-1130, U.S. Government Printing Office.

Dunlop, D. D., Song, J., Lyons, J. S., Manheim, L. M., & Chang, R. W. (2003). Racial/ethnic difference in rates of depression among preretirement adults. *American Journal of Public Health, 93*(11), 1945–1952.

Friedman, M. B. (2009). *Geriatric mental health 101* [Electronic slide presentation]. New York, NY: Author.

Harwood, D. G., Barker, W. W., Ownby, R. L., Mullan, M., & Duara, R. (1999) Factors associated with depressive symptoms in non-demented community-dwelling elderly. *International Journal of Geriatric Psychiatry, 14*(5), 331–337.

Hasin, D. S., Goodwin, R. D., Stinson, F. S., & Grant, B. F. (2005). Epidemiology of major depressive disorder: Results from the National Epidemiologic Survey on Alcoholism and Related Conditions. *Archives of General Psychiatry, 62*(10), 1097–1106.

Hybels, C. F., & Blazer, D. G. (2003). Epidemiology of late life mental disorders. *Clinics in Geriatric Medicine, 19*(4), 663–696.

Hybels, C. F., Blazer, D. G., & Pieper, C. F. (2001). Toward a threshold for subthreshold depression: An analysis of correlates of depression by severity of symptoms using data from an elderly community sample. *Gerontologist, 41*(3), 357–365.

Jeste, D. V., Blazer, D. G., & First, M. (2005). Aging-related diagnostic variations: Need for diagnostic criteria appropriate for elderly psychiatric patients. *Biological Psychiatry*, *58*(4), 265–271.

Kennedy, G. J. (2000). *Geriatric mental health care*. New York, NY: The Guilford Press.

Kessler, R. C., Berglund, P., Demler, O., Jin, R., Merikangas, K., & Walters, E. E. (2005). Lifetime prevalence and age-of-onset distributions of *DSM-IV* disorders in the national comorbidity survey replication. *Archives of General Psychiatry*, *62*(6), 593–602.

Kim, J., & Durden, E. (2007). Socioeconomic status and age trajectories of health. *Social Science & Medicine*, *65*(12), 2489–2502.

Kohn, R., Gum, A. M., & King-Kallimanis, B. (2009). The epidemiology of major depression in geriatric populations. In J. M. Ellison, H. H. Kyomen, & S. K. Verma (Eds.), *Mood disorders in later life* (pp. 37–64). New York, NY: Informa Healthcare USA, Inc.

Krishnan, K. R., Delong, M., Kraemer, H., Carney, R., Spiegel, D., Gordon, C., McDonald, W., et al. (2002). Comorbidity of depression with other medical diseases in the elderly. *Biological Psychiatry*, *52*(6), 559–588.

Kroenke, K. (2006). Minor depression: Midway between major depression and euthymia. *Annals of Internal Medicine*, *144*(7), 528–530.

Krout, J. A., Cutler, S. J., & Coward, R. T. (1990). Correlates of senior center participation: A national analysis. *The Gerontologist*, *30*(1), 72–79.

Lyness, J. M., Heo, M., Datto, C. J., Ten Have, T. R., Katz, I. R., Drayer, R., et al. (2006). Outcomes of minor and subsyndromal depression among elderly patients in primary care settings. *Annals of Internal Medicine*, *144*(7), 496–504.

McGuire, L. C., Strine, T. W., Vachirasudlekha, S., Mokdad, A. H., & Anderson, L. A. (2008). The prevalence of depression in older U.S. women: 2006 behavioral risk factor surveillance system. *Journal of Women's Health*, *17*(4), 501–507.

Mojtabai, R., & Olfson, M. (2004). Major depression in community-dwelling middle-aged and older adults: Prevalence and 2- and 4-year follow-up symptoms. *Psychological Medicine*, *34*(4), 623–634.

Mui, A. C. (2003). Physical health, mental health and quality of life. In Asian American Federation of New York (Ed.), *Asian American elders in New York City: A study of health, social needs, quality of life and quality of care* (pp. 30–46). New York, NY: Asian American Federation of New York.

Pardasani, M. (2004). Senior centers: Increasing minority participation through diversification. *Journal of Gerontological Social Work*, *43*(2–3), 41–56.

Pardasani, M., Sporre, K., & Thompson, P. (2009). *New models taskforce: final report*. Washington, DC: National Institute of Senior Centers, National Council on Aging. Retrieved March 1, 2009, from http://www.ncoa.org/assets/files/pdf/pdf/FullReport.pdf

Ryzin, J. (2005). Senior centers on the cutting edge. *Innovations in Aging*, *34*(2), 15–20.

Sneed, J. R., Kasen, S., & Cohen, P. (2007). Early-life risk factors for late-onset depression. *International Journal of Geriatric Psychiatry*, *22*(7), 663–667.

Turner, K. W. (2004). Senior citizens centers: What they offer, who participates, and what they gain. *Journal of Gerontological Social Work*, *43*(1), 37–47.

Unützer, J., Katon, W., Callahan, C. M., Williams, J. W., Hunkeler, E., Harpole, L., et al. (2003). Depression treatment in a sample of 1,801 depressed older adults in primary care. *Journal of American Geriatrics Society*, *51*(4), 505–514.

U.S. Department of Health and Human Services. (1999). *Mental health: A report of the surgeon general—executive summary*. Rockville, MD: U.S. Department of Health and Human Services, Substance Abuse and Mental Health Services Administration, Center for Mental Health Services, National Institutes of Health, National Institute of Mental Health.

U.S. Department of Health and Human Services. (2001). *Older adults and mental health: Issues and opportunities*. Rockville, MD: Author.

VanItallie, T. B. (2005). Subsyndromal depression in the elderly: Underdiagnosed and undertreated. *Metabolism, 54*(Suppl. 1), 39–44.

Vink, D., Aartsen, M. J., & Schoevers, R. A. (2008). Risk factors for anxiety and depression in the elderly. *Journal of Affective Disorders, 106*(1–2), 29–44.

Wang, P. S., Lane, M., Olfson, M., Pincus, H. A., Wells, K. B., & Kessler, R. C. (2005). Twelve-month use of mental health services in the United States: Results from the National Comorbidity Survey Replication. *Archives of General Psychiatry, 62*(6), 629–640.

Weyerer, S., Eiffilaender-Gorfer, S., Köhler, L., Jessen, F., Maier, W., & Fuchs, A., et al. (2008). Prevalence and risk factors for depression in non-demented primary care attenders aged 75 years and older. *Journal of Affective Disorders, 111*(2–3), 153–163.

Williams, J. W., Jr., Barrett, J., Oxman, T., Frank, E., Katon, W., Sullivan, M., Cornell, J., et al. (2000). Treatment of dysthymia and minor depression in primary care: A randomized controlled trial in older adults. *The Journal of the American Medical Association, 284*(12), 1519–1526.

Wu, L. T., & Anthony, J. C. (2000). The estimated rate of depression mood in US adults: Recent evidence for a peak in later life. *Journal of Affective Disorders, 60*(3), 159–171.

Yang, Y. (2006). How does functional disability affect depressive symptoms in late life? The role of perceived social support and psychological resources. *Journal of Health and Social Behavior, 47*(4), 355–372.

2

Evidence-Based Models of Intervention for Older Adults With Depression

Increasingly, evidence-based practice has become the norm in various human service fields, including aging services. Whether you are interested in learning more about what evidence-based programs exist so that you can incorporate them into your current programming, or to otherwise inform your work, it is important to have a better understanding of what makes a program evidence based and what currently exists for older adults with depression.

In these days of waning resources, agencies do not have the luxury of the time and money it takes to develop new programming. Evidence-based programs and practices (EBPs) can be helpful resources in infusing effective programming into the aging services network. However, although effective mental health service models currently exist, there is a lack of models for aging services programs seeking to educate older adults about mental health, identify those who are at risk for depression, and connect them to care in community-based settings.

This chapter will review evidence-based models for addressing depression among older adults and the advantages and disadvantages of incorporating evidence-based models into community-based aging service settings. Additionally, this chapter will provide a rationale for incorporating Educating About and Screening Elders for Depression (EASE-D), the model of mental health education, depression screening, and linkage to treatment introduced in chapter 1, into community-based aging service programs to address the mental health needs of older adults at-risk for depression.

WHAT IS AN EVIDENCE-BASED PROGRAM AND PRACTICE?

All of us who work with older adults know, deep in our hearts, when the work we are doing has made an impact. However, it is often difficult to articulate exactly what part of the intervention or program was the most helpful in affecting change. Alternately, EBPs are able to identify the methods that create the most impact. EBPs clearly instruct professionals on the specific methods to use and articulate the impact they will have on the older adults' life. Although many people use the terms "evidence-based program" and "evidence-based practice" interchangeably, they actually refer to different concepts. *Evidence-based programs* are those that are

> comprised of a set of coordinated services and activities that demonstrate effectiveness based on research. Criteria for ratings as such depend upon organization or agency doing the rankings. EBPs may incorporate a number of evidence-based practices in the delivery of services. (Williams-Taylor, 2007, p. 4)

Most evidence-based programs incorporate at least one evidence-based practice in their approach. *Evidence-based practices* are "skills, techniques, and strategies that can be used when a practitioner is interacting directly with a customer" (Fixsen, Naoom, Blase, Friedman, & Wallace, 2005, p. 82). The New York State Office of Mental Health (2008) defines EBP as "interventions for which there is consistent, scientific evidence showing that they improve consumer outcomes" (p. 10).

Evidence-based practice grew out of evidence-based medicine (EBM). EBM is, "the conscientious, explicit and judicious use of current best evidence in making decisions about the care of the individual patient. It means integrating individual clinical expertise with the best available external clinical evidence from systematic research" (Sackett, Rosenberg, Gray, Haynes, & Richardson, 1996, p. 71). In 1972, Dr. Archibald Cochrane was to shape history with his book, *Effectiveness and Efficiency: Random Reflections on Health Services*, which encouraged the need for developing a strong research base in the practice of medicine. Although Dr. Cochrane never witnessed the creation of The Cochrane Collaboration in 1993, it emerged to produce and disseminate systematic reviews of health care (The Cochrane Collaboration, 2010).

Many evidence-based practices are extremely beneficial in working with older adults. Examples of evidence-based practices for older adults with depression are cognitive behavior therapy (CBT; Thompson, Gallagher, & Breckenridge, 1987), problem solving therapy (PST), and interpersonal therapy (IPT) for late life depression (Bartels, 2008). Examples of evidence-based programs in mental health are (a) Improving Mood-Promoting Access to Collaborative Treatment (IMPACT; Hunkeler et al., 2006), (b) Program to Encourage Active, Rewarding Lives for Seniors (PEARLS; Ciechanowski et al., 2004), and (c) Identifying Depression, Empowering Activities for Seniors (Healthy IDEAS; Quijano et al., 2007). We will discuss each of these evidence-based programs in more detail later in the chapter (see "How Do I Find an Evidence-Based Model and What Will It Involve?").

There are no universal definitions for evidence-based programs; there are also no standard criteria for establishing an evidence-based program. Currently, there are approximately 23 different organizations rating evidence-based programs. Each organization maintains its own criteria on establishing EBPs. The following are two examples of different organizational criteria for EBPs.

Substance Abuse and Mental Health Services Administration

Substance Abuse and Mental Health Services Administration (SAMHSA) incorporates very specific standardized criteria to rate interventions and the evidence supporting their outcomes. All reviewers receive training on these criteria and are required to use them to calculate their ratings. Each reviewer independently evaluates against the readiness for dissemination. Reviewers examine the research for its reliability, validity, fidelity, missing data, potential confounding variables, and appropriateness of analysis. Reviews look at readiness for dissemination in terms of the availability of implementation materials, availability of training and support resources, and availability of quality assurance procedures (SAMHSA's National Registry of Evidence-Based Programs and Practices [NREPP], 2008).

SAMHSA is a federal agency established in 1992 to support substance abuse and mental health services in the United States. SAMHSA does this through distributing block grants and special programmatic funding, as well as disseminating up-to-date information about behavioral health issues and prevention or treatment approaches. SAMHSA also maintains the NREPP, which is a database of all EBPs on the prevention and treatment of mental health and substance use disorders. According to SAMHSA's Web site, NREPP contains reviews of 150 interventions and adds 3–5 new reviews each month (SAMHSA's NREPP, n.d.).

Blueprints for Violence Prevention

The University of Colorado's Center for the Study and Prevention of Violence (CSPV) was one of the first to apply specific criteria to establish effectiveness of programs and practices. Reviews examine the strength of the research design in showing deterrent effects for violence, delinquency, and drug use. Programs must show sustained effects for at least 1 year and must show success in diverse populations. Reviewers also consider program cost (CSPV, n.d.).

Although there are no uniform criteria for EBPs, most reviews focus on common elements such as strength in research design and strong evidence of effectiveness. For the most part, all reviews share the belief that EBPs should encompass a meticulous design, with clearly defined goals, outcomes, and procedures. To consider a program or practice evidence-based, it must have undergone rigorous scientific evaluation, usually using either experimental or quasi-experimental research techniques. It must be clear in the research that the results from the program are attributed to the model and not other possible outside factors (American Psychological Association [APA] Presidential Task Force on Evidence-Based Practice, 2006; Cooney, Huser, Small, & O'Connor, 2007). Moreover, all certifying organizations must make use of expert peer-reviewers to confirm the methodology is appropriate.

What Does It Take to Conduct Evidence-Based Research?

Many programs involve some type of research, but simply infusing research into your programmatic design will not ensure a certification for being evidence based. A fundamental component of all evidence-based programs is their adherence to methodologically solid research. Research designs can be experimental, quasi-experimental, or even preexperimental. The following sections describe these methods in detail.

What Is an Experimental Design?

Experimental design, lauded as the gold standard in research, is the best method at isolating the direct impact of the experimental variable. For our purposes, the experimental variable is the treatment or intervention given to older adults (de Vaus, 2001). In experimental designs, researchers randomly assign people to one of two groups, the treatment group (the model program) or the control group (those not participating in the model program, which can be individuals not receiving any treatment or receiving treatment as usual). What sets experimental designs apart from other methods is their ability to ensure that both the treatment and the control group are as similar as possible. By randomly assigning individuals from one general pool, experimental designs rely on the probability that both groups will be similar; thus, if neither group received the program, we would observe the same outcomes in both groups (Anastas, 2000; Trochim, 2006). In this way, one can attribute any differences between the two groups to the intervention or, in the case of evidence-based research, the program model.

Although most researchers strive to achieve an experimental design, in practice, there are multiple factors that often stand in the way of this occurring. Achieving random assignment can become ethically challenging in human services, as one group will be "denied" a service that would benefit them. Moreover, there is always the problem of individuals refusing to participate or dropping out of the program, limiting the sample size and making it more difficult to gauge the impact of a program or practice. Finally, by design, the experiment creates an artificial situation, which limits the ability to generalize the results to a real-world situation (Trochim, 2006). For these reasons, researchers often choose to or are obliged to rely on designs that are less robust.

What Is a Quasi-Experimental Design?

A quasi-experimental design is very similar to experimental design but does not have random assignment. Because of the problems listed previously, it may not be possible to assign individuals randomly to either a treatment or an experimental group. Quasi-experimental designs range from situations where the researcher has no control over how individuals are assigned to the treatment and control group, to cases where the researcher can assign individuals based on a predetermined criteria, such as a cutoff score on a depression screening instrument (Trochim, 2006). There are many different types of quasi-experimental designs, each with their own strengths and weaknesses. One of the common criticisms of the quasi-experimental design is its inability to eliminate possible confounders, reducing one's ability to draw causal inference (Trochim, 2006). As it is difficult to know with any certainty what differentiates the individuals assigned to the two groups, one cannot confidently attribute the differences in outcomes to the treatment.

Although seen as a weaker research design than experimental, statistical techniques can often control for the differences between the two groups (Salzberg, 1999). Interestingly, this lack of assignment can also be viewed as a strength; as quasi-experimental designs are more naturalistic in their approach, they have a greater ability to generalize their results to the natural environment than is the case with experimental designs. Additionally, quasi-experimental designs are stronger methods to use than preexperimental techniques.

What Is a Preexperimental Design?

A preexperimental design is beneficial when you are unable to study two independent groups. However, as preexperimental designs are unable to control for outside factors that could be influencing results, one cannot attribute any changes to the treatment condition. Although these methods are nonexperimental, it does not mean that they are unscientific and without value. Rather, preexperimental techniques are usually exploratory in approach and can be useful when conducting a study in a setting where using a stronger design is not feasible (Rubin & Babbie, 2001). Although useful, evidence-based programs are unlikely to rely on preexperimental designs.

What Is a Promising Program or Practice?

Although specific designations vary, organizations use their own rating systems to distinguish between the strongest programs, often called "effective" or "model" programs, from "promising" programs. Although having a lesser rating, experts believe these promising programs will someday prove to be evidence based with more time and rigorous evaluation. These programs usually have quantitative data showing positive results but have not illustrated sufficient results at such time as to gain evidence-based designation (Kyler, Bumbarger, & Greenberg, 2005).

A promising practice differs from programs that undertake evaluations as part of the requirements of their funder. Although program evaluations examine the impact of the work, one positive result will not qualify a program for even promising practice status. Program evaluations, although often rigorous, usually do not include a comparison group, making it difficult to attribute change to those participating in the program. However, a positive result on one program evaluation can lay the foundation for future research into those programs, leading the way to a potential designation as a promising practice.

WHY USE AN EVIDENCE-BASED PROGRAM TO WORK WITH OLDER ADULTS WITH DEPRESSION?

There has been a plethora of research in the past 10 years, all pointing to the benefits of evidence-based models, specifically for their use with individuals who are depressed. Research has shown that evidence-based models can successfully treat depression among older adults (Ayalon, Areán, Linkins, Lynch, & Estes, 2007; Ell, 2006; Snowden, Steinman, & Frederick, 2008). In 2003, the President's New Freedom Commission on Mental Health released a report recommending the use of evidence-based programs to improve care. More recently, the SAMHSA made available resources specifically for implementing evidence-based programs for the treatment of depression in the form of five Resource Kits to encourage the use of evidence-based practices in mental health. These toolkits are available to download by accessing their Web site at http://mentalhealth.samhsa.gov/cmhs/CommunitySupport/toolkits/about.asp.

In these days of scarce resources, coupled with the increasing emphasis on using evidence-based programming, aging services providers might find that it is easier to secure funding when using an evidence-based program, in great part because foundations and federal grants often insist on the use of these models. Even if the funding source does not demand the use of evidence-based programs, it is still advantageous to explore their utility. When used, agencies can be confident that the chosen model works; it has been tested and proven successful in keeping with program fidelity (the extent to which the delivery of the program adheres to the original design). Additionally, you might find that it takes less time to put such a program in place, because there is no need for a design phase. Because evidence-based programs are so structured, once you have selected the one to use, you can be up and running as soon as you train staff to undertake the program design.

Are There Tradeoffs or Concerns in Using an Evidence-Based Program?

Although there has been a groundswell of enthusiasm for EBPs, they are not without criticism. Concerns surrounding implementing EBPs usually center on the following (Williams-Taylor, 2007):

- Maintaining fidelity can be unachievable in the natural setting of a community program.
- Evidence-based programs can be expensive to implement.
- An evidence-based program may not exist for a specific population.
- Providers may lack the capacity needed to implement.

Evidence-based programs demand that agencies follow rigid guidelines to maintain program fidelity and ensure a successful implementation. Even slight variations in program implementation could disrupt the integrity of the model and its effectiveness. By design, EBPs maintain specific protocols, evaluation tools, manuals, and handouts, reducing an agency's ability to customize the model to the specific populations they serve. Often these programs offer little guidance in how an agency might adapt the original design in the natural setting. Modifying an EBP may not result in an ineffective program; however, because the adaption was not part of the evaluation design, one does not know if it will be as successful. There is a growing body of research that suggests, "sensitivity and flexibility in administering interventions produces better outcomes than rigid application of manuals or principles" (APA Presidential Task Force on Evidence-Based Practice, 2006, p. 278). When considering adapting an EBP, it is essential to contact the architect of the program to discuss how any modifications to the design can be made while maintaining program integrity.

Evidence-based programs often enjoy the benefits of generous funding to acquire the necessary levels of educated staff, manuals, resources, and ongoing coaching and monitoring to ensure integrity to method (The Iowa Consortium for Substance Abuse Research and Evaluation, 2003). Programs attempting to implement these EBPs without the same funding levels could find it difficult to locate necessary resources for training of staff, purchasing manuals, and treatment costs (if they are not covered through insurance). One might even need to employ additional staff to ensure the fidelity of the EBP. In addition, evidence-based programs sometimes charge a fee for training and program implementation.

Although there are multitudes of evidence-based programs, you might not find one to match the needs of your community. For example, there are few evidence-based programs with a specific focus on mental health education and services to link at risk older adults to treatment. If this is the focus of your program, there will be few EBP options. Instead, you will need to either develop your own model or, perhaps, employ the one suggested in this book. In addition, EBPs are effective for specific populations; if your cohort differs from those within the EBP, this may not be an effective model for your agency, because its effectiveness is unknown. If the population that you are working with represents a different culture, ethnic population, or setting from the one for which the evidence-based model was originally designed, it is recommended that you contact the program designers to discuss their model's applicability to the population your agency plans to serve. The authors of the program could see this as an opportunity to examine the benefits of expanding their program into other population and may assist you with implementation in your community.

When considering undertaking an EBP, an agency should first examine whether they have the capacity to do so, because it will commonly require some organizational change. Successful implementation of an EBP rests on the ability of executive management to create enthusiasm and commitment among staff. Embarking on an evidence-based program often requires a change in organizational norms and prior functions of staff. It has been said that, "to be effective, any design process must intentionally be, from the beginning, a redesign process" (Felner et al., 2001).

The following factors are necessary for successful implementation (Fixsen et al., 2005):

- Commitment of leadership to the implementation process;
- Involvement of stakeholders in planning and selection of programs to implement;
- Creation of an implementation task force made up of consumer and stakeholders;
- Suggestions for "unfreezing" current organizational practices;
- Resources for extra costs, effort, equipment, manuals, materials, recruiting, access to expertise, and retraining for new organizational roles;
- Alignment of organizational structures to integrate staff selection, training, performance evaluation, and ongoing treatment;
- Alignment of organizational structures to achieve horizontal and vertical integration; and
- Commitment of ongoing resources and support for providing time and scheduling for coaching, participatory planning, exercise of leadership, evolution of teamwork.

HOW DO I FIND AN EVIDENCE-BASED MODEL
AND WHAT WILL IT INVOLVE?

Be aware that not all evidence-based programs are equally effective. Just because an EBP has proven effectiveness through scientific rigor does not mean the impact is significant clinically. One program might statistically be able to show a reduction of depression in 2% of its clients, whereas another evidence-based program demonstrates a reduction of depression symptoms in 25% in the participants. Which program would you rather use? The answer may not be as straightforward as it might seem. In addition to examining the level of effectiveness of the EBP that you are considering, you should also contemplate your ability to replicate the program with fidelity. Additionally, you should also examine whether the EBP mirrors your population, because the target audience and setting for the EBP may not be the same as the context for your program or older adults with whom you work.

These days, using the Internet, it is easy to locate numerous evidence-based models within federal and trade organizations. A list of such Web sites is given in Table 2.2 on page 47. If you determine an EBP to have merit for your organization, you should reach out to the program architects to get a better sense of what would be involved in implementing it at your particular agency. Most are quite accessible by e-mail and phone and can explore with you whether their program model would be a good fit for your situation.

Which Model Is Right for My Organization?

The evidence-based programs discussed later all combine mental health screening using a validated instrument, a known evidence-based therapeutic technique, and involve partnerships with health and/or mental health institutions. The following EBPs are well-known for their effectiveness in reducing depression among older adults: (a) IMPACT, (b) PEARLS, and (c) Healthy IDEAS.

The purpose of all three models is to identify and treat older adults with depression and to engage older adults in their treatment plans. These models are similar in their strong reliance on collaboration and teamwork. In all three program models, the older adult is central to this team approach and is an active participant in their care. Other members of the team include a depression case manager and a consulting psychiatrist. Often, the primary care physician (PCP) is also a crucial member of the team. Intervention takes place in a health care clinic or in the older adult's own home. Additionally, each of these models incorporates evidence-based therapeutic techniques such as behavior activation (BA), or PST. As well as using a clearly delineated therapeutic technique, they all involve the use of standardized screening tools (for more information about depression screening tools, refer to chapter 4, under "What Depression Screening Tools Exist?") and some include educational components for staff and/or older adults being served. Monitoring and tracking the older adult's progress in their treatment is also a critical component in each of these programs. This chapter will briefly discuss each of programs, but if you are interested in finding out more about them, refer to Table 2.1 on page 40 for a brief summary, or visit their respective Web sites presented in Table 2.2 on page 47.

Improving Mood-Promoting Access to Collaborative Treatment (IMPACT)

Developed in 1998 with support from the John A. Hartford Foundation and the California HealthCare Foundation, IMPACT was originally designed for use as a colocation model for adults in primary care. Since then, the modality has changed over the years to include other populations and settings. IMPACT has been successful for use with adults of all ages, adolescents, people with diabetes, and people with cancer. IMPACT encourages organizations to adapt the model for use in diverse settings, such as case management and home health organizations, and even senior centers. IMPACT was one of the first evidence-based models to illustrate that trained professionals could significantly reduce depression among older adults through education, screening, use of PST, BA techniques, and, when needed, pharmacological treatment administered by psychiatrists or other medical doctors.

The structure of the model consists of a strong partnership between primary care and mental health services. The older adult with depression is central to the model and is a collaborator who helps to shape his or her own treatment plan. There are three key professionals working with the older adult with depression, including a PCP, a depression care manager (DCM), and a consulting psychiatrist. The DCM may come from various disciplines but is often either a social worker or a nurse.

In IMPACT, the PCP initiates a referral of an elderly patient with depression to a DCM. The DCM will then complete the initial assessment, educate the older adult about depression and treatment options, and engage him or her to become an active member in the treatment plan by helping to choose the treatment modality (PST and/or psychotropic medication). All older adults are also encouraged to take part in BA and pleasant activity scheduling (more information on these techniques is discussed later under "Therapeutic Models: Problem Solving Therapy and Behavior Activation"). The DCM then discusses the treatment plan with the PCP and the consulting psychiatrist and a recommended plan of action is determined. The treatment plan could consist of initiating or changing a course of medication and/or starting a brief behavioral intervention. The DCM then closely monitors the progress of the treatment. If the older adult does not seem to be improving, the team reevaluates and adapts the treatment plan as needed.

The DCM will use specially designed instruments and tools in their work with older adults who have depression. The authors of IMPACT have designed scripted brochures and videos to use in educating older adults about depression. In addition, IMPACT makes use of the Patient Health Questionnaire 9 (PHQ-9), a screening instrument that both identifies depression in the older adult and tracks his or her improvement during the course of treatment. The consulting psychiatrist also meets with the DCM regularly, ideally on a weekly basis, for consultation sessions regarding clients who are not responding to the set course of treatment.

The treatment protocol consists of three main components. First, all older adults with depression are involved in BA and pleasant activity scheduling with their DCM at every session. Second, the older adult may be prescribed antidepressant medication and/or PST and lastly, at the conclusion of the treatment, their DCM guides the older adult through a relapse prevention protocol.

The DCM usually delivers evidence-based counseling during the treatment phase. Service delivery occurs every 2 weeks, either in person or over the phone. These biweekly contacts eventually taper off to a monthly contact during the maintenance phase of treatment. If it is not possible for the DCM to conduct counseling, the primary care practice arranges a partnership with a mental health organization to provide treatment. In the ideal situation, the DCM or mental health provider is actually colocated in office space with the PCP. In this way, the DCM can consult in person with the doctor. However, colocation is not always possible; instead, follow-up phone calls are made to facilitate contact between the PCP and the DCM. Collaboration between the DCM and the PCP is critical; whether the model is administered in person or over the phone, the PCP *must* be available to consult with the DCM on the patient's mental health treatment.

IMPACT offers a range of training options. They maintain a user-friendly and accessible Web site with an online training option available free of charge. However, if you would prefer face-to-face trainings, they also offer that at a cost (at the time of this writing) of approximately $750 per participant. If your organization requires training on the evidence-based counseling modalities of PST, BA, or pleasant activity scheduling, that will be an additional $1,000–$1,500 per participant.

IMPACT represents the ideal treatment situation for the older adult. In addition to receiving coordinated treatment for depression, older adults learn concepts of self-empowerment that they can continue to use on their own, well after formal treatment ends. The short-term nature of this program could also make it attractive for older adults, because they are not required to commit to a long-term process. However, reliance on a strong partnership with PCPs, although a laudable goal, could be difficult to foster in the "real world." Primary care providers often do not screen their older patients for depression and securing an interactive collaboration could be challenging. In addition, although a range of professionals can function as the DCM, in many cases, Medicare, Medicaid, or third-party insurers may not reimburse for the cost of counseling.

Program to Encourage Active, Rewarding Lives for Seniors (PEARLS)

PEARLS was developed in 2000 through funding by the Washington State Aging and Disability Services Administration and the Mental Health Transformation State Incentive Grant award from the SAMHSA. The program emerged out of a research study at the Health Promotion Research Center at the University of Washington. PEARLS is a community-based program using PST as its core intervention; it aims to reduce depression among homebound older adults with minor depression or dysthymia (for more information about types of depressive disorders, refer to chapter 1, under "Defining Depression"). In addition to the techniques of PST, PEARLS also uses concepts from BA and pleasant activity scheduling in their therapeutic approach. Older adults who participated in PEARLS significantly reduced their depression, improved their quality of life, and even reduced their health care use compared to a similar population of homebound that received standard care (Ciechanowski et al., 2004).

PEARLS is a short-term program, which involves work with a PEARLS counselor (who can be a case manager) in the home for up to eight sessions over a 19-week period. Each counseling session lasts for about 60 minutes. The sessions are scheduled frequently at first, and then taper off over time because older adults integrate the therapeutic techniques to use on their own. The first two sessions are weekly, the second two are biweekly, and all of the remaining sessions are monthly. Following the face-to-face encounters are weekly follow-up phone calls for about 6 months. A script guides each session and includes standardized depression screening tools, which document the successes of the process. These instruments and protocols are available to download from the PEARLS Web site.

PEARLS expands on concepts from IMPACT and demonstrates the effectiveness of training case managers to provide similar treatment to homebound seniors with minor depression or dysthymia. As in IMPACT, the PEARLS counselor uses the techniques of PST, as well as BA and pleasant activity scheduling to reduce depression. Moreover, the older adults learn the concepts so that they are able to continue using the therapeutic techniques once the structured program is completed.

What sets this model apart from IMPACT is its use of preexisting staff in the screening, identification, and treatment of the older adults. For example, case managers already employed in an aging services agency act as PEARLS counselors. However, case managers should not be a PEARLS counselor for an older adult who is already assigned to their caseload, because this could potentially confuse roles. Additionally, it is important to identify the "right" person to become a PEARLS counselor. Although the techniques are easy to learn, for some individuals already possessing a strong clinical background, the structured nature of this process may be difficult to follow. Not all staff will embrace PST, because they may be wedded to techniques that they have been using for years, or because implementing PST is such a significant culture shift from their usual responsibilities. Once the "right" staff learns the techniques of PST, this model embeds itself into the standard agency procedure.

PEARLS is not without its limitations, however. PEARLS is not to be used with older adults having major depression, those with a psychiatric disorder other than depression, older adults who abuse substances, and those with cognitive impairments. In addition, there could be significant costs built into this program, because staff will often require training on PST, because they are unlikely to have this skill prior to program implementation. In addition, local aging organizations will be unable to bill Medicaid, Medicare, or third-party insurers for this service and could find its implementation to be a burden on top of their existing caseload. Finally, funds must be located to hire a part-time psychiatrist to consult on cases, because effective use of this model requires that programs have a psychiatric consultant to supervise the PEARLS case managers.

PEARLS offers a 2.5-day training in Seattle, Washington. As of April 2009, the cost of the training was $500, which covers the tuition, course materials, and breakfast or lunch. Continuing education unit (CEU) credits are available. For ease of instruction, the authors of PEARLS have also developed a user-friendly toolkit that is available free of charge on the Internet.

Identifying Depression, Empowering Activities for Seniors (Healthy IDEAS)

Healthy IDEAS was developed in 2007 by Baylor College of Medicine's Huffington Center on Aging in Houston, Texas. The John A. Hartford Foundation funded the initial project; the U.S. Administration on Aging funded the research to develop the model's evidence base. Similar to other evidence-based models relying on strong scientific evidence, Healthy IDEAS is highly effective in reducing depression among older adults (Quijano et al., 2007).

In developing Healthy IDEAS, the authors borrowed approaches from both PEARLS and IMPACT. Healthy IDEAS uses case managers working within their own caseloads of homebound clients to employ the therapeutic techniques. These case managers are not required to have previous training in mental health. Partnership is a necessary component of Healthy IDEAS. For this model to be successful, staff must have knowledge of and good relationships with the medical and mental health resources in the community. Experts in the technique of BA are necessary to act as supervisors and coaches to case management staff. These experts can be outside consultants or can be trained supervisory staff from within the organization.

The four key principles behind Healthy IDEAS are (a) screening, (b) education, (c) linkage, and (d) empowerment. Program monitoring and evaluation is part of each of these components. The Healthy IDEAS Web site discusses each of these concepts in detail.

The first key principle in the model is *screening*. Case managers, working with their own homebound clients, screen their clients for depression using a standardized instrument such as the Geriatric Depression Scale (GDS) or the PHQ-9. The model does not dictate the use of a specific instrument; rather, it simply requires that the screening tool should be a standardized instrument to detect depression. Case managers screen their clients for depression at their usual reassessment period, according to their agency's protocols.

The second key principle is *education*. Case managers spend time educating their clients about depression, treatment options and self-care principles. The Healthy IDEAS project team provides brochures and handouts that the case managers distribute to their clients. All information is in both English and Spanish. The material includes information about depression, local treatment resources and self-care strategies. There is also a video that the project team has put together that can be given to older adults if they are interested in getting even more information.

The third key principle is *linkage to service*. If older adults are at risk for either moderate or severe depression, they are encouraged to get a more extensive assessment from their primary care provider and/or mental health provider. For this reason, it is imperative that the agency conducting this project makes alliances with local mental health providers. As agencies create these necessary linkages, they usually find that their relationships with health and mental health providers strengthen at a community-based level.

The fourth and final principle involves the use of *empowerment*. The case managers follow a strict protocol and use the therapeutic techniques of BA to motivate older adults for positive life changes. Integral to the process is the tracking of outcomes to ensure that older adults are improving. This model rests on concepts of self-management; older adults learn skills that they can use within their daily life to help themselves feel better and be more proactive in their own care. The program involves two or three face-to-face visits and at least five telephone contacts. Interaction with older adults can be arranged to follow scheduled meeting times. It is important to the success of the intervention that case managers establish solid working relationships with their clients; for this reason, they should conduct all interventions after they have been working with their elderly clients for at least 6 months prior to beginning the program.

There is good on-line support from the Healthy IDEAS project team. At the time of this writing, the organization charged $3,000, plus travel expenses, to implement this model. The fees cover on-line training of staff, telephone support, use of their evaluation tools, use of their program materials, and 80-minute training DVD, and more. The materials include specific protocols, evaluation instruments, and scripts that case managers can follow when implementing the program. Additionally, the Healthy IDEAS project team offers training, either on-site or through a video, all for a fee.

Healthy IDEAS shares some of the strengths of the other two models in that it, too, relies on the principle of the self-empowerment for older adults. However, this model differs from IMPACT and PEARLS in various ways. First, the case manager conducts the intervention with his or her own client during their regular appointment schedules. Second, unlike the other models, the case managers do not implement PST, but instead use the less intensive approach of BA.

IMPACT and PEARLS rely significantly on the use of psychiatrists for medication management. Psychiatrists have weekly or biweekly supervision with the case manager or DCM to discuss cases. Although psychiatrists are an important part of the team with Healthy IDEAS, they help with staff training and are available on more of an "as needed" basis for supervision. Rather than psychiatrists, other licensed mental health professionals provide ongoing coaching and supervision, when needed. Case managers refer any client in need of pharmacologic assistance to their PCP, a psychiatrist, or the local mental health provider organization. Although knowing the resources in the community is helpful, communication with the PCP is not a major component of Healthy IDEAS. Both IMPACT and Healthy IDEAS are appropriate to use with older adults having varying levels of depression. As with both IMPACT and PEARLS, it is also a short-term intervention, which may increase its appeal to older adults.

Like the previously reviewed models, Healthy IDEAS also has its limitations. It is the most costly of the three models as the developers insist on conducting general on-site training. In addition, there are costs associated with bringing specific trainers to teach BA to the case managers and to act as skills-building coaches on an ongoing basis. Although it is helpful that this model becomes one component of the organization's routine practice, it shares the same limitation as the other two EBPs, because the local aging organizations will be unable to bill for this service. Additionally, integrating the Healthy IDEAS process will require case managers to spend more time with each client. If an aging services provider is already struggling with ballooning caseloads, they could find implementing this model cumbersome.

For easy reference, see Table 2.1, which compares these three programs.

TABLE 2.1   Comparing Evidence-Based Mental Health Programs

	IMPACT	PEARLS	Healthy IDEAS
Date program created	1998	2000	2007
Target population	Older adults with major depression or dysthymia	Older adults with minor depression or dysthymia	Older adults with major depression or dysthymia
Setting	Primary care settings; however, has expanded to other settings	Case management programs; implemented in the client's home	Case management programs; implemented in the client's home
Essential partners (those partners where routine consultation is built into the model, more than linkage and referral)	Client Specialized DCM primary care physician Consulting psychiatrist	Client PEARLS counselor Consulting psychiatrist	Client Case managers Behavioral health experts to help coach case managers (behavioral activation)
Evidence-based	At 12 months, patients receiving IMPACT reported at least a 50% reduction in depression symptoms, compared with only 19% of those in usual care	Study participants were three times more likely than nonparticipants to reduce their depressive symptoms (43% vs. 15%) or completely eliminate their depression (36% vs. 12%)	At 6 months, participants had significantly reduced depression severity scores (9.0 vs. 5.5). Additionally, more participants who knew how to get help for depression (68% vs. 93%) reported that increasing activity helped them feel better (72% vs. 89%), and reported reduced pain (16% vs. 45%)
Program Web sites	www.impact-uw.org	www.depts.washington.edu/pearlspr	www.careforelders.org/healthyideas
Program component 1: Screening	Use of PHQ-9 for screening and tracking outcomes	Use of PHQ-9 for screening and tracking outcomes	Use of GDS (programs may also opt for the PHQ-9) for screening and tracking outcomes

continued

	IMPACT	PEARLS	Healthy IDEAS
Program component 2: **Education of staff**	Staff is already knowledge-able about depression and therapeutic techniques	Staff requires training on techniques	Conducted on-site by Healthy IDEAS program staff for a fee
Program component 3: **Education of seniors**	Education of clients by DCM	No formal education of clients	Case managers educate clients and their caregivers about depression, treatment, and self-care techniques The program makes brochures available to give to clients and caregivers about depression
Program component 4: **Psychotherapeutic intervention**	BA Brief PST for a total of 6–8 sessions Psychotropic medication (when needed)	Social and activity planning PST for a total of 8 sessions Pleasant event planning and scheduling	BA Referral to mental health experts for other therapeutic techniques
Who identifies clients?	Primary care physician—refers to DCM	Usual case managers	Usual case managers
Who conducts interventions?	On-site DCM or staff in mental health local clinic	PEARLS counselors (but not the senior's own case manager)	Case managers' referrals for more intensive treatment
Background of counselors	Social work or a related field, such as nursing	Social work or a related field recommended, but not necessary	No specified background needed
Linkage to mental health services or primary care physician	Use of consulting psychiatrist (regular consultations with DCM)	Use of consulting psychiatrist (works with case managers)	Use of consulting mental health professionals (work with case managers)

continued

TABLE 2.1 Comparing Evidence-Based Mental Health Programs *(continued)*

	IMPACT	PEARLS	Healthy IDEAS
Treatment modality	In person and on the phone	In person and on the phone	In person and on the phone
Intensity and duration of treatment	**Intervention:** 6–8 sessions total **Follow-up:** Every 2 weeks during intensive intervention, moving to monthly follow-up until senior is ready to move into mainte-nance stage, which lasts for about 3 months	**Intervention:** 8 sessions **Follow-up:** 3–6 telephone contacts	**Intervention:** 3 face-to-face visits and 3–6 telephone contacts over a 3–6-month period. **Follow-up:** No particular follow-up indicated
Time frame	Short term	Short term	Short term
Training	Free, online 2–3 day course at cost of approximately $750 per participant Specific training on PST and BA is an additional cost of approxi-mately $1,000 per participant	Free, online Offers classes at a cost of $395 per person	Free consultation Training package of $3,000 plus travel expenses from Houston includes program manual, training DVD; on-site train-ing at organization

BA = behavior activation; DCM = depression care manager; GDS = Geriatric Depression Scale; Healthy IDEAS = Identifying Depression, Empowering Activities for Seniors; IMPACT = Improving Mood-Promoting Access to Collaborative Treatment; PEARLS = Program to Encourage Rewarding Lives for Seniors; PHQ-9 = Patient Health Questionnaire 9; PST = problem solving therapy.

All of these programs are excellent and share the strengths that have been delineated earlier; they all also share some common limitations, which will be relevant to providers of aging service programs. None of the programs was constructed to work specifically in group settings. Although some of these programs have expanded beyond their initial settings, their results with reaching out to congregate settings, such as senior centers, have been mixed. Even when expanded to group settings, the therapeutic work occurs on an individual level and as such necessitates senior centers locating private space for sessions.

Additionally, the programs will not recuperate the costs through traditional reimbursement mechanisms, such as Medicare or Medicaid. Although the mental health programs, the PCPs, and the psychiatrists involved could be reimbursed for their services (and this could be seen as an incentive for their participation), aging service programs themselves are unable to seek reimbursement and, as result, will need to find a source of funding to offset start-up and additional administrative costs. Finally, Healthy IDEAS is the only program that pays closer attention to the importance of education as a way to address stigma and engage older adults in treatment; it is also the only program that integrated into its design the tracking of older adults' knowledge about managing depressive symptoms.

THERAPEUTIC MODELS: PROBLEM SOLVING THERAPY AND BEHAVIOR ACTIVATION

PST and BA are both therapeutic models used within the EBPs discussed previously. Both IMPACT and PEARLS implement PST for clients, whereas all three of the models implement BA.

Problem Solving Therapy

PST, first introduced in 1991 for use in primary care settings, has since found utility in other service sectors. Since its beginnings, PST has been included in numerous evidence-based models. In 2002, PST was included in IMPACT and then again in 2004 in PEARLS. Evaluations are underway to determine if practitioners can employ PST in different modalities, such as over the telephone or via computer-based models in which a counselor would not be required.

PST is based on the premise that there is a strong connection between an individual's depression and being overwhelmed by unsolved problems. Accordingly, this method of treatment assumes that if an older adult can solve his or her own problems, he or she will gain a sense of mastery, which will help to reduce depression. In this approach, the older adult, with the help of the counselor, defines a problem or set of problems to resolve. Together, the older adult and the counselor determine ways in which these problems can be resolved. The older adult is encouraged to meet weekly or biweekly with the counselor to discuss progress toward resolving identified problems. It is a short-term approach, usually lasting from four to eight sessions over a period of no more than 6 months. Each session lasts about 30 minutes.

This treatment method is extremely interactive, with the older adult determining which problem he or she would like to work on each week and then completing weekly homework assignments, which help him or her focus on resolving the problem. It is important that the problem chosen to address in PST be both objective and something that the older adult has the capacity to change. In PST interventions, the counselor does not focus on the past, but rather, specifically encourages the older adult to address current problem areas. In this collaborative process, the ultimate goal is to enable the older adult to apply the PST concepts to his or her daily life long after the formal sessions have ended. Through learning PST techniques, older adults gain a better understanding of how unresolved problems contribute to depressive symptomatology, are better able to delineate their problems and set realistic goals, integrate this approach into daily life, and increase their sense of mastery and control.

The seven major steps involved in implementing PST are available for download on the PEARLS Web site (www.depts.washington.edu/pearlspr) and include:

1. Defining the problem or problems;
2. Articulating an achievable goal or resolution for the problem;
3. Brainstorming multiple resolutions to the problem;
4. Working through the pros and cons of each of these resolutions;
5. Identifying the preferred resolution to the problem;
6. Creating an action plan for how that resolution will be achieved; and
7. Evaluating the outcome.

PST has several advantages as a therapeutic model: it is collaborative, client centered, and brief intervention. All of these factors make PST attractive for use in a therapeutic setting. However, PST is not suitable for everyone. This approach will only work for those older adults who are motivated to participate actively in the therapeutic process and is not appropriate with clients who have some form of dementia. Aging service programs seeking training in PST can obtain it online on the IMPACT Web site.

Behavior Activation, Social and Physical Activation, Pleasant Activity Scheduling

BA and pleasant activity scheduling are easy-to-use techniques that case managers can implement with their older adult clients. Although these techniques often supplement other therapeutic methods, such as PST or CBT, one can also implement them independently. IMPACT and PEARLS both use BA and pleasant activity scheduling in combination with PST. Healthy IDEAS implements BA alone and refers clients to mental health professionals if they require PST or other forms of therapy.

In BA, clients learn to engage in healthy behaviors and to develop better strategies for coping with difficulties. For a more detailed description, you can go to the IMPACT's Web site and sign up for their free online training (www.impact-uw.org). The goals of BA include (Haverkamp, n.d.):

1. Establishing a positive routine for the client;
2. Increasing the number of positive behaviors in which the client engages;
3. Reducing any disruptive avoidance patterns; and
4. Exploring ways in which the client will be distracted from their problems or unpleasant events.

It is important to note that *distraction* is a different concept than *avoidance*. BA teaches one to take positive action. Older adults learn to identify their own avoidance patterns and to engage in behavior that can become more positive. Distraction involves the older adult turning their attention away from unpleasant thoughts or events with the aim of reducing negative feelings. Rather than avoiding difficult life circumstances, older adults learn, through BA, better coping strategies for managing these difficulties. Specific treatment strategies in BA are rating mastery and pleasure of activities, assigning activities to increase mastery and pleasure, mental rehearsal of assigned activities, role-playing behavioral assignments, therapist modeling, and periodic distraction from problems or unpleasant events (Hopko, Lejuez, Ruggiero, & Eifert, 2003).

During the interventions, the older adult creates a schedule of pleasant activities or physical activities in which he or she can easily engage and which he or she can do daily (examples might be reading a good book, talking to a friend, or working in the garden). The case manager can help the older adult to envision himself or herself taking part in this activity through visual imagery. As with PST, it is best for the older adult to select his or her own goals to increase the sense of empowerment and ownership in the therapeutic process. However, if the older adult has difficulty identifying pleasant activities, the case manager can be more active in helping the older adult select them. The case manager and the older adult write down all identified activities and make a connection between the specific activity and the activity's effect on mood. Like PST, BA is typically a short-term technique, which the older adult integrates into their daily lives, so that they can ultimately continue the process on their own, once the intervention has concluded.

HOW DO I PAY FOR AN EVIDENCE-BASED MODEL?

Finding the start-up money to implement these evidence-based models can be time consuming and create a barrier in the implementation of practice. Some tips to locating start-up funds for these models are reviewed here.

Locating Grant Money and Partnership With Academic Institutions

Various federal and state agencies offer grants specifically for implementing evidence-based models in the treatment of older adults. In addition, several foundations or philanthropic organizations offer grants for the start-up costs of these evidence-based programs. Although grants are often time limited, you might find that by receiving one grant, you can find matching funds with other grant makers. For example, this is how the Healthy IDEAS program got its start. Unless your organization has a development office or person dedicated for development and fund-raising, it is probably helpful to create linkages with your local academic institution to collaborate on such a grant.

It also might be helpful to think about funding components of these programs, rather than the models in their entirety. It is unlikely that any one funding source will offer enough resources to cover all aspects of these programs, but, by combining various funding sources, you may be able to fund the total program. IMPACT and PEARLS both include components of care that are billable under Medicare and Medicaid. Unfortunately, the very aspect that might make Healthy IDEAS attractive to a program (embedding the services within routine case management functions) could cause difficulty when it comes to reimbursement because aging programs usually do not bill for counseling services. There will always be a start-up cost; however, once a program is underway, Medicare and Medicaid will reimburse a licensed mental health facility, doctor, or psychiatrist for services.

It is important to highlight that at the current time, it is unlikely that an aging service provider (such as a case management agency, senior center, or Naturally Occurring Retirement Community [NORC]) could fund these programs themselves using federal reimbursement strategies. An aging service program that wanted to initiate an evidence-based program would need to find mental health and/or health care partners in the community to deliver the therapeutic services or obtain a license to provide mental health services within their own service settings.

Locating Federal Funding

Some programs have been able to take advantage of funds available through Titles III-B and III-E of the Older Americans Act of 1965 (Administration on Aging, 2006). These titles provide funding for home and community-based services (III-B) and caregiver services (III-E). Other possible funding sources would be Medicaid (targeted to those in financial need), Medicare (primarily funds serve for older adults), and the Department of Veterans Affairs. An unofficial listing of provisions within the Older Americans Act of 1965 can be accessed on the Administration on Aging's Web site (http://www.aoa.gov/aoaroot/AoA_Programs/OAA/oaa_full.asp#_Toc153957690).

TABLE 2.2   Web Sites to Locate Information on Evidence-Based Programs

Surgeon General—discussion on major funding sources of mental health in the
    United States
(http://www.surgeongeneral.gov/library/mentalhealth/chapter6/sec1.html)

Substance Abuse and Mental Health Services Administration (SAMHSA)
(http://samhsa.gov/grants/)

National Council on Aging (NCOA) web seminar—Money Matters: Funding and
    Sustaining Evidence-Based Depression Programming
(http://www.ncoa.org/calendar-of-events/webinars/depression-money-matters.html)

SAMHSA and Health Resources and Services Administration (HRSA)—way to fund
    mental health programs within primary care
(http://nmhicstore.samhsa.gov/cmhs/ManagedCare/pubs.aspx)

National Institute of Mental Health (NIMH)—funding research on mental health
(http://www.nimh.nih.gov/research-funding/index.shtml)

**Administration on Aging (AOA) resources on current evidence-based prevention
    grant programs**
http://www.aoa.gov/AoARoot/AoA_Programs/HCLTC/Evidence_Based/index.aspx

SAMHSA's National Registry of Evidence-Based Programs and Practices
(http://www.nrepp.samhsa.gov/)

National Council on Aging (NCOA)—Evidence-Based Programs
(http://www.healthyagingprograms.org/content.asp?sectionid=32)

Through Medicaid, some states have been able to access the 1915(c)
Home and Community-Based Services (HCBS) waiver. In doing so, these
states have been able to design specific programs and more specifically
embed evidence-based depression programs in their standard of care. It
is also useful to look for federal grants listed on the SAMHSA's Web site.
Table 2.2 lists several sources to help you locate special funding that might
be available.

EVIDENCE-BASED PROGRAMS ARE EFFECTIVE:
SO WHY USE EASE-D?

As discussed previously, there are several effective evidence-based models
for reducing depression among older adults. However, there is lack of evidence base when it comes to programming specifically targeted for use
within senior and community centers. Although EBPs, such as IMPACT,
PEARLS, and Healthy IDEAS encourage implementation in various programs, dissemination of these models into community-based settings is still

in its infancy. Most of the programs use therapeutic techniques for individual older adults, where senior and community centers promote group programming. Finally, there is little emphasis on the role of education and referral in these models, both of which are central functions of senior and community centers. Clearly, there is a need to develop innovative mental health models for use specifically within senior and community centers.

EASE-D is useful in filling the void that currently exists within evidence-based programming. Its model of mental health education, depression screening, and linkage to treatment can work in conjunction with the evidence-based programs described previously or can be implemented beneficially as an independent program. Unlike the evidence-based programs described earlier, EASE-D maintains a flexible approach to meet the needs of particular communities. Another significant advantage of the EASE-D model is the resource sharing it engenders between the aging service, mental health, and health care sectors to meet the mental health needs of older adults; such partnerships are increasingly essential as agencies struggle with the need for innovative programming and a concurrent lack of funds for implementation. Furthermore, EASE-D is a natural fit within senior center programming that continues to embrace concepts of health and wellness to foster successful aging among its members.

REFERENCES

Administration on Aging. (2006). *Unofficial compilation of the Older American's Act of 1965: As amended in 2006* (Public Law 109-365). Retrieved May 16, 2010, from http://www.aoa.gov/aoaroot/AoA_Programs/OAA/oaa_full.asp#_Toc153957690

American Psychological Association Presidential Task Force on Evidence-Based Practice. (2006). Evidence-based practice in psychology. *American Psychologist, 61,* 271–285.

Anastas, J. (2000). *Research design for social work and human services*. New York, NY: Columbia University Press.

Ayalon, L., Areán, P., Linkins, K., Lynch, M., & Estes, C. L. (2007). Integration of mental health services into primary care overcomes ethnic disparities in access to mental health services between black and white elderly. *American Journal of Geriatric Psychiatry, 15,* 906–912.

Bartels, S. (2008). *Effective programs to treat depression in older adults: Implementation strategies for community agencies* [PowerPoint slides]. Retrieved March 2, 2010, from www.prc-hanconferences.com/docs/2008-Day_1_Bartels.pdf

Center for the Study and Prevention of Violence. (n.d.). *Blueprints for violence prevention*. Retrieved March 2, 2010, from www.colorado.edu/cspv/blueprints

Cochrane, A. L. (1972). *Effectiveness and efficiency: Random reflections on health services*. London: Nuffield Provincial Hospitals Trust.

The Cochrane Collaboration. (2010). Retrieved March 2, 2010, from http://www.thecochranelibrary.com/view/0/index.html

Ciechanowski, P., Wagner, E., Schmaling, K., Schwartz, S., Williams, B., Diehr, P., et al. (2004). Community-integrated home-based depression treatment in older adults: A randomized controlled trial. *Journal of the American Medical Association, 291*(13), 1569–1577.

Cooney, S. M, Huser, M., Small, S., & O'Connor, C. (2007). *Evidence-based programs: An overview. What works, Wisconsin - Research to practice series.* Retrieved March 2, 2010, from www.uwex.edu/ces/flp/families/whatworks_06.pdf

de Vaus, D. (2001). *Research design in social research.* Thousand Oaks, CA: Sage Publishing, Ltd.

Ell, K. (2006). Depression care for the elderly: Reducing barriers to evidence-based practice. *Home Health Care Services Quarterly, 25*(1–2), 115–148.

Felner, R. L., Favazza, A., Shim, M., Brand, S., Gu, K., & Noonan, N. (2001). Whole school improvement and restructuring as prevention and promotion: Lessons from STEP and the project on high-performance learning communities. *Journal of School Psychology,* 39, 177–202.

Fixsen, D. L., Naoom, S. F., Blase, K. A., Friedman, R. M., & Wallace, F. (2005). *Implementation research: A synthesis of the literature.* Tampa, FL: University of South Florida, Louis de la Parte Florida Mental Health Institute, The National Implementation Research Network.

Haverkamp, R. (n.d.) *Treatments: Behavior activation.* Retrieved from IMPACT: Evidence-Based Depression Care Web site: www.impact-uw.org

Hopko, D. R., Lejuez, C. W., Ruggiero, K. J., & Eifert, G. H. (2003). Contemporary behavioral activation treatments for depression: Procedures, principles, and progress. *Clinical Psychology Review, 23*(5), 699–717.

Hunkeler, E., Katon, W., Tang, L., Williams, J. W., Jr., Kroenke, K., Lin, E. H. B., et al. (2006). Long term outcomes from the IMPACT randomized trial for depressed elderly patients in primary care. *British Medical Journal, 332*(7536), 259–263.

The Iowa Consortium for Substance Abuse Research and Evaluation. (2003). *Evidence-based practices: An implementation guide for community-based substance abuse treatment agencies.* Retrieved March 2, 2010, from http://www.uiowa.edu/~iowapic/files/EBP%20Guide%20-%20Revised%205-03.pdf

Kyler, S. J., Bumbarger, B. K., & Greenberg, M. T. (2005). *Technical assistance fact sheets: Evidence-based programs.* University Park, PA: Prevention Research Center, The Pennsylvania State.

New Freedom Commission on Mental Health. (2003). *Achieving the promise: Transforming mental health care in America. Final report* (DHHS Pub. No. SMA-03-3832). Rockville, MD: Author.

New York State Office of Mental Health. (2008). Commitment to quality: 2004–2008. In *Statewide comprehensive plan for mental health services 2004–2008* (p. 10). Retrieved May 15, 2010, from http://www.omh.state.ny.us/omhweb/Statewideplan/2004/5070408Chapter01.htm

Quijano, L. M., Stanley, M. A., Petersen, N. J., Casado, B. L., Steinberg, E. H., Cully, J. A., et al. (2007). Healthy IDEAS: A depression intervention delivered by community-based case managers serving older adults. *Journal of Applied Gerontology, 26*(2), 139–156.

Rubin, A., & Babbie, E. (2001). *Research methods for social work* (4th ed.). Belmont, CA: Wadsworth.

Sackett, D., Rosenberg, W. M, Gray, J. A., Haynes, R. B., & Richardson, W. S. (1996). Evidence based medicine: What it is and what it isn't. *British Medical Journal, 312,* 71–72.

Salzberg, A. (1999). Removable selection bias in quasi-experiments. *The American Statistician*, 53,103–107.

Snowden, Steinman, & Frederick. (2008). Treating depression in older adults: Challenges to implementing the recommendations of an expert panel. *Preventing Chronic Disease*, 5(1). Retrieved May 15, 2010, from http://www.cdc.gov/pcd/issues/2008/jan/07_0154.htm

Substance Abuse and Mental Health Services Administration's National Registry of Evidence-based Programs and Practices. (n.d.) Retrieved May 15, 2010, from http://www.nrepp.samhsa.gov

Substance Abuse and Mental Health Services Administration's National Registry of Evidence-Based Programs and Practices. (2008). *Quality of research*. Retrieved March 2, 2010, from http://www.nrepp.samhsa.gov/review-quality.asp

Thompson, L. W., Gallagher, D., & Breckenridge, J. S. (1987). Comparative effectiveness of psychotherapies for depressed elders. *Journal of Consulting and Clinical Psychology*, 55(3), 385–390.

Trochim, W. M. (2006). *The research methods knowledge base* [Electronic version]. Retrieved May 22, 2010, from http://www.socialresearchmethods.net/kb/

Williams-Taylor, L. (2007). *Evidence-based programs and practices: What does it all mean?* Published by Children's Services Council of Palm Beach County. Retrieved March 2, 2010, from http://cache.trustedpartner.com/docs/library/000238/EBP_Meaning.pdf

3

Educating About Depression: Approaches for Older Adults, Their Service Providers, and Community Members

"WHAT IS DEPRESSION, ANYWAY?"

It is 10:30 a.m. at an urban community senior center. A workshop about depression is underway with a group of 15 older adults. Early in the workshop, the workshop leader asks if anyone in the group would describe depression in his or her own words. A flurry of responses emerges.

"Depression is really about feeling sorry for yourself," says one group member. Some other participants quietly nod their heads in agreement. At the same time, others continue to speak up.

"When I was growing up, I was taught to be strong and to just deal with problems on my own. They call it 'depression,' but it's really just when people are weak in the head and let things get to them," says another.

"Look, I'm 82 years old," begins someone else. "Everyone my age has got problems—maybe they're worried about money, or maybe they're sick, or maybe they're lonely. Who wouldn't be depressed if they were dealing with all of that stuff? Isn't it normal to feel depressed sometimes, anyway, especially when you get old?"

"Wait a minute," interrupts another participant. "You see these commercials all the time on television for antidepressants. It seems like they're saying depression is some kind of disease or something and that if you have problems, you're crazy and need pills. I don't even think those things work—they probably just make you crazier."

These kinds of comments are likely to be familiar to anyone who has ever worked with older adults and broached the topic of depression. Some older adults believe depression is the result of a personal weakness that can be overcome through sheer willpower. Some may view it as the natural inheritance of late life, an expected consequence of growing older. Many older adults feel that depression is an effect of age-related health problems and is not, therefore, a real difficulty in its own right. Furthermore, many older adults are concerned about the possibility of a negative result from treatment, especially from psychotropic medications. Older adults' misunderstandings about depression, coupled with embarrassment and fear about acknowledging emotional difficulties, make addressing their mental health needs challenging. Engaging older adults in a productive discussion about mental health, although difficult, can be their first step in helping them improve their general well-being.

This chapter will highlight the role of education as a key component in the early identification of older adults at risk for depression. The model of mental health education in Educating About and Screening Elders for Depression (EASE-D) includes (a) the provision of interactive workshops for elderly members of community aging service agencies, such as senior and community centers and (b) depression screening. Although most of this chapter will focus on the role of mental health education for older adults, it will also highlight the importance of mental health education in raising the awareness of providers of aging services, health care providers, and members of the general community about depression among older adults. A checklist found at the end of the chapter will guide program staff through the process of planning the educational components of EASE-D.

THE ROLE OF EDUCATION FOR SERVICE PROVIDERS

Although the primary audience for mental health education in EASE-D is older adults, another audience for mental health education also includes providers within the aging service sector, such as program coordinators, case managers, transportation providers, and food service staff. Like older adults, aging service providers are not immune to stigma and can harbor their own misconceptions about depression in older age. Such misconceptions may exacerbate the challenges in identifying depression easily among the older adults they serve. Providers also may have difficulty knowing where to refer at-risk older adults for treatment if they are not aware of the mental health resources in the communities. Staff who provide services to older adults would benefit from mental health education to better understand their own perceptions of depression and aging, to recognize depression symptoms among older adults, and to encourage older adults to accept appropriate treatment. Educational interventions may include in-service and skills-building trainings to identify at-risk older adults and link them to treatment resources.

Wherever possible, it is also helpful to provide outreach and education to the health care professionals serving older adults, including primary care physicians, who will likely be the first to diagnose and treat clinical depression among their elderly patients. Increased knowledge about depression in later life enhances the ability of health care professionals to recognize depression and to provide or refer to clinically appropriate mental health treatment. Primary care physicians can be approached within their own practices using several educational models, including workshops, seminars, and academic detailing, among others.

In addition to aging service providers and health care professionals, community members can be educated to identify and refer older adults at-risk for depression or other mental disorders using the "gatekeeper" model of early identification. Educational methods for aging services providers, health care professionals, and community gatekeepers will be discussed in more detail in later sections of this chapter.

HEALTH AND MENTAL HEALTH LITERACY

A person's ability to comprehend information about health, illness, and resources for treatment or for maintaining their health is generally understood as *health literacy*. Research shows that older adults with insufficient levels of health literacy are more likely to have poorer outcomes in both their physical and mental health (Wolf, Gazmararian, & Baker, 2007). Despite these findings, health education for older adults focused on mental health has not proliferated. Although there have been some efforts to address mental disorders among older adults through the implementation of mental health education programs (Pratt, Schmall, Wilson, & Benthin, 1992; Schimmel-Spreeuw, Linssen, & Heeren, 2000), relatively more interventions targeting older adults' physical health, rather than mental health, are described in the literature.

Health education focusing on mental disorders, such as depression, aims to increase older adults' *mental health literacy*. Similar in concept to health literacy, mental health literacy is commonly described as "knowledge and beliefs about mental disorders which aid in their recognition, management or prevention" (Jorm et al., 1997, Introduction, para. 1). Increasingly, mental health literacy is understood to influence whether people are able to recognize mental disorders and to seek help for them (Chang, 2008). We believe that information about mental health can and should be an instrumental component of health education for older adults. Such information contributes to older adults' understanding of mental health as a vital component of their general well-being, functional capacity, and ability to age successfully.

Engaging older adults about their mental health and providing them with accurate, accessible information about depression and its treatment not only improves mental health literacy but also breaks down the barriers preventing at-risk older adults from reaching out for help. The mental health education model in EASE-D heightens older adults' awareness of the signs and symptoms of depression, increases their understanding of the various types and efficacies of depression treatment, and encourages older adults to participate in mental health screening and connect to evaluation and treatment services.

EDUCATING OLDER ADULTS ABOUT DEPRESSION

In a study conducted in the United Kingdom, researchers determined that ethnically diverse older adults largely believe depression to be the result of the physical and social challenges associated with aging and tend to attribute a person's depression symptoms to personal weakness, rather than to a diagnosable and treatable illness (Lawrence et al., 2006). Research from Australia also indicates that older adults typically have lower levels of mental health literacy than younger people and generally are more likely to associate mental disorders with personal flaws and less likely to recognize symptoms of mental illnesses (Farrer, Leach, Griffiths, Christensen, & Jorm, 2008). Additionally, in a study of the relationship between core beliefs and the ability to acquire new health-related information, researchers found that older adults struggle most with learning information that directly contradicts their previously held convictions about the health condition in question (Rice & Okun, 1994).

Because many older adults erroneously associate depression with the natural process of aging or to an internal character defect, it is helpful for educational interventions to address such beliefs, as well as to provide accurate information about depression and its treatment. Moreover, to encourage optimal engagement with information about mental disorders and their treatment, it is essential to align the structure and content of mental health education to the learning needs and preferences of older adults as much as possible.

DIFFERENT APPROACHES TO MENTAL HEALTH EDUCATION

Choosing the format for mental health education for older adults is dependent on various factors including, but not limited to, the learning needs and preferences of older adults, the personnel and other resources available to provide educational interventions, and the amount of time and space available to administer programs within any given site. Possibilities for designing mental health education interventions include both didactic and experiential approaches that may be adapted to the learning needs of the targeted community.

We have explored different approaches to mental health education throughout the development and implementation of EASE-D. Two of the approaches we have implemented include (a) playing psychoeducational games and (b) didactic presentations combined with group discussion and feedback. Each of these approaches has aspects to recommend them, as well as potential limitations, which will be discussed next.

Psychoeducational Games

In the first phases of designing EASE-D, we provided education for older adults in a familiar and entertaining format, believing this would be a nonstigmatizing approach to depression, a subject that older adults might feel particularly uncomfortable discussing directly. During its pilot phase, the mental health education session took the form of playing a psychoeducational game called Feel Good Bingo, originally developed by Screening for Mental Health, Inc. Played in a manner similar to traditional bingo, this game provides information about the signs and symptoms of depression and the contexts in which depression may occur. In addition to symptoms, the game highlights information about mental health services and the types of treatments available for depression. Because traditional bingo is virtually universally popular at the senior centers in which we work, the psychoeducational version of the game was a natural vehicle with which to engage older adults in a discussion about mental health (more information about Feel Good Bingo can be found on the Screening for Mental Health, Inc., Web site at http://www.mentalhealth-screening.org/events/ndsd/conduct_materials.aspx).

This format proved to be very popular and seemed to increase older adults' comfort with learning about depression. However, we eventually observed that many older adults were more focused on winning the bingo game than they were on exploring the topics of depression and mental health. Upon evaluating program data obtained through the administration of a pretest and a posttest before and after the game-playing session, we found that older adults were not demonstrating a significant change in their level of knowledge about depression and its treatment (for more information about program evaluation, refer to chapter 7, "Developing Program Evaluation Tools"). It soon became clear that a different educational intervention would be needed to support the program's goals.

Interactive Psychoeducation

Once we realized that the bingo game did not significantly improve older adults' mental health literacy, we adjusted our approach and created an educational intervention which resembled more traditional group psychoeducation. The critical elements of this secondary model include (a) an interactive workshop conducted by a group leader with mental health expertise and (b) the opportunity for participants to discuss the workshop material with the group leader and with each other, which the game-playing approach did not easily allow.

These adjustments made were in keeping with research findings that older adults prefer to learn health-related material in structured learning environments with a qualified person leading the discussion and significant peer interaction (Van Wynen, 2001). Unlike the game approach, which did not allow for instructional improvisation because of its structured approach, the revised educational format provided workshop leaders with the opportunity to tailor the workshop content to address the issues specifically brought up by each unique group of participants. Additionally, this new depression workshop enabled us to better engage older adults about their particular beliefs regarding mental health and mental illness. Consciousness-raising of this sort has been identified as an essential component of education seeking to help older adults change their health behaviors (Burbank, Padula, & Nigg, 2000).

For example, the workshop specifically addresses misconceptions older adults may have about depression, particularly with regard to the aging process. During the workshop, we engage older adults in a discussion about the role of depression in aging and particularly emphasize the point that depression is not normal in older age. The general content of the interactive workshop on depression also includes information about:

- Symptoms of depression;
- Risk factors associated with depression;
- Effective treatment options;
- Resources for treatment; and
- Self-care activities.

During the workshop, we also provide older adults with educational material summarizing the key points covered during the workshop so that they can review it again at their leisure and also distribute it to family members or friends (for more information about creating educational materials for older adults, refer to chapter 6 under "Educational Materials for Older Adults").

At first, the group psychoeducation model presented some challenges for recruitment. The workshop was explicitly marketed as a group discussion and did not initially draw as many participants as the bingo game. Unlike the bingo game, for which older adults readily signed up to participate, we often had to provide on-the-spot recruitment for the workshop. However, once the workshop got underway, this format proved to be equally as engaging to older adults as the bingo game had been. Older adults enjoyed taking part in an active discussion with the group leader and with each other, and many expressed their appreciation for the information and experience. Upon evaluation, this intervention also proved to be significantly more effective in increasing older adults' knowledge about depression and its treatment. Because of its success, this model became our main method of providing mental health education within EASE-D.

OTHER EDUCATIONAL APPROACHES

Other educational approaches may be suitable for older adults, particularly when considering the cultures of older adults being served. For example, in the early stages of program implementation, we began to work extensively in the Chinese community of New York City. The need to develop a model to work with this particular group of older adults became apparent after we convened a meeting of stakeholders in the Chinese community to determine an effective educational approach.

These stakeholders, all service providers working directly with Chinese older adults, alerted us that the bingo game format we were using with other groups would likely not suffice as an educational tool, because bingo was not a common activity in the senior centers serving Chinese older adults. Additionally, many stakeholders reflected that Chinese older adults experience depression differently from other groups of older adults, and we would need a different approach when designing our educational activities. They also emphasized that Chinese older adults with depression are more likely to experience physical symptoms associated with depression or difficulties with their family relationships, rather than the persistent feelings of sadness and lack of interest in pleasurable activities commonly described as the cardinal symptoms of depression. Finally, stakeholders felt that a singular focus on mental health would be difficult to market to older adults and that recruitment would be challenging as a result.

With consideration for all of these factors, the educational intervention about depression developed for Chinese older adults included psychoeducation with a particular focus on physical health and emotional well-being. The workshop developed included a combination of storytelling elements, as well as didactic presentations by the group leader, accompanied by group discussion. The storytelling workshop, delivered by a bicultural, bilingual Chinese social worker, recounted the story of a fictional Chinese older adult struggling to manage a chronic physical illness along with troubling emotional symptoms, all of which resulted in isolation from family and friends. Throughout the story, participating older adults were engaged in discussion about the difficulties faced by the older person in the story, and information about the relationship between chronic illness and depression was woven in throughout.

This storytelling example is just one approach that aging service programs may take. It is important to tailor your approach to the culture and learning needs of the intended audience. Programs with space and audiovisual equipment may choose to include special videos or DVDs about depression as part of your program about health and wellness. For example, at the request of one senior center director in the Chinese community, we adapted our usual workshop to include an electronic slide presentation. Although our approach usually does not incorporate slides, the director felt that using them would underscore the seriousness of the topic and would lend credibility to the presentation for those who attended, and indeed, this approach was successful.

SINGLE SESSION VERSUS MULTISESSION WORKSHOPS

Although the initial implementation of EASE-D entailed delivering a single, interactive workshop focused on clinical depression offered once at any given senior center, the response from both participating older adults and aging service program directors was positive enough to encourage the development of additional mental health education sessions. As we shifted our model from the game-playing format to a more traditional psycho-educational approach, we found that many participating older adults not only demonstrated gains in knowledge on the pretest and posttests but also approached the workshop leaders to remark on their enjoyment of the workshop and to comment on how much they felt they had learned.

Eventually, we began to notice how often group participants would ask questions at the end of depression workshops, such as, "When are you coming back again?" or "I have a friend who would love to hear this information—when can I tell her to see you?" Additionally, during the workshops, older adults commonly asked questions about depression that also indicated their other concerns about mental health, such as "Is depression the same as anxiety?," "Can depression cause dementia?," or "Can medications make you depressed?" It seemed that the explicit focus on depression as a legitimate health subject gave permission for older adults to express their interest in the material and to ask for even more information about mental health.

At the same time, many senior center directors noticed older adults enjoying the educational activities, and they began to ask for repeated workshops. Many were concerned that no single workshop, no matter how successful, could reach as many members as they would wish; many wanted to have additional opportunities to help more older adults access mental health–related information. We also believed that having more opportunities to engage with older adults about mental health would create increased trust in the workshop presenters and would encourage greater numbers of older adults to engage in the depression screening offered at the conclusion of the workshop. The repeated requests for additional sessions led to the creation of a series of health workshops focused on mental health and wellness.

DEVELOPING A MULTISESSION WORKSHOP SERIES

Depending on available resources, programs implementing EASE-D might begin by developing a single mental health workshop focusing on clinical depression as a pilot before embarking on a larger workshop series. Additionally, providers may find it helpful to survey their elderly members to see what other mental health topics may be of interest before they develop additional workshops (more information about program development and using surveys can be found in chapter 7 under "Conducting a Programmatic Needs Assessment"). Older adults who participate in the depression workshop should be asked what other topics may interest them. Other key groups such as members of the senior center advisory council or other peer leaders can be valuable sources of advice as you develop your workshop series. You might also consult community stakeholders, such as social service and mental health providers for their guidance, as well.

In our mental health education series, we generally offer each senior center several different workshops. The list of workshop offerings has changed from year to year, based on the feedback received from older adults and aging services providers. Although new workshops are often in development and workshop offerings may change from year to year, the program includes several established topics that are regularly available.

The workshop topics we typically include in a series are:

- Depression;
- Stress and anxiety;
- Memory loss; and
- Medication safety.

When designing your own workshop series, consider weaving mental health–related content into classes which incorporate information about physical health topics. A workshop about maintaining wellness in older age, for example, can include an educational component about the mental health benefits of regular physical activity, such as reduced depression and anxiety. Such an approach may attract greater numbers of participants and help cement the link between mental health, physical health, and general well-being. Depression screening could also be included as part of wellness-related classes, as well.

Each provider should consider various factors before they determine the number of workshops to give or the particular topics, other than depression, that are addressed. Important factors include the needs of a particular community of older adults, the personnel available to provide the program, and the costs associated with program development and implementation. EASE-D is best implemented by coalitions of stakeholders within the aging and mental health service sectors, so consultations with community partners to determine resources is especially important to program development and expansion.

Programs implementing a multisession mental health workshop series do not need to offer a specific number of sessions. However, conducting a minimum of two to three workshop sessions will not only provide older adults with more information than a single session on depression but also may have the added benefit of increasing older adults' trust of workshop leaders. More contact with workshop leaders, we have found, increases older adults' potential to participate in the depression screening that follows the workshop.

MARKETING A MENTAL HEALTH WORKSHOP

Whatever the method of instruction, the most effectively designed program of mental health education only works if older adults actually attend. Many providers of aging services are acutely aware of the challenges in recruiting older adults to participate in mental health education. Often, the concern about stigma is so great that program staff are reluctant even to mention the words "mental health" or "depression" to the older adults they serve for fear of discouraging workshop attendance. Providers working with older adults may also experience the effects of stigma and feel reluctant to market mental health workshops directly because of their own discomfort with the material being covered.

It may be helpful for aging service providers to remember that mental health education is *health* education focusing on the mind and includes information about the ways in which thoughts, feelings, and behaviors either support or hinder an older adult's well-being. By providing mental health education in the first place, and advertising it openly in the second, aging services organizations can send older adults the valuable message that mental health is worthy of discussion and is as important to well-being as is physical health.

We recommend that aging services organizations advertise mental health education in a manner similar to any other health education programs they offer, including providing information about the mental health workshops in the organization's calendar or newsletter, posting flyers to advertise the workshops, and using verbal announcements to draw attention to the program offerings. Given the sensitivities about mental health for both older adults and their service providers, it may be helpful to market the workshops without an explicit focus on mental disorders in the outreach material. Because mental health conditions have various emotional as well as physical symptoms and occur in various contexts, aging service providers may be able to use alternative titles for each workshop.

Truth in advertising is important; however, you also need to be appropriately creative in your approach to encourage participation. Titles of workshops should capture the essence of the particular mental health concept to be discussed, even if particular symptoms or mental disorders are not explicitly mentioned. For example, a workshop about depression may be entitled *Understanding the Blues*, or *How Our Emotions Affect Our Well-Being*. A workshop focused on anxiety may be marketed as *Understanding and Managing Stress*. A multisession workshop series about mental health may be entitled *The Emotional Wellness Workshop Series*. Advertising workshops with a dual health and mental health focus may be somewhat more straightforward—for example, a workshop about Alzheimer's disease or dementia could simply be titled *Memory Loss* (for more information about how to develop effective marketing materials, refer to chapter 6 under "Outreach Material for Older Adults"). At the beginning of each workshop, the leader should be sure to make an immediate connection to the workshop title and the purpose and outline of the workshop, so that participants do not feel confused or misled by the advertising. Once the workshop has begun, stigma can be addressed by calling depression, or any other mental disorder, explicitly by its name, avoiding euphemisms, which may downplay the seriousness of the condition or which may inadvertently convey the idea that mental disorders are shameful and should not be discussed openly.

RECRUITING PARTICIPATION

Schedule the workshops enough in advance to allow time for the program staff to recruit participating older adults. When staff are generally enthusiastic and encouraging about the mental health workshops, participation tends to be greater, particularly if staff have ample time to remind older adults about upcoming events. Additionally, if program staff are particularly concerned about certain older adults who they suspect may be with depression, they can also use the additional time before the workshop to encourage those individuals to attend. However, workshop attendance should be completely voluntary; no one should feel compelled to participate if they do not wish to do so.

Generally, we do not set group minimums or maximums when planning the workshops. Groups have been conducted successfully with as few as 5 participants and as large as 30 or more. However, our experience leads us to believe that groups are ideally sized somewhere between 10 and 20 participants. Groups of these sizes offer more opportunities for peer interaction and often permit a greater diversity of opinions and knowledge to be shared among participants. If interest in a particular workshop is significant, it may be helpful to preregister participants to guarantee a space in the workshop for all of the older adults who are interested. If a workshop looks as if it will be overcrowded, it may be beneficial to schedule additional sessions of that particular topic to ensure maximum participation within a particular organization.

If attendance is lackluster for a given workshop, it may be necessary to recruit participation on the day of the event. Workshop leaders and other staff should make announcements about the workshop early in the day and should be available to answer any questions older adults may have about the event. During on-the-spot recruitment, some older adults may state they are not interested or may express their concerns about the workshop content. Evidence of concern about the workshops may take the form of statements, such as "I don't need that class, I feel fine," "I don't want anybody getting into my personal business," or "Why should I go to that class? I'm not crazy!"

Strategies to address older adults' concerns include emphasizing that the workshop is a health-related information session related to how thoughts and feelings affect well-being, and clearly stating that no one will be asked to disclose personal information during the group discussion. Staff can also inform older adults that although they may have no particular concerns about their own emotional well-being, the information they learn and share in the workshop may help them to help others in their lives, such as friends and family.

If group leaders have any interesting promotional items to give away during the workshop, these can also be displayed in advance to pique interest. Some aging service programs with which we have worked have also provided extra incentives to encourage attendance, such as holding a special raffle for workshop participants or providing additional items for older adults to take home after they have attended the workshop. Offering refreshments can also help boost workshop attendance.

ADDITIONAL TIPS FOR SUCCESS

Planning successful mental health education sessions will also include creating a conducive learning environment and developing educational resource material to disseminate to older adults during the workshop. Additionally, it will be important to develop effective tools to collect program data to evaluate the effectiveness of the educational interventions. During planning for each of these program components, pay special consideration to those older adults with special language needs or vision impairments.

When preparing the space for a workshop, it is important to focus attention on the following environmental factors:

- **Workshop space.** Is the workshop located in a space that older adults can and will access easily? We have found that in some senior centers, older adults may be unwilling or unable to move from where they are sitting to another location where the workshop will be given. Often, we have chosen to conduct workshops in the senior center's main space, such as a dining room or lobby, rather than a private activity room because of the reluctance of some older adults to single themselves out by being seen going to a mental health related workshop.

  An additional benefit to holding a workshop in a communal area is that older adults who are not ready to fully participate in the workshop can still benefit by listening from the margins of the room. We have often found that older adults who are initially reluctant will actively participate in a workshop when they have the option of joining after the workshop has started in the shared space.

- **Signage.** Consider the use of signage throughout the program site to help guide older adults to the workshop location. In particular, it is helpful to locate signage as close to eye level as possible and to use high color contrast to ensure that older adults with vision impairment are better able to read the signs. It is also helpful for the workshop leader and other involved staff to be available just before the workshop begins to guide older adults to the workshop room or area.

- **Seating and workspace.** In addition to an accessible location, the workshop space requires ample seating and workspace. Chairs and tables should already be set up for participants in advance and should be configured in a manner that allows easy viewing of the workshop leader. Although seating is the most critical element of leading a workshop, tables will also be important if you are going to be administering any type of paper work, such as pretests or posttests and the depression screening tools. If tables are not available, another possible option would be to provide older adults with clipboards so that they will have a surface on which to write.

- **Lighting.** Is there sufficient light in the workshop room or area to promote successful viewing of the workshop leader, other participants, and any distributed paper work or materials? Some older adults with vision impairment are particularly sensitive to glare, so ensuring both adequate light and shading in the room may be especially helpful. If possible, workshop leaders should not stand in front of a window on a sunny day when giving their presentation. Doing so may cause the workshop leader to be silhouetted by incoming sunlight and may make it difficult to be seen by participants.

■ **Sound.** In addition to considering vision impairment, workshop leaders should also remember that some participants might have diminished hearing capacity. If available, workshop leaders should use a microphone to address workshop participants, especially if the group is large and participants cannot easily gather around the workshop leader. Those with hearing impairments can be encouraged to sit closer to the workshop leader so that they might hear the presentation better. Some older adults with hearing impairments may be more comfortable sitting close to the workshop leader, but somewhat apart from fellow participants, to minimize any distraction from cross talk within the group.

■ **Temperature.** It is important to regulate the temperature to ensure participants' comfort. Many older adults are particularly sensitive to changes in temperature and may leave a workshop early if they are too warm or too chilled. Although the temperature of a room may not entirely be in the workshop leader's control, it may be possible to open or close windows or doors to help warm or cool the workshop area.

■ **Language.** Many senior or community centers serve older adults who speak several languages. Remember that workshops are most effective when given in a single language; if your program serves older adults who speak several languages, it is better to repeat the workshop in each of the predominant languages than to use a translator.

In addition to giving the workshops in the language older adults are most comfortable speaking, all signage, outreach, data collection, and educational materials should also be written in the language(s) that older adults most easily read. Resource information should also be written in the same language(s) as the other materials distributed at the workshop (for more information about ensuring the correct translation of documents, refer to chapter 6 under "The Culture and Language of Target Audience of Older Adults").

Be sure to use easy to understand words when discussing mental health–related topics. Avoid the use of jargon wherever possible. For example, when discussing signs of depression, instead of using a clinical term like *anhedonia*, the workshop leader should use more ordinary language, such as "having little pleasure or interest in doing things," to describe symptoms.

When working with older adults who have vision impairments, clarity in giving directions is paramount. Workshop leaders and other staff should be especially sure to introduce themselves when addressing the group and should reintroduce themselves when they work one-on-one with an older adult to administer paperwork, assist with the depression screening instrument, or explain the resources available for evaluation and treatment. Additionally, it is helpful to avoid terms such as "over there," or "over here," when directing an older adult with vision impairment; using directions such as "to your right/left" or using the "clock method," such as "I am to your right at three o'clock," is usually more helpful.

DEPRESSION SCREENING: A COMPONENT OF MENTAL HEALTH EDUCATION

Depression screening is an intervention apart from education, used to identify older adults who may be experiencing symptoms of depression. However, the depression screening process also serves as an additional opportunity to reinforce the knowledge gained during a mental health education workshop. Supporting these educational gains during a depression screening may help encourage at-risk older adults to seek out a mental health evaluation.

For example, when discussing the results of a depression screening with older adults, it can be useful to refer back to information discussed during the workshop, particularly when a referral for a clinical evaluation is warranted. Options for following up on the depression screening can be reviewed using the same framework discussed in the workshop. For example, we might say, "In the group discussion earlier today, someone mentioned that a doctor can be a good source of information about depression. How would you feel about going to see your own doctor to discuss your depression screening?" The continuation of psychoeducation throughout the screening process may help older adults make the link between their knowledge of depression's effects in the abstract and the impact of depression symptoms in their daily lives (for a thorough discussion on depression screening instruments refer to chapter 4 under "What Depression Screening Tools Exist?").

EDUCATING PROVIDERS OF HEALTH CARE, AGING SERVICES, AND COMMUNITY GATEKEEPERS

There have been increasing efforts to help health care and aging service providers better understand how older adults are affected by depression, so that they may increase their ability to identify and assist older adults who are at risk. These professionals are often the first line of defense for older adults with depression, as many older adults visit their doctors on a regular basis and many receive services from community-based organizations, such as senior and community centers.

Formal methods of training physicians to recognize and treat depression have grown over the last decade or more, because the medical profession increasingly recognizes the negative impact of untreated depression on physical health and its impact on health care costs. Although the aging services system may be a natural setting for the early identification of at-risk older adults, there are few models of mental health education specifically designed for aging services professionals. However, mental health training for aging services providers can be provided through linkages with local mental health agencies, particularly if aging service and mental health organizations are collaborating to implement EASE-D. Finally, there are those older adults who are at risk for depression or other mental disorders that are not connected to either the health care or aging services systems, who may be identified by "community gatekeepers," or community members who, during the course of their usual business, come in contact with older adults.

Primary Care Physicians

Many older adults who are initially intimidated by the idea of seeking a consultation with a mental health professional may feel more at ease discussing their depression symptoms with their own primary care physician. Geriatric medical and mental health professionals are also in short supply, necessitating primary care physicians to have at least some training in geriatric mental health (Kaplan, Adamek, & Martin, 2001), because more older adults with depression will be seen by a general practitioner than a geriatric specialist.

Both the health care and the mental health service systems recognize that primary care physicians are usually the first professionals that older adults seek for a mental health consultation; as a result, there have been significant developments in training health care providers, particularly primary care physicians, to recognize depression among their patients. Research indicates that physician education is central to helping primary care doctors increase their knowledge about the depression as well as to gain the skills necessary to effectively identify, refer, and treat patients with depression (Katzelnick et al., 2000; Lin, Simon, Katzelnick & Pearson, 2001).

Physicians have recognized the importance of understanding and recognizing depression and have reported the need for comprehensive training about depression in medical schools and during residency training (Glasser & Gravdal, 1997). Experts have recommended the increased development of continuing medical education (CME) courses to provide an accessible forum to train physicians about depression; such courses offer a particularly useful opportunity to teach physicians about state-of-the-art clinical guidelines for identifying and assessing depression (Kaplan et al., 2001). These courses can increase doctors' knowledge about specific aspects of treatment, including algorithms for prescribing medication, monitoring medication adherence and referring patients with depression for consultations with mental health specialists, when warranted (Yeung, Overstreet, & Albert, 2007).

Different types of physician education about depression include short- and long-term in-service training, academic detailing, and the dissemination of clinical guidelines and toolkits physicians may use to incorporate the identification of depression as a routine component of medical practice. Specialized educational programs have been shown to improve the ability of physicians to recognize depression and have been especially effective for doctors who do not have extensive knowledge about mental health; however, physician education also benefits family physicians who already have significant knowledge about depression (Kutcher, Lauria-Horner, MacLaren, Bujas-Bobanovic, & Karlovic, 2003).

Educational interventions can help primary care physicians communicate more effectively with their patients to solicit information about depression symptoms they may be experiencing (Gerrity, Cole, Dietrich, & Barrett, 1999). Additionally, mental health training can help primary care physicians change their routine behaviors to treat depression successfully, particularly if the primary care setting is equipped with effective practice tools, such as routine depression screening, longer appointments for at-risk patients, and protocols to monitor patients' treatment adherence over time (Brody, 2003; Lin et al., 1997).

In New York City, where we implement EASE-D, the New York City Department of Health and Mental Hygiene (DOHMH) has identified depression as 1 of 10 key health indicators in its public health policy agenda, entitled *Take Care New York 2012* (DOHMH, 2009). In addition to raising public awareness about depression through its public health campaign, DOHMH also provided outreach to physicians to improve their ability to recognize and treat clinically significant depression. As part of its goal to "increase depression screening and effective management by primary care physicians" (DOHMH, 2009), DOHMH developed and disseminated a *City Health Information (CHI)* bulletin entitled *Detecting and Treating Depression in Adults* (DOHMH, 2007). The *CHI* serves as a clinical guideline for physicians to enable them to provide effective depression screening and treatment services, including referrals to mental health specialists, as needed. The *CHI* particularly notes the tendency of many adults in primary care settings, particularly older adults, to lack awareness of the signs and symptoms of depression, necessitating primary care doctors to routinely screen their patients for the illness (DOHMH, 2007). The DOHMH guidelines for the detection and treatment of depression are available for review at the following Web site: http://www.nyc.gov/html/doh/downloads/pdf/chi/chi26-9.pdf.

To support the use of the clinical guidelines disseminated in the *CHI*, DOHMH also began a program of academic detailing about depression to physicians throughout the city, including those practicing within primary care settings. Academic detailing is a procedure in which professionals from within the health care field educate physicians about a particular medical topic. The goal of academic detailing is to promote physician behaviors that are the most consistent with state-of-the-art practice for a given medical issue.

In New York City, the trained detailers disseminating the *CHI* conducted outreach to physicians to promote the practices of routine depression screening, initiation of pharmacologic treatment and medication monitoring, and referral to a mental health specialist when indicated. During the implementation of its academic detailing program, DOHMH conducted outreach to more than 1,400 doctors. More than 60% of primary care physicians visited by academic detailers agreed to use the resources provided, including the *CHI* guidelines for screening and treating depression (DOHMH Office of Public Health Detailing, 2007; for more information about the history and practice of academic detailing and to learn more about academic detailing programs in states other than New York, refer to chapter 6, under "Engaging Physicians to Treat Depression: Academic Detailing").

We were fortunate to be able to synergize our outreach to older adults and providers of aging services with DOHMH's outreach to local area physicians. When we began implementing EASE-D, we conducted outreach to senior centers located within the same neighborhoods as the doctors who received training from DOHMH's academic detailers. We were able to refer at-risk older adults for clinical follow-up with their regular primary care physicians, many of whom had previously been contacted by the academic detailers. During our own follow-up with older adults who accepted referrals, we determined whether doctors conducted further clinical evaluation or made a referral to a mental health specialist. If they did not, we were able to request that DOHMH send an academic detailer to that particular doctor, to increase the opportunity for a better result with future patients.

Despite the documented benefits of mental health education for physicians, research also indicates that overall, education alone does not enable doctors to improve the detection and treatment of depression among their patients. To ensure physician competence in detecting and treating depression, primary care practices will need to be restructured to incorporate key practices, including routine depression screening to patients, providing longer appointments to at-risk patients to provide adequate counseling and treatment services, and increasing the capacity of primary care practitioners to appropriately monitor treatment compliance to ensure optimal outcomes.

Such changes have not yet been universally implemented in primary care, despite the existence of successful evidence-based identification and treatment models. As a result, older adults may not encounter uniformly receptive responses from their doctors regarding their concerns about clinical depression. Although some older adults may receive adequate screening, counseling, and treatment services, others may be frustrated by their attempts to raise this issue with their doctors. Until the routine practice of screening for treating depression becomes institutionalized in primary care, educational programs such as EASE-D may be able to help bridge the gap between at-risk older adults and their physicians.

By educating older adults about depression and screening them for depression, older adults visit their health care providers with a greater level of awareness about their symptoms and their options for treatment. Because of their increased awareness, older adults may become more proactive consumers of medical and mental health services. As one older person with whom we worked told us, "When I went to my doctor about my depression screening, he told me not to worry, because it was normal for me to feel this way at my age. I didn't think that answer was right, so I went for a second opinion, because I don't want to have to feel this way [depressed] any more!"

Education for Providers in the Aging Services Sector

Although the majority of older adults seek mental health consultations from their primary care physicians, they may also discuss their concerns about depression with the providers they encounter in aging services programs. Personnel such as senior center program coordinators, case managers or case assistants can benefit from education about late-life depression, both to help identify older adults who may be struggling with depression and to help link older adults to mental health services, if necessary.

There is minimal information available about formal models of mental health education for providers of aging services. However, educational interventions for service providers can be created to meet several different end goals, ranging from raising general awareness about depression and available treatments, to enabling service providers to screen older adults for depression, link them to treatment, and even to provide depression interventions from within their own program. If aging service providers are collaborating with mental health agencies to implement EASE-D, education for aging services staff could be delivered by the same mental health staff educating or screening older adults for depression.

In-Service Presentations to Build General Knowledge
An efficient way to provide training is through in-service presentations for staff members. Although in-service trainings may be provided during a special training period carved out of the regular workday, they may also be

conducted during staff meeting times, minimizing the time workers spend away from their usual duties. In-service trainings may consist of a single presentation or a series of presentations, depending on the designated educational goals.

At a minimum, in-service trainings can help to raise staff awareness of depression among older adults and provide useful information about how and where to refer at-risk older adults for mental health evaluation and treatment services. If possible, these presentations should be provided on a regularly scheduled basis, because staff turnover may create knowledge gaps within organizations. Additional training on other mental or behavioral disorders can also be incorporated into an in-service training model and can likely be delivered by the mental health agencies that are collaborating on the implementation of EASE-D.

Skills Building Trainings to Implement Interventions

In addition to general in-service trainings, providers of aging services may find it helpful to implement skills building training for staff who work directly with older adults. Skills building trainings can address various training and technical assistance needs. If a provider of aging services is interested in receiving training in specific evidence-based intervention models, such as behavioral activation, it is best to contact those organizations that provide training on those models (for additional information about early intervention models for older adults with depression, refer to chapter 2, under "How Do I Find an Evidence-Based Model and What Will It Involve?").

For other mental health training tailored to meet the needs of specific aging service agencies, skills building sessions can be coordinated through partnerships with local mental health organizations. Mental health providers can train staff about effective engagement techniques, referral strategies, and how to incorporate depression screening into routine service provision. They also may be able to provide ongoing case consultation or coaching services to aid staff in their work with at-risk older adults.

We have conducted both general in-service trainings to impart basic knowledge about depression among older adults, available treatments for depression, and local referral information. We have also trained case managers to engage older adults in depression screening, provide information and referral services and to conduct follow-up with at-risk older adults. Each type of training required consultation with the aging service provider agencies to determine the particular learning needs and to ensure that the intended goals of the training could be easily incorporated into the agency's regular program operations.

We have found that general in-service presentations about depression may take place during single sessions of about 45–60 minutes in length. Skills building trainings require more time to implement and require extending the training session by several hours or conducting a series of two to three training sessions. To ensure that staff successfully implement their recently obtained skills, the initial training sessions should be followed by subsequent coaching and supervision sessions. Such an approach works particularly well when staff providing services to older adults are learning how to implement specific interventions, such as depression screening, into their repertoire of regular services. Multiple training sessions and coaching sessions allow staff to review their success and to troubleshoot difficulties they may experience as they employ newly acquired techniques.

Mental Health Education for Community Gatekeepers

Mental health education for professionals within medical or social service settings is designed to help identify older adults with depression who are already receiving services for other reasons. How, then, can we identify older adults at risk for depression or other mental disorders who are not being seen within health care or aging services? One answer to this question is to provide mental health education to individuals within other community-based organizations and businesses who regularly encounter older adults. These individuals, otherwise known as "community gatekeepers," can identify older adults who are potentially at-risk and refer them to sources of treatment and support.

Perhaps the best known model of mental health education and outreach for community gatekeepers is the one created by the Elder Services program of Spokane Mental Health, a nonprofit mental health organization located in Spokane, WA. Developed in 1978, the Spokane model is designed to help identify socially isolated older adults who may be at risk for mental illness and refer them to a team of professionals who can provide follow-up interventions, such as psychosocial evaluations and mental health assessments, and connect at-risk older adults to clinical and other services, which they may need to live safely within the community.

The Spokane model defines community gatekeepers as people who interact with older adults through their regular courses of business, such as postal service workers, maintenance workers, meter readers, bank tellers, property managers, police and fire department personnel, pharmacy staff, and cable television company workers, among others. These individuals are those who are the most likely to encounter isolated older adults who are not identified within other systems of service provision.

Community gatekeepers are trained to identify key physical, cognitive, emotional, and behavioral signs of mental disorders in older adults and to refer those older adults demonstrating these symptoms to a central intake source within the community. Training for gatekeepers occurs on-site at their regular places of business, usually within a single 60-minute session. The gatekeeper curriculum incorporates various educational techniques, such as the use of manuals and training videos to help participants understand the basics of case finding and making a referral (Florio & Raschko, 1998).

The Spokane gatekeeper model has been studied for efficacy and has been shown to successfully engage isolated at-risk older adults who are not well integrated within health care and other social service settings. Research conducted on this model indicates that the gatekeeper approach is effective in identifying at-risk older adults, who generally are more likely to be women, socially isolated, struggling financially, and are less likely to be connected to a regular health care provider (Florio et al., 1996). Additionally, because of its success, the federal Substance Abuse and Mental Health Services Administration (SAMHSA) has recognized the Spokane model as a "promising practice." More information about the specific components of the model is found on the Spokane Mental Health Web site at http://www.smhca.org and by contacting their Elder Services division directly.

FINAL WORDS ABOUT MENTAL HEALTH EDUCATION

Offering mental health education to older adults, their service providers and to community gatekeepers increases the likelihood of identifying older adults who are at risk for depression. Education for older adults raises their mental health literacy and provides them with an opportunity to learn more about how to effectively treat depression and other mental disorders. It also paves the way for the administration of on-site depression screenings, which can reinforce knowledge gain during educational activities while simultaneously helping to link older adults to mental health services. Mental health education can also equip older adults with the knowledge and tools to seek treatment when needed and to advocate for themselves if they receive an ageist or otherwise inappropriate response to their efforts to obtain help.

Both aging service and health care providers can benefit from education to dismantle any misconceptions they hold about depression among older adults, as well as to help them build the necessary skills to identify and assist older adults who are depressed. Depression education for primary care providers and other health care practitioners can help them better recognize at-risk older adults, particularly if, in addition to learning more about depression, they are also incorporating recommended protocols for the identification and treatment of depression. Mental health education can also benefit providers of services to older adults in community and can raise their awareness of depression among the older adults they serve. Aging services providers can build on the collaborative partnerships they create with local mental health organizations to implement EASE-D to receive specialized training about depression.

Mental health programs, too, can benefit from collaborating with aging services providers. Mental health providers working with older adults in clinical settings may not have had much training in gerontology; in addition, they may not be familiar with the array of community-based services for older adults. Cross-training with aging services programs will broaden mental health providers' fund of knowledge about aging and the important roles aging services programs can play in the lives of their elderly clients to reduce social isolation and facilitate community engagement.

Community gatekeepers, like health care practitioners and social service providers, can also identify at-risk older adults and help them access treatment for depression or other mental disorders. Community gatekeepers, through training, can recognize the signs of cognitive dysfunction and psychological distress among the older adults they encounter during their routine course of business. Providing mental health education to community members can help them to link older adults to sources of evaluation, treatment, and psychosocial support. In these ways, mental health education can help to create a larger safety net for those older adults who may be at risk for depression or other treatable mental disorders.

CHECKLIST FOR PROVIDING EDUCATION TO OLDER ADULTS AND THEIR PROVIDERS

Education for Older Adults

- Designate staff to provide workshops
  - Mental health staff   _____
  - Aging services staff   _____

Workshop Format

- Single session on depression   _____
- Multisession series   _____
  Additional topics for series
    - Anxiety
    - Memory loss
    - Substance abuse
    - Medication safety
    - Other

Educational Approach

- Psychoeducational game   _____
- Interactive psychoeducation   _____
- Additional approach   _____
- Story telling   _____
- Using media   _____
- Other (to be determined)   _____

Learning Environment

- Location
  - Is space accessible?   Yes/No
  - Are tables available?   Yes/No
  - Is signage accurate and legible?   Yes/No
- Lighting
  - Is there adequate lighting in the room?   Yes/No
  - Is glare minimized?   Yes/No
  - Is the workshop leader able to avoid silhouetting?   Yes/No
- Sound
  - Is there a microphone available?   Yes/No
  - Can participants sit close to the workshop leader?   Yes/No
  - Is there space to sit away from the group, to aid hearing?   Yes/No
- Temperature
  - Is the room a comfortable temperature?   Yes/No
  - Are there doors and windows to open/close if necessary?   Yes/No
- Language
  - Is workshop given in language older adults are
    comfortable speaking?   Yes/No
  - Are all materials in the language spoken by older adults?   Yes/No
  - Is the workshop crafted to avoid overly technical jargon?   Yes/No
  - Are verbal directions clear for older adults with
    vision impairments?   Yes/No

Education for Health Care Providers

- Determine which providers will receive outreach:
  - Primary care physicians   _____
  - Family practice offices   _____
  - Geriatric specialists   _____
  - Other   _____

- Materials for providers:
  - General information about implementing EASE-D   _____
  - Toolkit about depression   _____
  - Clinical guidelines for identifying and treating depression   _____

Education for Providers of Aging Services

- Determine who will conduct training:
  - Mental health staff collaborating on EASE-D   _____
  - Other mental health professionals brought in for training   _____
- Type of training provided:
  - In-service training on depression   _____
  - In-service training on other behavioral health issues   _____
  - Skills building training to identify depression   _____
  - Skills building training to provide interventions for depression   _____

Education for Community Gatekeepers

- Determine what model of outreach will be used
  - Spokane model   _____
  - Other   _____

REFERENCES

Brody, D. S. (2003). Improving the management of depression in primary care: Recent accomplishments and ongoing challenges. *Disease Management and Health Outcomes, 11*(1), 21–31.

Burbank, P. M., Padula, C. A., & Nigg, C. R. (2000). Changing health behaviors of older adults. *Journal of Gerontological Nursing, 26*(3), 26–33.

Chang, C. (2008). Increasing mental health literacy via narrative advertising. *Journal of Health Communication, 13*(1), 37–55.

Farrer, L., Leach, L., Griffiths, K. M., Christensen, H., & Jorm, A. F. (2008). Age differences in mental health literacy. *BioMed Central Public Health, 8*(125), 1–8.

Florio, E. R., & Raschko, R. (1998). The gatekeeper model: Implications for social policy. *Journal of Aging and Social Policy, 10*(1), 37–55.

Florio, E. R., Rockwood, T. H., Hendryx, M. S., Jensen, J. E., Raschko, R., & Dyck, D. G. (1996). A model gatekeeper program to find the at-risk elderly. *Journal of Case Management, 5*(3), 106–114.

Gerrity, M. S., Cole, S. A., Dietrich, A. J., & Barrett, J. E. (1999). Improving the recognition and management of depression: Is there a role for physician education? *Journal of Family Practice, 48*(12), 949–957.

Glasser, M., & Gravdal, J. A. (1997). Assessment and treatment of geriatric depression in primary care settings. *Archives of Family Medicine, 6*(5), 433–438.

Jorm, A. F., Korten, A. E., Jacomb, P. A., Christensen, H., Rodgers, B., & Pollitt, P. (1997). "Mental health literacy": A survey of the public's ability to recognise mental disorders and their beliefs about the effectiveness of treatment. *Medical Journal of Australia, 166*(4), 182–186.

Kaplan, M. S., Adamek, M. E., & Martin, J. L. (2001). Confidence of primary care physicians in assessing the suicidality of geriatric patients. *International Journal of Geriatric Psychiatry, 16*(7), 728–734.

Katzelnick, D. J., Simon, G. E., Pearson, S. D., Manning, W. G., Helstad, C. P., Henk, M. S., et al. (2000). Randomized trial of a depression management program in high utilizers of medical care. *Archives of Family Medicine, 9*(4), 345–351.

Kutcher, S., Lauria-Horner, B., MacLaren, C., Bujas-Bobanovic, M., & Karlovic, Z. (2003). Short-term educational intervention improves family physicians' knowledge of depression. *The Journal of Continuing Education in the Health Professions, 23*(4), 239–243.

Lawrence, V., Murray, J., Banerjee, S., Turner, S., Sangha, K., Byng, R., et al. (2006). Concepts and causation of depression: A cross-cultural study of the beliefs of older adults. *The Gerontologist, 46*(1), 23–32.

Lin, E. H., Katon, W. J., Simon, G. E., Von Korff, M., Bush, T. M., Rutter, C. M., et al. (1997). Achieving guidelines for the treatment of depression in primary care: Is physician education enough? *Medical Care, 35*(8), 831, 842.

Lin, E. H. B., Simon, G. E., Katzelnick, D. J., & Pearson, S. D. (2001). Does physician education on depression management improve treatment in primary care? *Journal of General Internal Medicine, 16*(9), 614–619.

New York City Department of Health and Mental Hygiene. (2007). Detecting and treating depression in adults. *City Health Information, 26*(9), 59–66. Retrieved February 15, 2010, at http://www.nyc.gov/html/doh/ downloads /pdf/chi/chi26-9.pdf

New York City Department of Health and Mental Hygiene. (2009). *Take care New York 2012: A policy for a healthier New York City.* New York, NY: Author. Retrieved February 15, 2010, from http://www.nyc.gov/html/doh/downloads/pdf/tcny/tcny-2012.pdf

New York City Department of Health and Mental Hygiene Office of Public Health Detailing. (2007). *Expanded depression detailing campaign 1/22/07–5/7/07.* New York, NY: Author.

Pratt, C. C., Schmall, V. L., Wilson, W., & Benthin, A. (1992). Alcohol problems in later life: Evaluation of a model community education program. *Community Mental Health Journal, 28*(4), 327–335.

Rice, G. E., & Okun, M. A. (1994). Older readers' processing of medical information that contradicts their beliefs. *Journal of Gerontology, 49*(3), P119–P128.

Schimmel-Spreeuw, A., Linssen, A. C., & Heeren, T. J. (2000). Coping with depression and anxiety: Preliminary results of a standardized course for elderly depressed women. *International Psychogeriatrics, 12*(1), 77–86.

Van Wynen, E. A. (2001). A key to successful aging: Learning-style patterns of older adults. *Journal of Gerontological Nursing, 27*(9), 6–15.

Yeung, A., Overstreet, K. M., & Albert, E. V. (2007). Current practices in depression care. *The Journal of Continuing Education in the Health Professions, 27*, S9–S17.

Wolf, M. S., Gazmararian, J. A., & Baker, D. W. (2007). Health literacy and health risk behaviors among older adults. *American Journal of Preventive Medicine, 32*, 19–24.

4

Implementing Depression Screening

As you have seen, all of the evidence-based models in chapter 2 include depression screening as one of their major components, as this is a proven way to identify older adults who are at risk. In Educating About and Screening Elders for Depression (EASE-D), voluntary depression screenings are offered to all older adults who attend mental health education sessions. It is worthwhile to offer depression screenings immediately following depression workshops, because older adults have already engaged in an active discussion about depression, its symptoms, and treatment options. Their raised awareness about depression's impact on health and well-being fosters participation in screening and creates an opportunity to identify older adults who are at risk and to connect them to treatment, if warranted.

This chapter will address using depression screening to address depression among older adults seen in community-based aging service programs, such as senior centers. We will review common concerns about conducting depression screenings, common depression screening instruments used in the general population and those specifically for use with older adults, how to determine which depression screening tools are most useful when implementing EASE-D, as well as how to identify suicide risk among older adults and what should be done if risk is present.

CONCERNS ABOUT DEPRESSION SCREENINGS IN COMMUNITY-BASED SETTINGS

Although conducting screenings can be extremely helpful in detecting older adults in need of services, aging service professionals may not always see the value in such efforts. It is common for them to remark, "Why should I screen for depression? I have a good sense who among my older adults are depressed and in need of treatment." Many of us who first hear of screening tools for depression jump to the conclusion that this could end up being a tremendous amount of work for little payoff. Concerns about depression screening that we sometimes hear from aging service staff who works individually with older adults in the community include the following:

- It will extend the length of my assessment and I do not have the time.
- The older adult will be insulted if I ask them personal questions.
- If I ask these questions, the older adult will become emotional, and then I will not know what to do.
- What if we find out they are thinking of suicide? I am not prepared to handle this.
- My older adult client is already in mental health treatment; do I need to screen them?
- I already know who is depressed; if I have to, I will screen those for whom I think it is an issue.

We will address each concern separately.

It Will Extend the Length of My Assessment and I Do Not Have the Time

Of course, if you ask more questions to someone, you will spend more time speaking with that person. However, most assessment scales for depression take only about 10 minutes to complete, are self-administered, and usually require your active assistance just for those that are most in need. It may not seem obvious, but you might find that uncovering depression that has gone undiagnosed will save you time in the long run, because the older adult with depression who obtains treatment can become more motivated in following your suggestions for care, more involved in programming, and be more pro-active about their own self-care.

The Older Adult Will Be Insulted if I Ask Them Personal Questions

Often aging services staff articulate this concern, but it is likely they are expressing their own discomfort, not necessarily that of the older adults they serve. In our experience, when an older adult does not have depression, he or she quickly answers the questions without uneasiness or indignation. On the other hand, older adults who have depression usually welcome the opportunity to speak with someone about their emotional pain and other symptoms. However, it can happen that older adults with depression, especially if they are harboring serious suicidal thoughts, may feel uncomfortable during a depression screening, at least at first. However, these are the very older adults we are trying to help, so it is worthwhile to try to tolerate any discomfort you or older adults feel during the process. Also, the more experience you have administering depression screening questions over time, the easier this task will become. Moreover, when you provide older adults an opportunity to routinely share their thoughts in a nonjudgmental way, they will become more comfortable about sharing their feelings, as well. Remember, questions about emotional well-being are no more personal than other questions we ask of our elderly clients, such as about their personal finances, ability to care for themselves, or their memory.

If I Ask These Questions, the Older Adult Will Become Emotional and Then I Will Not Know What to Do

Emotional reactions can certainly happen during a depression screening, but one should not interpret them as a problem. In truth, our questions may well elicit an older adult's feelings because the process of depression screening allows older adults to speak openly about their thoughts and emotions. However, this is no more the case than most questions that we ask of our elderly clients.

To gauge how to react to an older adult's emotionality during a depression screening, it might be valuable to think about how you have managed similar situations in the past. What has been helpful with clients that are emotional during your questioning about issues other than depression? Most likely, you have used active and supportive listening as a pivotal intervention to help older adults manage their difficult feelings. This is exactly the type of intervention needed when an elderly client becomes emotional during a depression screening. In fact, many older adults we have worked with have said that it has felt almost therapeutic being asked the questions on the depression screening instrument, because it has allowed them to talk about the circumstances of their lives. This might have been their first and only opportunity to talk to someone about their emotional pain; many older adults have told us how freeing it is to be able to talk to someone who is nonjudgmental and will listen.

What if We Find Out They Are Thinking of Suicide? I Am Not Prepared to Handle This

The possibility of suicide can be extremely intimidating for the person conducting a depression screening. We will be devoting more discussion to the topic of suicide assessment and intervention further in this chapter, and in chapter 5, under "Suicide Risk and Emergency Interventions." However, for now, know that many people, even those who talk about suicide, do not necessarily have an active plan to harm themselves. There are many different reasons that an older adult might communicate their desire to die, without the actually wishing to harm themselves. At times, as older adults reflect on their lives, they may articulate their belief that when their time to die comes, they will be ready for it. Do not confuse reflection on mortality in older age with active suicidal ideation or intent; this can be a product of an older adult's own "life review," a process for which the older adult reviews the events and choices they have made in their life. In fact, life review can be a useful therapeutic technique to use with older adults. In life review therapy, the clinician encourages their elderly client to reminisce as a way to examine, understand, and come to terms with the meaning of his or her own life (McMordie & Blom, 1979).

For older adults who are enduring a significant degree of physical or emotional pain, they might not be conveying their true wish to die, but rather, their desire to be relieved of the pain. Others fantasize about dying or are just hoping they would die to join deceased family members. However, significant preoccupation with death or dying, reported thoughts of self-harm and all statements concerning suicide, and an older adult's desire to take his or her own life should be taken seriously. We will be talking at greater length about how to identify active suicidal ideation later in this chapter (under "Screening Tools for Suicide").

Remember, that although it is potentially daunting to think about discussing suicide with an older adult, if you do uncover a more active ideation through depression screening, you may be instrumental in saving a life.

My Older Adult Client Is Already in Mental Health Treatment; Do I Still Need to Screen Them?

When depression screenings follow mental health education sessions, it is beneficial to invite everyone in the group to participate in depression screening. In this way, you will not single out an individual, making him or her feel self-conscious among his or her peers, and you will identify those older adults previously not known to be depressed. Even if you already know that an older adult is participating in mental health treatment, it is still helpful to screen for depression. A high score on a depression screening instrument could mean that an older adult's treatment is not working adequately, that he or she is not following the treatment protocol correctly, or perhaps that he or she has not been in treatment long enough to experience a clinically significant effect. This information would be important to share with his or her health or mental health provider, so that the provider can revise the treatment plan, if necessary.

Why Should I Screen for Depression? I Have a Good Sense Who Among My Older Adult Clients Are Depressed and in Need of Treatment

Depression symptomatology varies significantly for each individual. People display depressive symptoms all very differently. You may suspect depression if you notice easily observed signs, such as tears or agitation; but at other times, it is not easy to tell who might have depression symptoms. By only screening those with the most blatant symptoms, you will surely be missing those individuals who are better at masking their symptoms. In older adults, symptoms may be unspoken; other symptoms may be obvious but may manifest somatically. For example, changes in sleep or eating patterns may be troubling an older adult, but if he or she does not speak of these, there is no easy way to detect them. It is not possible to detect depression simply by looking at someone or after having a brief conversation with them; the most accurate way to know if someone is depressed is to ask through a standardized depression screening tool.

WHAT IS DEPRESSION SCREENING?

In general, screening is a way to detect illnesses in individuals even before they have been officially diagnosed. It is especially helpful to screen for problems that often go undetected, misdiagnosed, or ignored by individuals, which is often the case for depression among older adults.

So, you might ask why this is helpful for aging service professionals. We know that many times, older adults are not even cognizant that they have a problem. Recognizing depression in older adults is quite challenging because they rarely communicate the emotional symptoms of depression and instead tend to focus on the physical symptoms, such as fatigue, pain, or vague feelings of malaise (Sharp & Lipsky, 2002). Physical manifestations of depression are difficult to diagnose because both the primary care physician and the older adult focus on possible underlying health conditions, often missing the potential cause of depression (Gallo & Rabins, 1999; Gallo, Ryan, & Ford, 1999; Katon, Sullivan, & Walker, 2001). Health care and aging service professionals alike may easily dismiss somatic presentations of depression as a function of normal aging (U.S. Department of Health and Human Services, 1999).

Without building in routine screenings, the depression will often go undiagnosed and untreated, because neither older adults nor their providers are asking about or otherwise discussing it. Depression screening frees aging service providers from having to wait for the older adult to approach them, which is unlikely to happen without prompting. In addition, by building in depression screening routinely after conducting mental health education, people do not feel singled out as having a problem, because everyone is invited to participate. Normalizing detection through ongoing and universal screening, either through implementation of EASE-D or in some other customary agency practice, will become routine to the older adult, just like the regular blood pressure screenings or other health-related screenings are. It is important to emphasize that depression screening does not substitute for diagnostic evaluation for depression. Administering a depression screening tool does not allow you to definitively diagnose a person with depression. Even the best tools give probabilities of depression, and these can sometimes be wrong. Depression screening does enable providers to identify those older adults for whom depression might be a problem and provides a rationale for helping them connect with evaluation and treatment resources in the community.

There are different ways to approach depression screening. One can conduct a universal screening where all older adults in the program are routinely screened. Another method consists of case finding, a more targeted approach. Case finding involves screening a smaller group of people who are at high risk for depression. Although universal screening is more time-consuming because you are covering more individuals, we recommend this approach for screening for depression with your older adults so as not to inadvertently miss anyone that could be at risk. Research yields mixed results in screening for depression; however, generally, universal screenings are more effective than case findings (Freudenstein, Arthur, Matthews, & Jagger, 2002; Morrow-Howell et al., 2008).

It is clear from the research that depression screenings alone are not an effective prevention strategy, unless they include education of older adults (Saver, Van-Nguyen, Keppel, & Doescher, 2007) and follow-up for treatment (Bartels, 2003). Because EASE-D incorporates depression screening as part of a model including mental health education and linkage to treatment services, it is more likely that depression screenings conducted as part of this model will result in a diagnostic evaluation and treatment for at-risk older adults.

EVALUATING DEPRESSION SCREENING TOOLS

There is a plethora of screening tools, so it is important to understand what makes a screening tool effective and how to select the right one from your program. You want a tool that will accurately predict depression, without underdiagnosing or misdiagnosing individuals who are not at risk.

The best screening tool is one that accurately differentiates those with and those without depression. Researchers discuss these qualities as the sensitivity and specificity of the measure. A measure that has good *sensitivity* is one that can correctly identify older adults with depression (the statistical measure will indicate the proportion of actual positives). A measure that has good *specificity* is one that correctly identifies older adults without depression (the statistical measure will indicate the proportion of actual negatives).

Determining Whether an Instrument Is Helpful Using Concepts of Specificity, Sensitivity, Reliability, and Validity

Creators of screening tools employ sophisticated scientific techniques to ensure their utility. The tools are developed not only to be easy to use and understand but also to achieve their goal of identifying at risk older adults. Scientific concepts of specificity, sensitivity, reliability, and validity communicate the quality of the measure. Although a comprehensive discussion of instrument design is outside of the scope of this chapter, it is important to familiarize yourself with these concepts and measures as you decide which screening tool to use within your organization.

Specificity and Sensitivity
Of course, it makes sense to be concerned about the sensitivity of the screening tool, so that you can be sure it is accurately detecting cases of depression. However, it may not be as obvious why there should be a concern over also detecting individuals *without* depression. A person having some of the symptoms of depression may or may not actually have depression. Some of the same depressive symptoms can be caused by vitamin deficiencies, dementia, or another underlying medical condition. Although it might be valuable clinically to identify these problems for referral to a primary care physician, it is important not to label them as depression erroneously. A specificity of 100% indicates that the screening tool is able to detect accurately those older adults that do not have depression.

However, this score alone is not enough to know that the screening tool is useful. We would also need to know the sensitivity of the test to know whether we are also accurately picking up cases of depression. A screening tool for depression will not be useful if it is unable to detect actual cases of depression. If the tool misses many individuals with depression, it would be inefficient to use with older adults in the community. A sensitivity of 100% indicates that the screening tool is able to detect accurately all older adults that do have depression. However, as is the case with specificity, this score alone would not be enough to tell whether this will be a useful screening tool. Taken together, the two statistical tests, specificity and sensitivity, indicate the value of the screening tool. As you consider various instruments, scores for specificity and sensitivity are often available for your review.

Reliability and Validity

In examining different scales, you will undoubtedly come across two other terms, reliability and validity, that are extremely important in determining whether a tool is of good quality. *Reliability* refers to the extent that the results on the depression screening are the same if they are applied repeatedly, assuming that the person's severity on depression has not changed (Rubin & Babbie, 2001). An example of reliability would be if you were to weigh yourself on your bathroom scale at 9:30 a.m. and then return to that scale to weigh yourself at 9:35 a.m. (hoping, perhaps, to see some improvement). The scale would be a reliable measure of your weight, if your weight is the same at both times (even if you are not happy about the results).

Although reliability is important, a reliable measure does not ensure the accuracy of the measure. For a measure to be worthwhile, it must also be valid. *Validity* refers to the extent that the screening tool reflects the "actual concept"; in our case, the concept is depression (Rubin & Babbie, 2001). An instrument can have strong reliability but weak validity. For example, a bathroom scale has great reliability in that it will always give you the same weight, if you have not actually lost or gained weight, but it certainly would not be a valid measure of depression.

Validity is a more complex concept than reliability and, as such, more difficult to measure. There are two broad ways we can categorize how to measure validity: through observation and through statistical analysis. Before going through the rigorous process of proclaiming a measure is valid statistically, it must have strong face and content validity. *Face validity* is concerned with whether a measure seems, at face value, to measure the concept it is trying to capture. In our case, you would want to look at the questions in the depression screening tool. You would say a tool has good face validity if it seems to make sense to you, because all the questions seem to be measuring components of depression. *Content validity* is very similar to face validity, but instead of the measure seeming reasonable to you, it must look good at face value to experts in the field.

There are various ways to assess validity statistically. The more you are able to show validity based on these different measures, the more your measure possesses good construct validity. The ways we demonstrate construct validity is through measures of criterion validity, which includes predictive, concurrent, convergent, and discriminant validity (Nunnally & Bernstein, 1994).

In general, criterion validity compares the measure against some other criterion. The different measures of criterion related validity vary in terms of the specific criterion chosen. A thorough discussion of these different types of statistical techniques is beyond the aim of this chapter. However, concepts of specificity, sensitivity, reliability, and validity are helpful to keep in mind because you are examining various tools that exist. Rest assured that the tools that we will be discussing within this chapter are those that have proven merit based on the measures we have discussed.

WHAT DEPRESSION SCREENING TOOLS EXIST?

There are several excellent screening tools to detect depression among older adults; each has its own strengths and limitations. However, all of the screening tools listed within this chapter have merit. Although there is a great deal of depression screening tools available, we will highlight the ones that are the most frequently used with older adults. We will thoroughly review those tools that can be self-administered with some minor assistance, because these have the most versatility for use in senior and community centers. The tools we will review are:

- Beck Depression Inventory, 2nd Revision (BDI-II);
- Center for Epidemiological Studies Depression Scale (CES-D 20 item);
- Geriatric Depression Scale (GDS); and
- Patient Health Questionnaire (PHQ-9 and the PHQ-2).

At the end of this section we will briefly mention some additional tools you might have heard about but are not self-administered and used more frequently by professionals in clinical settings. Those tools are:

- Hamilton Depression Rating Scale (Ham-D); and
- Cornell Scale for Depression in Dementia (CSDD).

Beck Depression Inventory, 2nd Revision

Dr. Aaron Beck created the BDI in 1961 (Beck, Ward, Mendelson, Mock, & Erbaugh, 1961). It is appropriate to use with anyone older than the age of 13. Originally designed for use by trained health care professionals, over time it evolved into a self-administered tool. This inventory is consistent with the diagnostic criteria for depression in the *Diagnostic and Statistical Manual of Mental Disorders*, fourth edition (*DSM-IV*). There are three versions of the BDI—the original BDI (published in 1961), a revised version known as the BDI-1A (in 1978), and finally, the BDI-II (in 1996). In the BDI-II, an individual answers 21 questions about how they have been feeling in the past 2 weeks. Each question has a set of at least four possible answer choices, ranging in intensity. For example, a question pertaining to mood:

(0) I do not feel sad.
(1) I feel sad.
(2) I am sad all the time and I cannot snap out of it.
(3) I am so sad or unhappy that I cannot stand it.

This is a short screening, usually taking no more than 5–10 minutes. All iterations of the Beck are written at a 5th grade reading level for ease of use (Conoley, 1987). Unlike most of the other screening tools we will review in this chapter, the BDI-II is not in the public domain and the creators charge a fee for its use. As of this writing, the entire kit, the inventory and the scoring sheet, is for purchase for $109 on the Web site: http://www.pearsonassessments.com/HAIWEB/Cultures/en-us/Productdetail.htm?Pid=015-8018-370&Mode=summary. The forms are available in English and Spanish (there is a separate charge for the Spanish version).

How Do I Score the BDI?

The answers on the inventory range on a scale from 0 (*no indication of the problem*) to 3 (*the most extreme indication of the problem*). When scoring, you will find that the higher the total score, the more severe the depressive symptoms. The cutoffs used in the BDI-II indicate that when tallying up the answers to all the questions, a total score of 0–13 indicates minimal depression, 14–19 indicates mild depression, 20–28 indicates moderate depression, and 29–63 indicates severe depression (Beck, Brown, & Steer, 1996). However, these cutoffs differ for individuals already having a clinical diagnosis of depression. A strength of this screening tool is that it can distinguish between different subtypes of depressive disorders, such as major depression and dysthymia.

Is the BDI a Reliable and Valid Tool?

The new addition of the Beck Inventory has proved to be both more reliably valid and clinically sensitive than the original tool (Beck et al., 1996). The BDI-II also demonstrates strong content and construct validity. The BDI-II has content validity (the extent to which items of a test are representative of that which is to be measured) because it was constructed from a consensus among clinicians about depressive symptoms presented by psychiatric patients. At least 35 studies indicate high levels of validity between the BDI-II and other measures of depression (Beck et al., 1996).

Center for Epidemiological Studies Depression Scale (20 items)

Dr. Lenore Radloff developed the CES-D scale in 1977 to be a short, self-administered scale measuring depression in adults (Radloff, 1977). The development of this scale involved taking items from previously used validated scales, which would represent the major components of depression. Components included in the CES-D are depressed mood, feelings of worthlessness, feelings of hopelessness, loss of appetite, poor concentration, and sleep disturbance. The scale does not include items for increased appetite or sleep, anhedonia (loss of the capacity to experience pleasure), psychomotor agitation or retardation (states of overactivity and underactivity, respectively), guilt, or suicidal thoughts. An individual answers 20 questions about how they have been feeling in the past week. Each question has a set of at least four possible answer choices, with increasing degree of frequency. The response categories are listed as 0 = *rarely or none of the time* (less than 1 day), 1 = *some or little of the time* (1–2 days), 2 = *occasionally or a moderate amount of time* (3–4 days), and 3 = *most or all of the time* (5–7 days).

   Similar to other screening tools, the CES-D takes about 10 minutes to complete. The scale is in the public domain; you can reproduce and use the tool without cost and there is no copyright restriction. The instrument is available in multiple languages including Spanish, French, Greek, Japanese, Chinese, Dutch, Korean, German, and Russian. Table 4.1 is a reproduction of the CES-D.

How Do I Score the CES-D?
Scores range from 0–60; the higher the score, the greater the severity of depression. Before summing the scores, you must first reverse score questions 4, 8, 12, and 16. These questions are controlling for bias in the individual responses by placing certain questions in the positive, which then requires reverse scoring. A total score of 16–26 indicates mild depression, with scores of 27 or more indicating major depression (Ensel, 1986; Zich, Attkisson, & Greenfield, 1990).

Is the CES-D a Reliable and Valid Tool?
The CES-D has mixed results in terms of reliability and validity but, overall, has shown to be effective, especially within specific subgroups of the population. Research within the overall population demonstrates good-to-moderate results based on the different ways one can measure reliability (Radloff, 1977). Research demonstrates its reliability within various racial and ethnic groups (African American, Asian, French, Greek, Hispanic, and Japanese; Naughton & Wiklund, 1993). The CES-D also has mixed results when proving validity (DeForge & Sobal, 1988; Gerety et al., 1994; Weissman, Sholomskas, Pottenger, Prusoff, & Locke, 1977). However, it is

TABLE 4.1   Center for Epidemiologic Studies Depression Scale

Circle the number of each statement that best describes how often you felt or behaved this way DURING THE PAST WEEK.

	Rarely or None of the Time (Less Than 1 Day)	Some or a Little of the Time (1–2 Days)	Occasionally or a Moderate Amount of the Time (3–4 Days)	Most or All of the Time (5–7 Days)
During the past week:				
1. I was bothered by things that usually do not bother me.	0	1	2	3
2. I did not feel like eating; my appetite was poor.	0	1	2	3
3. I felt that I could not shake off the blues even with help from my family and friends.	0	1	2	3
4. I felt that I was just as good as other people.	0	1	2	3
5. I had trouble keeping my mind on what I was doing.	0	1	2	3
6. I felt depressed.	0	1	2	3
7. I felt that everything I did was an effort.	0	1	2	3
8. I felt hopeful about the future.	0	1	2	3
9. I thought my life had been a failure.	0	1	2	3
10. I felt fearful.	0	1	2	3
11. My sleep was restless.	0	1	2	3
12. I was happy.	0	1	2	3
13. I talked less than usual.	0	1	2	3
14. I felt lonely.	0	1	2	3
15. People were unfriendly.	0	1	2	3
16. I enjoyed life.	0	1	2	3
17. I had crying spells.	0	1	2	3
18. I felt sad.	0	1	2	3
19. I felt that people disliked me.	0	1	2	3
20. I could not get "going."	0	1	2	3

Source: Modified with permission from *Psychiatric Measures* by A. J. Rush, M. B. First, and D. Blacker, 2000, Washington, DC: American Psychiatric Publishing, Inc. Copyright 2000 by American Psychiatric Publishing, Inc.

specifically useful within specific subgroups; research conducted by Zich et al. (1990) demonstrates the validity of the CES-D with older adults.

There has been criticism of this scale in terms of its content validity. Some questions such as "I feel fearful" and "I feel that people dislike me" are criticized as not being accurate components of depression (Liang, Van Tran, Krause, & Markides, 1989). The CES-D demonstrates good-to-adequate results on construct validity, through examination of its concurrent validity (Gerety et al., 1994). Although the CES-D does have mixed results in establishing reliability and validity, it has been a popular and easy to use screening tool. However, there are a couple of significant limitations in the design of the CES-D, including its lack of assessment of suicidality and its limited focus on symptoms occurring only during the past week.

The screening tools previously mentioned are "first generation" instruments used to quickly assess for depression among the general population. Although they have their merits, we strongly recommend using one of the following two screening instruments with an older population. Both of the following two instruments are excellent and are considered gold standards for use with older adults.

Geriatric Depression Scale

The GDS is the only screening tool developed specifically for use by older adults. Dr. Jerome Yesavage constructed the GDS in 1982 at Stanford University Medical Center. There are two forms of the GDS, a long form (30 questions) and the short form (15 questions), developed in 1986 by Sheikh and Yesavage. The short form was developed by selecting the best (those showing the greatest validity) questions from the long-form version. Both the long and short forms of the instrument are meant to be self-administered. This is an easy to use screening tool with older adults selecting "yes" or "no" option to each of the questions on the tool.

How Do I Score the GDS?
The scores are tallied; the higher the score, the more likely the person is at risk for depression. Scores of 0–4 are considered *normal*, 5–8 indicate *mild depression*, 9–11 indicate *moderate depression*, and 12–15 indicate *severe depression*. The short form is particularly useful for frail older adults, those with mild-to-moderate cognitive impairments, and those that might be easily fatigued by the longer version (Kurlowicz & Greenberg, 2007). It takes from 5–7 minutes to complete. For clinical purposes, a score of more than 5 points is suggestive of depression and should warrant a follow-up interview, whereas scores of more than 10 are usually attributed to depression (Sheikh & Yesavage, 1986).

The GDS is useful in monitoring depression over time—a clinician can readminister the GDS throughout the course of treatment to assess whether the treatment is effective (Brink et al., 1982). This tool is in the public domain with no fee for its use. On the creator's Web site, they have developed an online version, which will give you immediate scoring and recommendations: http://www.stanford.edu/~yesavage/GDS.html. This tool is available in 28 different languages; although the creators cannot guarantee the accuracy of these translations, most come from trusted sources. You can access the following translated tools all on their Web site: Arabic, Chinese, Creole, Dutch, Farsi, French, German, Greek, Hebrew, Hindi, Hungarian, Icelandic, Italian, Japanese, Korean, Lithuanian, Malay, Maltese, Norwegian, Portuguese, Romanian, Russian, Spanish, Swedish, Thai, Turkish, Vietnamese, and Yiddish.

The15-item short scale GDS follows (see Table 4.2). Answers in capital letters are indicative of depression if they are circled.

TABLE 4.2   Short Form of the Geriatric Depression Scale

CHOOSE THE BEST ANSWER FOR HOW YOU FELT THIS PAST WEEK

Are you basically satisfied with your life?	yes	NO
Have you dropped many of your activities and interests?	YES	no
Do you feel that your life is empty?	YES	no
Do you often get bored?	YES	no
Are you in good spirits most of the time?	yes	NO
Are you afraid that something bad is going to happen to you?	YES	no
Do you feel happy most of the time?	yes	NO
Do you often feel helpless?	YES	no
Do you prefer to stay at home, rather than going out and doing new things?	YES	no
Do you feel you have more problems with memory than most?	YES	no
Do you think it is wonderful to be alive now?	yes	NO
Do you feel pretty worthless the way you are now?	YES	no
Do you feel full of energy?	yes	NO
Do you feel that your situation is hopeless?	YES	no
Do you think that most people are better off than you are?	YES	no

Score: _____ (Number of "depressed" answers—ones that are in capital letters)

Is the GDS a Reliable and Valid Tool?

Both the long and short forms of the GDS have undergone rigorous testing among various older populations. In all cases, this has proved to be an excellent tool, highly sensitive and with strong ratings in reliability and validity (Ertan, Ertan, Kiziltan, & Uyguçgil, 2005; Malakouti, Fatollahi, Mirabzadeh, Salavati, & Zandi, 2006; Sheikh & Yesavage, 1986). A telephone version of the GDS also demonstrates strong reliability and validity (Burke, Roccaforte, Wengel, Conley, & Potter, 1995).

Strengths of the GDS

This is an extremely easy to administer tool and has been used extensively. It comes in multiple languages, which older adults can easily complete themselves. It is also in the public domain, allowing open access without a charge.

Limitations of the GDS

Criticisms of the GDS involve its reliance on looking at symptoms within the past week, and its lack of inclusion of a question on suicidal ideation. Although widely used by the public, health care professionals are not as familiar with this tool and, for this reason, has less versatility when trying to connect with primary care (Kurlowicz & Greenberg, 2007).

Patient Health Questionnaire (PHQ-9 and PHQ-2)

The PHQ-9 consists of the nine questions on depression that were originally constructed for the Primary Care Evaluation of Mental Disorders Patient Health Questionnaire (PRIME-MD). Dr. Spitzer, Dr. Williams, Dr. Kroenke, et al. developed the PHQ-9 for use in health care. Although there is no cost to use this screening tool, Pfizer, Inc., holds the copyright and requires permission to use this instrument. MAPI Research Trust, on behalf of Pfizer, Inc., distributes the PHQ-9. For more information about the terms of use for the PHQ-9, visit http://www.mapi-trust.org/services/questionnairelicensing/catalog-questionnaires.

The PHQ-9 is extremely versatile, used for both screening purposes, as well as for use of monitoring the efficacy of treatment (Chen, Huang, Chang, & Chung, 2006; Kroenke & Spitzer, 2002; Löwe, Unützer, Callahan, Perkins, & Kroenke, 2004). The questions directly correspond to the nine symptoms of depression as specified in the *DSM-IV* (Kroenke, Spitzer, & Williams, 2001). In cases where even a briefer screen is preferred, professionals may administer the PHQ-2, which consists of the first two questions of the PHQ-9 (Whooley, Avins, Miranda, & Browner, 1997). If an older adult responds positively to either of these questions, he or she then completes the remaining seven questions. The rationale of first administering the PHQ-2 is that these first two questions represent the cardinal symptoms of depression; if one does not present with either of these symptoms, it is unlikely that depression will be the cause of the other symptoms. This shorter screening can be quite helpful if you are trying to screen a large number of people with few resources. The individual is asked to rate their symptoms in terms of frequency of occurrence in the past 2 weeks; the greater the frequency, the greater the score.

The PHQ-9 is available for use in diverse populations. The instrument has been translated into various languages, including Arabic, Assamese, Chinese (Cantonese and Mandarin), Czech, Dutch, Danish, Finnish, French, French Canadian, German, Greek, Gujarati, Hindi, Hebrew, Hungarian, Italian, Korean, Malay, Malayalam, Norwegian, Oriya, Polish, Portuguese, Russian, Spanish (U.S.), Swedish, and Telugu (The MacArthur Initiative on Depression Primary Care, 2010).

How Do I Score the PHQ-9?

The process of scoring the PHQ-9 is rather straightforward; the differences emerge in the interpretation of the scoring. To score the PHQ-9, one simply adds up the scores within each column, and then, to get the final score, one adds the column scores. For clinical purposes, an individual is unlikely to have depression unless one of the first two questions is checked in the grayed out boxes (more than half the days or nearly every day), regardless of their total score. In general, the higher the total score, the greater the likelihood of depression (The MacArthur Initiative on Depression Primary Care, 2010).

You might find varying interpretations on scoring the PHQ-9 based on whether you are using the instrument as a clinical tool versus a screening tool. For use as a screening tool, we have found the following guidelines to be most helpful: Scores of 5–9 indicate *mild depression*, 10–14 *moderate depression*, 15–19 *moderately severe depression* and 20–27 *severe depression*. In our experience, a score of 10 or greater will warrant an evaluation by a medical doctor or a mental health professional to assess for depression or some other medical condition. Research has shown this cutoff to be the strongest marker for possible depression (Kroenke & Spitzer, 2002).

In addition to scoring for risk, one can also use this tool to measure the individual's response to treatment. Guidelines suggest that a drop of 5 points from the baseline score is an adequate response to treatment, with no change needed to the treatment protocol. A drop of 2–4 points from baseline may warrant some change in treatment and a drop of 1 point, no change, or even an increase in scores, indicates an inadequate treatment response, which definitely warrants a change in treatment strategy (The MacArthur Initiative on Depression Primary Care, 2010). The PHQ-9 in Figure 4.1 is reprinted with permission.

Over the <u>last 2 weeks</u>, how often have you been bothered by any of the following problems? *(Use "✔" to indicate your answer)*	Not at all	Several days	More than half the days	Nearly every day
1. Little interest or pleasure in doing things..	0	1	2	3
2. Feeling down, depressed, or hopeless...	0	1	2	3
3. Trouble falling or staying asleep, or sleeping too much............................	0	1	2	3
4. Feeling tired or having little energy..	0	1	2	3
5. Poor appetite or overeating.................	0	1	2	3
6. Feeling bad about yourself — or that you are a failure or have let yourself or your family down...............	0	1	2	3
7. Trouble concentrating on things, such as reading the newspaper or watching television...........................	0	1	2	3
8. Moving or speaking so slowly that other people could have noticed? Or the opposite — being so fidgety or restless that you have been moving around a lot more than usual..............	0	1	2	3
9. Thoughts that you would be better off dead or of hurting yourself in some way...	0	1	2	3

(For office coding: Total Score _____ = ___ + ___ + ___)

If you checked off <u>any</u> problems, how <u>difficult</u> have these problems made it for you to do your work, take care of things at home, or get along with other people?

Not difficult at all	Somewhat difficult	Very difficult	Extremely difficult
❏	❏	❏	❏

Source: Primary Care Evaluation of Mental Disorders Patient Health Questionnaire (PRIME-MD PHQ), developed by Robert L. Spitzer, Janet B. W. Williams, Kurt Kroenke, and colleagues. Copyright 1999 by Pfizer Inc. Reprinted with permission.

FIGURE 4.1 Patient Health Questionnaire-9

As you can see, an additional item is included in this screening tool. Although not part of the screening of symptoms, Question 10 asks individuals to rate the difficulty the problems make it for them to do work, take care of things at home, or get along with other people (not difficult at all, somewhat difficult, very difficult, extremely difficult). The architects of the PHQ-9 find a strong relationship between this item and quality of life and functional impairment (Kroenke et al., 2001).

In addition to functioning as a screening tool for depression, this instrument can also identify individuals with thoughts of suicide. A positive score of anything to Question 9 ("thoughts you would be better off dead or of hurting yourself in some way") should automatically trigger your organization's protocol for suicide assessment and intervention. If you are using the PHQ-9 and your organization does not have a clearly delineated strategy for working with individuals with suicidal ideation, it is important to put one in place. Specific screening instruments for suicide will be reviewed later in this chapter; however, there is no universally accepted gold standard screening tool for suicide. In spite of this, there are some simple assessment questions that we recommend asking older adults to explore suicidality during a depression screening:

1. **What are your specific thoughts about suicide?** You should find out the content of suicidal thoughts, as well as, when and how often they occur. Has the older adult been experiencing these thoughts for some time?
2. **Do you have a plan for hurting or killing yourself?** Can the older adult articulate specific a plan for self-harm? What method of self-harm is the older adult planning to use? Does the older adult have access to the means of self-harm they wish to use?
3. **Have you ever made any past suicide attempts?** If so, did the older adult receive medical and/or mental health treatment because of the attempt? Does the older adult feel that treatment was effective?
4. **What, if anything, prevents you from self-harm or killing yourself?** This question is very important in determining an older adult's risk. Is the older adult able to articulate a reason for living, or at least, a reason not to hurt or kill himself or herself? Is the older adult able to give verbal assurance that he or she will not harm himself or herself until he or she receives professional assistance?

The goal of asking follow-up questions is to identify suicidal desire, suicidal capability, and suicidal intent and buffers against suicide (Joiner et al., 2007). It is important to assess for each of these domains, for it is not desire alone that should trigger emergency intervention; rather, your decision about how to proceed will depend on an older adult's answer about desire, in combination with any of these other domains. In practice, we use the preceding questions to delineate whether an individual is referred for outpatient counseling, a visit with a mobile crisis team, or to 911. For example, a person that has a desire to die but cannot articulate a plan or has little means to carry out a plan (talks about shooting themselves but does not have a firearm or know how to get one), coupled with buffers in their life that would prevent them from carrying out their plan (religious beliefs against suicide), would definitely trigger a mental health referral but probably not a call to 911.

Discussing the individual's attitude toward suicide is particularly important when working with older adults with diverse ethnic and cultural backgrounds. It is natural for aging service or other professionals to be initially uncomfortable asking these questions, especially for new workers or those who have had little experience in discussions concerning suicide. The more experience one has in asking these questions, the more comfortable and skilled one will become at asking them, even those without formal clinical training. Staff may be concerned that asking questions about suicide could create or exacerbate a dangerous situation for their elderly client, but this is simply not the case. Asking about suicide will not provoke a person into attempting suicide. Often, asking these questions of an older adult who is struggling with suicidal thoughts can offer comfort, because the questions enable him or her to communicate his or her feelings with someone who can offer support and help in a nonjudgmental way. There is more discussion of screening tools for suicide at the end of this chapter.

Is the PHQ-9 a Reliable and Valid Tool?

Both the PHQ-2 and the PHQ-9 have been tested extensively and have been found to be excellent tools in assessing the risk of depression (Cannon et al., 2007; Kroenke & Spitzer, 2002; Löwe et al., 2004; Williams et al., 2005). They have excellent internal reliability in numerous studies and in diverse populations. There are studies validating the usefulness of the PHQ-9 with Chinese adults (Chen et al., 2006), with Asian Indians (Poongothai, Pradeepa, Ganesan, & Mohan, 2009), with Koreans (Han et al., 2008), and of course with older adults (Ell, Unützer, Aranda, Sanchez, & Lee, 2005). Validity of the measure has been shown in comparison to other measures through concurrent validity (Adewuya, Ola, Afolabi, 2006; Kroenke et al., 2001).

Strengths of the PHQ-9

There are many advantages of this screening tool as compared to other screening tools. First, it is the shortest instrument with comparable sensitivity and specificity. It is quite versatile in implementation and can be used through a face-to-face interview, by telephone, or even self-administered. This is one of the only tools that directly corresponds with the criteria for depressive disorders in the *DSM-IV*. It can be used both as an assessment tool and to help in the monitoring of treatment. It has gained widespread use in the medical community. Finally, the inclusion of a question on suicide (Question 9) is indispensable in gauging a person's risk to self.

Limitations of the PHQ-9

Although this is a short screening tool, we have found that the response categories can be confusing for some people to complete without staff assistance. Older adults sometimes struggle with the response categories of "several days" and "more than half the days," because these categories can seem ambiguous. When older adults struggle with these categories, we find it helpful to review them with the older adult, often breaking down the categories into easier groupings. For example, if an older adult were struggling with the response categories in Question 1 we might ask: "Over the last 2 weeks have you had little interest or pleasure in doing things? Yes or no."

If the older adult says "no," we confirm that he or she has not experienced this specific problem at all in the last 2 weeks. If the older adult answers "yes," we go on to see how often this problem has occurred in the last 2 weeks, sometimes breaking it down into the number of days contained within each response category, if necessary.

Often, an older adult knows if he or she experiences this problem every day and is easily able to acknowledge if this is the case. It is usually when the problem has been intermittent over the last 2 weeks that the older adult may have some difficulty differentiating between "several days" and "nearly every day." To help the older adult, we quantify each of these response categories, so that "more than half the time" would be about 8–11 days, whereas "several days" would be fewer than 7 days in the last 2 weeks.

Table 4.3 compares the self-administered screening tools we have reviewed in this chapter.

As you can see, all of these tools are quite good, with solid reliability and validity, and success in implementing them with older adults. They are all considered to be brief screening tools, the shortest being the PHQ-9 at nine questions. Most are in the public domain or are free with the exception of the BDI- II. All of the instruments are valid to use in diverse populations and are available in multiple languages, although the BDI-II is only available in English and Spanish. Only the BDI-II and the PHQ-9 include a question on suicide.

TABLE 4.3   Self-Administered Screening Tools

SCREENING TOOLS	BDI-II	CES-D 10 ITEM	GDS	PHQ-9
Reliable/valid	High reliability and validity	Good reliability with some mixed results for validity	High reliability and validity	High reliability and validity
Validated to use with older adults	Yes	Yes	Yes; specific for older adults	Yes
Number of items	21 questions	20 questions	Short form has 15 questions	9 questions
Time to complete	5–10 minutes	10 minutes	5–7 minutes	2–5 minutes
Cost	$109	None—public domain	None—public domain	None—but need permission
Multiple languages	Yes, only Spanish	Yes	Yes	Yes
Ages used with	Anyone older than 13	Adult	Older adults	Adults
Time frame in answering questions	2 weeks	1 week	1 week	2 weeks
Suicide question included	Yes	No	No	Yes

The next two instruments differ from the others in that they are not self-administered tools but administered by trained clinicians. A brief review follows.

Hamilton Depression Rating Scale

Dr. Max Hamilton originally developed the HAM-D in 1960. It is a 21-question multiple-choice tool that is used by clinicians to rate the severity of depression among individuals. It was, at one time, considered the gold standard as a screening tool for use by clinicians. This is not a self-administered instrument; instead, the clinician guides their client through the questions and records their answers. Each question has between three and five responses, with increasing severity. Only the first

17 questions contribute to the total score. The second half of the screening tool identifies aspects of the depression, but is not a part of the screen (Hamilton, 1980). The following is an example of one of the questions:

1. Depressed mood (sadness, hopeless, helpless, worthless)
   0 = *Absent.*
   1 = *These feeling states indicated only on questioning.*
   2 = *These feeling states spontaneously reported verbally.*
   3 = *Communicates feeling states nonverbally* (i.e., through facial expression, posture, voice, and tendency to weep).
   4 = *Patient reports virtually these feeling states in his spontaneous verbal and nonverbal communication.*

   For the 17-item version, scores can range from 0–54. Scores between 7 and 17 indicate *mild depression*, scores between 18 and 24 indicate *moderate depression*, and scores more than 24 indicate *severe depression*. This tool takes about 30 minutes to administer.

   An interview guide for the questionnaire is available for purchase. This tool can measure outcomes and used throughout the course of treatment to assess the client's improvement. Some of the criticisms surrounding this instrument relate to its reliance on interviewer skill and its lack of proven reliability and validity (Bagby, Ryder, Schuller, & Marshall, 2004). The format of the response items has been criticized as difficult to use (Evans, Sills, DeBrota, Gelwicks, Engelhardt, & Santor, 2004). Moreover, because anxiety is included as a question, it is not always possible to separate symptoms related to anxiety from symptoms related to depression (Bagby et al.). Finally, researchers caution the usefulness of this tool in assessing for depression with older adults (Lichtenberg, Marcopulos, Steiner, & Tabscott, 1992).

The Cornell Scale for Depression in Dementia

The CSDD detects depression among patients with dementia. The CSDD obtains information from various sources because the patient may not be the best informant due to cognitive decline. In this way, the clinician will gather information directly from both the patient and an informant who is in frequent contact with the patient, such as a caregiver, home care worker, or staff in the nursing home. The information will be gathered in two separate interviews; the first is with the person rating the patient based on change in symptoms in the past week.

   The patient receives three different scores for this screening: one from the patient, one from the informant, and one from the clinician, based on professional judgment. Each interview takes about 20 minutes to administer. Each item is rated for severity on a scale from 0–2 (a score of 0 = *no depression*, 1 = *mild depression*, 2 = *severe depression*). All items are then added together. A score of 10 indicates *probable major depression*; a score of 18 indicates *definite major depression*. A total score of 8 or more suggests depressive symptoms.

The CSDD is touted as the gold standard when assessing depression among dementia patients. It has both good validity and good reliability (Alexopoulos, Abrams, Young, & Shamoian, 1988). However, even this tool has been found to show a greater degree of validity with patients having mild-to-moderate dementia than with severe dementia (Herrmann, Bartels, & Wallesch, 1993; Katz, 1998). It is helpful in that it can assess for both depression and the severity of depression.

SCREENING TOOLS FOR SUICIDE

As discussed earlier, although there are several standardized screening tools that exist to identify an individual's risk for suicide, no universal gold standard has emerged and the efficacy of these tools has shown mixed results (U.S. Preventive Services Task Force, 2004). Perhaps the most well-known of these screening tools is the Scale for Suicide Ideation (SSI; Beck, Kovacs, & Weissman, 1979). Interviewers ask between 5 and 21 questions depending on the response to the initial 5 questions. Three of these five screening items assess the individual's wish to live or to die, and the remaining two screening items assess the individual's desire to attempt suicide. It takes approximately 10 minutes to administer. The questions measure the individual's attitudes, behaviors, and plans to commit suicide on the day of the interview. Extensive research points to the high reliability and validity of the SSI (Beck, Brown, & Steer, 1997; Beck et al., 1979; Beck, Steer, Kovacs, & Garrison, 1985; Hawton, 1987; Mann, Waternaux, Haas, & Malone, 1999; Molock, Kimbrought, Lacy, McClure, & Williams, 1994).

Moreover, the SSI is one of the few suicide assessment instruments to have documented the predictive validity for completed suicide (Beck, Brown, Steer, Dahlsgaard, & Grisham, 1999; Brown, Beck, Steer, & Grisham, 2000). Specifically, Brown found that patients scoring in the high risk category of the SSI (two or more) were seven times more likely to commit suicide than those who scored in the lower risk category (Brown et al.). There are two modified versions of the SSI, the Scale for Suicide Ideation–Worst (SSI-W) and the Modified Scale for Suicide Ideation (MSSI). Both have solid reliability and validity; however, they not used as often as the original SSI (Beck et al., 1979; Clum & Yang, 1995; Miller, Norman, Bishop, & Dow, 1986). A modified SSI, the Beck Scale for Suicide Ideation (BSI) is available as a 21-item self-report measure (Beck & Steer, 1991). Similar to the SSI, the BSI contains an initial five screening items and depending on the score an additional 14 items are completed. The BSI takes approximately 10 minutes to administer.

In addition to screening tools for older adults at-risk for suicide, there are several interesting tools to use with your staff in assessing their comfort and skill level in identifying individuals at risk of suicide. The Quiz on Depression and Suicide in Late Life (QDSLL; Pratt, Wilson, Benthin, & Schmall, 1992) assesses the knowledge level of community service providers about depression and suicide in older persons. The QDSLL consists of 12 true–false items. The Suicide Opinion Questionnaire (SOQ; Domino, Gibson, Poling, & Westlake, 1980; Domino, Moore, Westlake, & Gibson, 1982) consists of 100 self-report items that assess the attitudes of health care professionals about suicide. The Suicide Potential Rating Scale, also called the Suicide Lethality Scale (SPLS; Holmes & Howard, 1980; Litman & Farberow, 1961), is a self-report questionnaire that assesses general knowledge about suicide. The SPLS consists of 13 items. Each item has four possible choices. An example of one of the items is the following: Persons who are most likely to succeed in committing suicide are (a) female and younger than 50 years of age, (b) female and older than 50 years of age, (c) male and younger than 50 years of age, or (d) male and older than 50 years of age. Individuals respond by answering either correct or incorrect.

An excellent resource for these and other screening tools for suicide is available by accessing http://www2.endingsuicide.com/TopicReq?id=1918. In addition, the National Institute of Mental Health has funded a Web site called EndingSuicide.com. They offer online education courses on suicide prevention for professions. These courses are available by accessing www.endingsuicide.com.

CAN I MODIFY SCREENING INSTRUMENTS?

The creation of all screening tools takes a tremendous amount of care to ensure that they are reliable and valid. Before they are available for public use, they generally undergo rigorous testing in multiple populations. There are many facets to depression and the instruments that we have just examined include questions from each domain. If you took one question from one source and another from another source, you might not be capturing all the aspects you need to adequately screen for depression.

What Does It Mean When a Tool Complies With *DSM-IV* Diagnostic Criteria?

You will find that when you review the various screening tools that they mention that their instrument corresponds with the *DSM-IV* (American Psychiatric Association [APA], 2000). The *DSM-IV* is a manual for psychiatric diagnoses published by the APA. The *DSM* has had five revisions since its first publication in 1952. The most recent version and the one that we currently use, *DSM-IV*, was published in 1994 with a slight "text revision" in 2000. The fifth edition is due to be available in 2013. There are 297 disorders listed in the 886 page long manual, which lists all of the currently used criteria for mental disorders for adults, adolescents, and children. This manual is considered the "bible" for mental health practitioners because they diagnose and develop a treatment plan for their clients. It also contains codes used in insurance reimbursement. This manual is intended for use by trained medical and mental health clinicians and not for paraprofessionals or nonclinical professionals, because it takes extensive training to be able to accurately interpret the categories. The diagnostic categories are simply guidelines for professionals as individuals with the same diagnosis may not share the same underlying etiology and as such may require different treatment strategies.

METHODS OF ADMINISTERING A SCREENING INSTRUMENT

As you read in the discussion previously, some tools are clearly designed to be self-administered, some to be administered by trained clinicians, and some can be used by both methods. When using a self-administered tool such as the GDS or the PHQ-9, it is important that trained staff are available to ensure that the older adults answer all questions correctly and completely and to discuss the results with the older adult. Although it is certainly preferential that these staff are social workers or trained health care workers, this is not a necessity as long as the staff has received adequate training in what to look for, particularly with regard to suicidal ideation. We have had success in training case managers, nutritionists, nurses, public health practitioners, and graduate social work interns to assist with screening. It is important that the staff administering depression screenings are nonjudgmental, patient, and able to listen to the older adult's verbal and nonverbal cues. As long as there is at least one clinically trained individual to assist with questions or issues that may come up during depression screenings, this strategy can work well with limited resources.

There are advantages and disadvantages to using internal staff from your agency to conduct screening, versus external staff from another agency, such as a mental health service provider. Ultimately, it will probably depend on the resources you have at your disposal. If you have several clinically trained staff available at your agency, using these existing resources can work well. However, sometimes we find that some older adults would rather talk with someone that they do not see on a daily basis. There is that concern, often the case in senior centers, about people "knowing their business." At the same time, being screened by someone they know can be an advantage to some older adults, because they might have a trusting relationship with a particular staff person, and over time, be willing to disclose more information about depression to that person. In general, the more that a depression screening tool can be incorporated into regular agency practice, especially within intake and assessment questionnaires, the better. We find the strength of using any tool as a part of routine agency practice is that it normalizes the concept of depression. It becomes just another test with a number that could warrant a medical and/or clinical intervention, similar to finding out about your cholesterol, blood pressure, or sugar levels.

However, many programs are very short-staffed or do not have the right configuration to be able to use internal staff for screenings. Implementing EASE-D in partnership with mental health providers can help to ameliorate these difficulties; indeed, the model is designed with collaborative partnerships in mind. Possible partners may include schools of social work, a mental health provider in the community, or a local clinic. Together with additional institutional resources, you might be able to implement depression screening more easily within your aging service program.

WHAT SHOULD YOU DO WHEN SOMEONE IS AT RISK FOR DEPRESSION?

Once you have decided on which screening tool to administer, you should develop a referral protocol if the individual is at risk for depression. A screening is only helpful if, once identified, the older adult has assistance in obtaining the help they need. Of course, the best possible program design would be to offer identified at-risk older adults on-site treatment by a trained counselor. However, most organizations will not have this luxury and will need to identify resources in the community for referrals when an individual requires follow-up. In terms of referral options for older adults, we believe that the best option is to allow for individual preference, offering older adults the options of seeking help from specialty mental health clinics or from their primary care physician. Most older adults would never consider going to a mental health clinic for help, but virtually all older adults go to a doctor on a regular basis, and many will consider speaking with their doctors about psychological symptoms long before seeking specialty mental health services.

Our model includes giving an older adult a copy of the results of his or her depression screening, which they can take to their doctor or to a mental health professional. The benefit of older adults seeing their doctor is that the screening tools do not give a definitive diagnosis and it is possible that an underlying medical condition is causing the symptoms. Of course, this strategy works best when the primary care physician is knowledgeable about depression and engages the older adult to obtain the treatment that they need. Unfortunately, we have found that this is not always the case and, at times, the older adult may go without care because of a primary care physician missing the symptoms and the doctor's own ageist beliefs that depression is a normal part of aging.

This is one of the reasons it is beneficial to conduct follow-up (other reasons to conduct follow-up will be discussed in chapter 5, under "Pretreatment Care Management in the EASE-D Model") with older adults so that if their doctors have not been responsive, then a referral to a mental health clinic or another medical professional for follow-up could be warranted. Moreover, although most older adults initially prefer going to their own doctor for evaluation and/or treatment, some will prefer going to a mental health provider, so it is important to have those resources available for older adults as well. Wherever the referral, it is important to make a copy of their screening tool that they can bring to the appointment. This can allow for a freer discussion, as without a concrete reason for bringing up the subject of depression, it may be difficult or uncomfortable for some older adults to volunteer information about their depression symptoms.

In general, an older adult who scores in the mild-to-moderate category should receive a referral from either their doctor or mental health practitioner for follow-up. However, when an older adult scores positive in a category indicating severe depression or is indicating suicidal ideation, then it is likely that the older adult will require both medical and mental health intervention as a treatment plan. In these cases, the older adult may require both counseling and the use of antidepressants for their symptoms to improve.

WHAT ARE IMPORTANT FACTORS TO CONSIDER WHEN CHOOSING A SCREENING TOOL?

At this point, you might be thinking that because there are so many good screening tools to choose from, it can be difficult to determine which would be the best to use. When looking at these screening tools, you should keep the following checklist in mind:

- Is this tool reliable and valid?
- Has this tool been used successfully in the population I work with?
- Has this tool been used successfully in the culture that I work with?
- Is it available in the language I need?
- How long is the instrument (all things being equal shorter could be better)?
- How much time will it take to complete?
- Does it look confusing to answer or straightforward?

- Who administers the tool (can it be self-administered or will I need to use staff)?
- Is there a cost to administer the tool?
- Will you be communicating the findings of the tool to a particular service system (for example, the PHQ-9 was developed specifically for primary care doctors so they are most familiar with this instrument)?

After answering these questions, you will probably find that one tool emerges as the best for your situation. The two screening tools that we have found the most helpful in working with older adults are the GDS and the PHQ-9. You cannot go wrong in choosing either one of these two tools. The PHQ-9 may be a bit more difficult for an older adult to complete than the GDS; however, the inclusion of the item on suicidal ideation and the fact that the medical community is most familiar with it has made it a more desirable tool for us in implementing EASE-D.

FINAL WORDS ABOUT DEPRESSION SCREENING

Whatever instrument you choose, providing depression screening following mental health education is an effective way for aging service providers to identify older adults who are at risk. Depression screening can build on the knowledge that older adults gain in mental health education sessions and provides an opportunity for older adults to disclose symptoms in a familiar environment. As with all aspects of EASE-D, depression screening can be offered through collaborative partnerships between aging service and mental health agencies, and can be an essential first step toward treatment for older adults.

REFERENCES

Adewuya, A. O., Ola, B. A., & Afolabi, O. O. (2006). Validity of the patient health questionnaire (PHQ-9) as a screening tool for depression amongst Nigerian university students. *Journal of Affective Disorders, 96*(1–2), 89–93.

Alexopoulos, G. S., Abrams, R. C., Young, R. C., & Shamoian, C. A. (1988). Cornell Scale for Depression in Dementia. *Biological Psychiatry, 23*(3), 271–284.

American Psychiatric Association. (2000). *Diagnostic and Statistical Manual of Mental Disorders* (text revision). Washington, DC: Author.

Bagby, R. M., Ryder, A. G., Schuller, D. R., & Marshall, M. B. (2004). The Hamilton Depression Rating Scale: Has the gold standard become a lead weight? *American Journal of Psychiatry, 1612*(12), 2163–2177.

Bartels, S. J. (2003). Improving the system of care for older adults with mental illness in the United States. Findings and recommendations for the President's New Freedom Commission on Mental Health. *American Journal of Geriatric Psychiatry*, *11*(5), 486–497.

Beck, A.T., Brown, G. K., Steer, R. A., Dahlsgaard, K. K., & Grisham, J. K. (1999). Suicide Ideation at its Worst Point: A Predictor of Eventual Suicide in Psychiatric Outpatients. *Suicide and Life-Threatening Behavior*, *29*, 1–9.

Beck, A. T., Brown, G., & Steer, R. A. (1996). *Manual for Beck Depression Inventory-II*. San Antonio, TX: Psychological Corporation.

Beck, A. T., Brown, G. K., & Steer, R. A. (1997). Psychometric characteristics of the Scale for Suicide Ideation with psychiatric outpatients. *Behavior Research and Therapy*, *35*(11), 1039–1046.

Beck, A. T., Kovacs, M., & Weissman, A. (1979). Assessment of suicidal intention: The Scale for Suicide Ideation. *Journal of Consulting and Clinical Psychology*, *47*(2), 343–352.

Beck, A., & Steer, R. (1991). *Manual for the Beck Scale for Suicidal Ideation*. San Antonio, TX: Psychological Corporation.

Beck, A. T., Steer, R. A., Kovacs, M., & Garrison, B. (1985). Hopelessness and eventual suicide: A 10-year prospective study of patients hospitalized with suicidal ideation. *American Journal of Psychiatry*, *142*, 559–563.

Beck, A. T., Ward, C. H., Mendelson, M., Mock, J., & Erbaugh, J. (1961). An inventory for measuring depression. *Archives of General Psychiatry*, *4*, 561–571.

Brink, T. L., Yesavage, J. A., Lum, O., Heersema, P, Adey, M. B., & Rose, T. L. (1982) Screening tests for geriatric depression. *Clinical Gerontologist*, *1*, 37–44.

Brown, G. K., Beck, A. T., Steer, R., A., & Grisham, J. R. (2000). Risk factors for suicide in psychiatric outpatients: A 20-year prospective study. *Journal of Consulting and Clinical Psychology*, *68*, 371–377.

Burke, W. J., Roccaforte, W. H., Wengel, S. P., Conley, D. M., & Potter, J. F. (1995). The reliability and validity of the Geriatric Depression Rating Scale administered by telephone. *Journal of American Geriatrics Society*, *43*(6), 674–679.

Cannon, D. S., Tiffany, S. T., Coon, H., Scholand, M. B., McMahon, W. M., & Leppert, M. F. (2007). The PHQ-9 as a brief assessment of lifetime major depression. *Psychological Assessment*, *19*(2), 247–251.

Chen, T. M., Huang, H. Y., Chang, B. S., & Chung, H. (2006). Using the PHQ-9 for depression screening and treatment monitoring for Chinese Americans in primary care. *Journal of Psychiatric Services*, *57*, 976–981.

Clum, G. A., & Yang, B. (1995). Additional support for the reliability and validity of the Modified Scale for Suicide Ideation. *Psychological Assessment*, *7*(1), 122–125.

Conoley, C. W. (1987). Review of the Beck Depression Inventory (revised edition). In J. J. Kramer & J. C. Conoley (Eds.), *Mental measurements yearbook* (11th ed., pp. 78–79). Lincoln, NE: University of Nebraska Press.

DeForge, B. R., & Sobal, J. (1988). Self-report depression scales in the elderly: The relationship between the CES-D and ZUNG. *International Journal of Psychiatry and Medicine*, *18*(4), 325–328.

Domino, G., Gibson, L., Poling, S., & Westlake, L. (1980). Students' attitudes towards suicide. *Social Psychiatry*, *15*, 127–130.

Domino, G., Moore, D., Westlake, L., & Gibson, L. (1982). Attitudes toward suicide: A factor analytic approach. *Journal of Clinical Psychology*, *38*(2), 257–262.

Ell, K., Unützer, J., Aranda, M., Sanchez, K., & Lee, P. J. (2005). Routine PHQ-9 depression screening in home health care: Depression prevalence, clinical and treatment characteristics and screening implementation. *Home Health Care Services Quarterly*, 24(4), 1–9.

Ensel, W. M. (1986). Measuring depression: The CES-D scale. In N. Lin, A. Dean, & W. M. Ensel (Eds.), *Social support, life events, and depression* (pp. 51–70). New York, NY: Academic Press.

Ertan, F. S., Ertan, T., Kiziltan, G., & Uyguçgil, H. (2005). Reliability and validity of the Geriatric Depression Scale in depression in Parkinson's disease. *Journal of Neurological Psychiatry*, 76, 1445–1447.

Evans, K. R., Sills, T., DeBrota, D. J., Gelwicks, S., Engelhardt, N., & Santor, D. (2004). An Item Response analysis of the Hamilton Depression Rating Scale using shared data from two pharmaceutical companies. *Journal of Psychiatric Research*, 38(3), 275–284.

Freudenstein, U., Arthur, A., Matthews, R., & Jagger, C. (2002). Can routine information improve case finding of depression among 65 to 74 year olds in primary care? *Family Practice*, 19(5), 520–522.

Gallo, J. J., & Rabins, P. V. (1999). Depression without sadness: Alternative presentations of depression in Late Life. *American Family Physician*. Retrieved March 2, 2010, from http://www.aafp.org/afp/990901ap/820.html

Gallo, J. J., Ryan, S. D., & Ford, D. E. (1999). Attitudes, knowledge, and behavior of family physicians regarding depression in late life. *Archives of Family Medicine*, 8, 249–256.

Gerety, M. B., Williams, J. W., Jr., Mulrow, C. D., Cornell, J. E., Kadri, A. A., Rosenberg, J., et al. (1994). Performance of case-finding tools for depression in the nursing home: Influence of clinical and functional characteristics and selection of optimal threshold scores. *Journal of American Geriatrics Society*, 42, 1103–1109.

Hamilton, M. (1980). Rating depressive patients. *Journal of Clinical Psychiatry*, 41(12 Pt 2), 21–24.

Han, C., Jo, S. A., Kwak, J. H., Pae, C. U., Steffens, D., Jo, I., et al. (2008). Validation of the Patient Health Questionnaire-9 Korean version in the elderly population: The Ansan Geriatric study. *Comprehensive Psychiatry*, 49(2), 218–223.

Herrmann, M., Bartels, C., & Wallesch, C. W. (1993). Depression in acute and chronic aphasia: Symptoms, pathoanatomical-clinical correlations and functional implication. *Journal of Neurology, Neurosurgery, and Psychiatry*, 56, 672–678.

Hawton, K. (1987). Assessment of suicide risk. *British Journal of Psychiatry*, 150, 145–153.

Holmes, C. B., & Howard, E. (1980). Recognition of suicide lethality factors by physicians, mental health professionals, ministers, and college students. *Journal of Consulting and Clinical Psychology*, 48, 383–387.

Joiner, T., Kalafat, J., Draper, J., Stokes, H., Knudson, M., Berman, A. L., et al. (2007). Establishing standards for the assessment of suicide risk among callers to the national suicide prevention lifeline. *Suicide and Life-Threatening Behavior*, 37(3), 353–365.

Katon, W., Sullivan, M., & Walker, E. (2001). Medical symptoms without identified pathology: Relationship to psychiatric disorders, childhood and adult trauma, and personality traits. *Annals of Internal Medicine*, 134, 917–922.

Katz, I. R. (1998). Diagnosis and treatment of depression in patients with Alzheimer's disease and other dementias. *Journal of Clinical Psychiatry*, 59(9), 38–44.

Kroenke, K., & Spitzer, R. L. (2002). The PHQ-9: A new depression diagnostic and severity measure. *Psychiatric Annals, 32*(9), 1–7.

Kroenke, K., Spitzer, R. L., & Williams, J. B. (2001). The PHQ-9: Validity of a brief depression severity measure. *Journal of General Internal Medicine, 16*(9), 606–613.

Kurlowicz, L., & Greenberg, S. A. (2007). The Geriatric Depression Scale. *Try This: Best Practices* in *Nursing Care to Older Adults,* (4).

Liang, J., Van Tran, T., Krause, N., & Markides, K. S. (1989). Generational differences in the structure of the CES-D scale in Mexican Americans. *Journal of Gerontology, 44*(3), 110–120.

Lichtenberg, P. A., Marcopulos, B. A., Steiner, D. A., & Tabscott, J. A. (1992). Comparison of the Hamilton Depression Rating Scale and the Geriatric Depression Scale: detection of depression in dementia patients. *Psychological Reports, 70,* 515–521.

Litman, R. E., & Farberow, N. L. (1961). Emergency evaluation of self-destructive behavior. In N. Farberow & E. Schneidman (Eds.), *The cry for help* (pp. 52–74). New York, NY: McGraw-Hill.

Löwe, B., Unützer, J., Callahan, C., Perkins, A. J. & Kroenke, K. (2004). Monitoring depression treatment outcomes with the Patient Health Questionnaire-9. *Medical Care, 42*(12), 1194–1201.

The MacArthur Initiative on Depression Primary Care. (2010). *Patient Health Questionnaire.* Retrieved March 2, 2010, from http://www.depression-primarycare.org/clinicians/toolkits/materials/forms/phq9/

Malakouti, S. K., Fatollahi, P., Mirabzadeh, A., Salavati, M., & Zandi, T. (2006). Reliability, validity and factor structure of the GDS-15 in Iranian elderly. *International Journal of Geriatric Psychiatry, 21*(6), 588–593.

Mann, J. J., Waternaux, C., Haas, G. L., & Malone, K. M. (1999). Toward a clinical model of suicidal behavior in psychiatric patients. *American Journal of Psychiatry, 156*(2), 181–189.

McMordie, W. R., & Blom, S. (1979). Life review therapy: Psychotherapy for the elderly. *Perspectives in Psychiatric Care, 17*(4), 162–166.

Miller, I. W., Norman, W. H., Bishop, S. B., & Dow, M. G. (1986). The Modified Scale for Suicide Ideation: Reliability and validity. *Journal of Consulting and Clinical Psychology, 54*(5), 724–725.

Molock, S. D., Kimbrough, R., Lacy, M. B., McClure, K. P., & Williams, S. (1994). Suicidal behavior among African American college students: A preliminary study. *Journal of Black Psychology, 20*(2), 234–251.

Morrow-Howell, N., Proctor, E., Choi, S., Lawrence, L., Brooks, A., Hasche, L., et al. (2008). Depression in public community long-term care: Implications for intervention development. *The Journal of Behavioral Health Sciences and Research, 35*(1), 37–51.

Naughton, M. J., & Wiklund, I. (1993) A critical review of dimension-specific measures of health-related quality of life in cross-cultural research. *Quality of Life Research, 2,* 397–432.

Nunnally, J., & Bernstein, I. (1994). *Psychometric theory* (3rd ed.). New York, NY: McGraw-Hill.

Poongothai, S., Pradeepa, R., Ganesan, A., & Mohan, V. (2009). Reliability and validity of a modified PHQ-9 item inventory (PHQ-12) as a screening instrument for assessing depression in Asian Indians (CURES-65). *Journal of Association of Physicians of India, 57,* 147–152.

Pratt, C. C., Wilson, W., Benthin, A., & Schmall, V. (1992). Alcohol problems and depression in later life: Development of two knowledge quizzes. *Gerontologist, 32*(2), 175–183.

Radloff, L. S. (1977). The CES-D Scale: A self-report depression scale for research in the general population. *Applied Psychological Measurement, 1*, 385–401.

Rubin, A., & Babbie, E. (2001). *Research methods for social work.* Belmont, CA: Wadsworth.

Saver, B. G., Van-Nguyen, V., Keppel, G., & Doescher, M. P. (2007). A qualitative study of depression in primary care: Missed opportunities for diagnosis and education. *The Journal of American Board of Family Medicine, 20*(1), 28–35.

Sharp, L., & Lipsky, S. (2002). Screening for depression across the lifespan: A review of measures for use in primary care settings. *American Family Physician, 66*(6), 1001–1008.

Sheikh, J. I., & Yesavage, J. A. (1986). Geriatric Depression Scale (GDS): Recent evidence and development of a shorter version. In T. L. Brink, *Clinical Gerontology: A Guide to Assessment and Intervention* (pp. 165–173). New York, NY: The Haworth Press, Inc.

U.S. Department of Health and Human Services. (1999). *Mental health: A report of the surgeon general.* Rockville, MD: Author, Substance Abuse and Mental Health Services Administration, Center for Mental Health Services, National Institutes of Health, National Institute of Mental Health.

U.S. Preventive Services Task Force. (2004). *Screening for suicide risk: Recommendation and rationale.* Rockville, MD: Agency for Healthcare Research and Quality. Accessed March 2, 2010 at http://www.ahrq.gov/clinic/3rduspstf/suicide/suiciderr.htm

Weissman, M. M., Sholomskas, D., Pottenger, M., Prusoff, B. A., & Locke, B. Z. (1977). Assessing depressive symptoms in five psychiatric populations: A validation study. *American Journal of Epidemiology, 106*, 203–214.

Whooley, M. A., Avins, A. L., Miranda, J., & Browner, W. S. (1997). Case-finding instruments for depression: Two questions are as good as many. *Journal of General Internal Medicine, 12*(7), 439–445.

Williams, L. S., Brizendine, M. S., Plue, L., Bakas, T., Tu, W., Hendrie, H., et al. (2005). Performance of the PHQ-9 as a screening tool for depression after stroke. *Stroke, 36*(3), 635–638.

Zich, J. M., Attkisson, C. C., & Greenfield, T. K. (1990). Screening for depression in primary care clinics: The CES-D and the BDI. *International Journal Psychiatry and Medicine, 20*(3), 259–277.

5

Connecting Older Adults to Treatment: Pretreatment Care Management

If you work with older adults, you have probably noticed that simply giving a referral for services may not be the most effective way to ensure that they get the help they need. In our experience, we have found that the approach of providing mental health referrals without offering any additional follow-up or support is not usually enough to facilitate an older adult's connection to treatment for depression.

The ultimate goal of Educating About and Screening Elders for Depression (EASE-D) is to identify older adults at risk for depression and to help them connect to appropriate clinical evaluation and treatment services. Mental health education raises awareness of the signs and symptoms of clinical depression, addresses stigma, and provides information about effective treatment options. Depression screening identifies individuals who may be at risk for depression and generates a referral for mental health treatment. However, the EASE-D model does not stop there, because at the point of identification and referral, the work is only partially complete. The next step involves helping an older adult connect with a qualified health care or mental health professional for a clinical evaluation for depression, through an intervention we call *pretreatment care management*.

This chapter will help service providers understand the basics of providing supportive follow-up services for at-risk older adults and will address (a) the difference between standard models of depression care management and pretreatment care management, (b) determining what types of staff should provide pretreatment care management, (c) the roles of pretreatment care managers, (d) designing a pretreatment care management protocol and data collection instrument, and (e) using program incentives to facilitate older adults' connection to a provider. Additionally, the end of this chapter includes a short checklist to help program managers think through each aspect of building the pretreatment care management component of EASE-D.

DEPRESSION CARE MANAGEMENT IN THE HEALTH CARE AND AGING SERVICES SECTORS

Care Management in Primary Care Settings

Depression is increasingly recognized as a public health problem, resulting in higher rates of morbidity and mortality, decreased capacity to maintain optimal functioning and well-being, increased use of the health care system, and increased disability (Dobscha et al., 2006). Although effective treatments for depression exist, many people with depression do not adhere easily to treatment and, as a result, may experience little meaningful improvement in symptoms and functioning.

Increasingly, health care and other service providers recognize that mental health treatment recommendations, such as prescriptions for antidepressants or referrals to psychotherapy, are only the beginning of the process of helping someone overcome depression. The professional literature speaks to the need for follow-up services for individuals diagnosed with depression to ensure better treatment adherence. One such service, *clinical care management*, is defined as "patient education and activation, symptom and treatment adherence monitoring, and self-management reinforcement" (Dobscha et al., 2006, p. 477). The need for care management to ensure treatment adherence is particularly noted for patients with depression in primary care settings who may not otherwise receive adequate follow-up in the traditional practice of primary care (Bollini, Pampallona, Kupelnick, Tibaldi, & Munizza, 2006).

In addition to being used for the general population of adult patients with depression, care management strategies have also been employed as a strategy to improve physical and mental health outcomes among older adults (Counsell et al., 2007), who are particularly at risk for complications associated with untreated depression, such as increased disability, poorer health outcomes, and a heightened risk for suicide (Unützer et al., 2002). Depression care management programs are typically located within primary care settings and are usually staffed by nurses, social workers, or other highly trained personnel. Their duties range from patient education to more complex case coordination and counseling (Belnap et al., 2006; Nutting et al., 2008; Simon, Ludman, & Operskalski, 2006; Unützer et al., 2002).

Pretreatment Care Management in the EASE-D Model

In EASE-D, pretreatment care management is a goal-oriented and time-limited intervention, consisting of weekly follow-up contact with at-risk older adults for a designated period to encourage their initial connection with a qualified service provider for an evaluation for depression.

Although conceptually similar to the type of depression care management already conducted as part of the health care sector, pretreatment care management differs slightly in its goals. The goal of depression care management in health care settings is to help patients diagnosed with depression follow a treatment regimen to alleviate their symptoms. In contrast, the goal of pretreatment care management is to increase the chances that at-risk older adults will connect to a qualified professional for an evaluation for depression in the first place. Traditional care management is a postdiagnostic intervention, whereas pretreatment care management is a prediagnostic intervention.

Unlike traditional depression care management, pretreatment care management is not yet an evidence-based intervention for depression. However, we consider pretreatment care management to be a useful intervention that encourages older adults to use their referrals to make the first step toward the treatment of clinical depression. To our knowledge, there has only been one study to date that has explored the efficacy of prediagnostic care management as a strategy to engage individuals in mental health treatment. Zanjani, Miller, Turiano, Ross, and Oslin (2008) conducted a study to examine whether telephonic follow-up services could improve the rates of engagement in mental health treatment for veterans who were at risk of mental disorders, such as depression. The data from this study indicates that care management, as a pretreatment intervention, improved the rate of engagement in mental health treatment; however, there has not yet been a similar study of such an intervention to engage older adults.

WHO SHOULD CONDUCT PRETREATMENT CARE MANAGEMENT?

In health care settings, clinical case managers, registered nurses, or social workers conduct depression care management, contacting patients on a regular basis to support treatment adherence and effective depression self-management. EASE-D is an early intervention designed to help older adults make the initial connection to treatment providers, so the staff conducting follow-up do not need to have extensive training in the management of clinical depression to help at-risk older adults. With training and when guided by a standardized protocol and data collection instrument, staff such as case managers, program coordinators, or others working in aging services agencies can provide follow-up services to older adults following a depression screening.

Our design of pretreatment care management is flexible in terms of staffing pattern. In New York City, where we implement EASE-D in senior centers, pretreatment care management is conducted by the same staff who provide mental health education or depression screening services. We believe that when the same people who originally provided mental health education and depression screening services offer pretreatment care management, older adults begin to build up a relationship that began on the day of the depression workshop and may be more likely to use that relationship to help them connect to services.

However, we recognize that the way we implement the program is not the only way to provide pretreatment care management services, and we encourage providers to construct education and screening programs that best fit their older adults' needs and their own program realities. For example, aging services organizations may not be able to provide each aspect of EASE-D on their own, but they may be able to partner with a community-based mental health agency to provide on-site mental health education, depression screenings, and information and referral services for identified at-risk older adults. Because mental health programs may not be able to provide pretreatment care management services to older adults who are not yet clients of their own mental health program, a case manager, program assistant or other staff within the aging services program may be well positioned to provide this service. This type of task-sharing arrangement could prove to be beneficial, because many older adults have trusting relationships with aging service program staff and may be more comfortable receiving follow-up from them than from another person located outside of the agency where they usually receive services.

Regardless of their credentials or program location, pretreatment care managers should be empathic, knowledgeable about accessing treatment resources in the community, and willing to make sustained efforts to stay in contact with at-risk individuals who may be ambivalent about seeking help or who may be struggling with depression symptoms or psychosocial difficulties significant enough to hamper their progress. Additionally, pretreatment care managers should have the necessary skills to follow through on program protocols, including knowing when to conduct or arrange for additional depression screenings, when to assess for suicidal ideation, and when to access mental health crisis services or other emergency interventions, if older adults require them.

If pretreatment care managers are staff members of aging services agencies, they may require initial training to become familiar with the mental health system and to know when an older adult is in need of an additional depression screening or emergency intervention. If providers of aging services are collaborating with a local mental health agency to implement EASE-D, it is likely that the staff of the mental health agency can provide such training. If there is not an explicit collaboration with a mental health agency to implement the project, it is likely that preliminary training can still be arranged through partnerships with local mental health agencies in the community.

DEVELOPING THE PRETREATMENT CARE MANAGEMENT PROTOCOL

Successful outcomes will depend, in part, on designing a program protocol that provides a framework for the pretreatment care manager to encourage older adults to follow through with their referrals. When developing a pretreatment care management protocol, program directors will need to consider several questions, which includes the following:

- Will services be provided in person or on the telephone?
- How often and for how long will services be carried out?
- When should pretreatment care management services end?
- What is the role of the pretreatment care manager?
- Should older adults have additional depression screenings during pretreatment care management?
- What should be done if older adults report suicidal thinking?
- What kinds of information should be included in data collection?
- When and how should incentives be used to enhance program outcomes?

The answers to these questions will help program managers create their protocol for pretreatment care management and will inform the development of a useful data collection instrument.

PRETREATMENT CARE MANAGEMENT: BY PHONE OR IN PERSON?

Pretreatment care management can be provided either over the phone or in person, and the decision to proceed depends largely on the organization implementing EASE-D. For example, if a single agency, such as a senior center or geriatric case management program, is conducting the program using their own staff, and the older adults are regular clients of the agency, it is possible that pretreatment care management can be conducted easily in person, either during the course of regular service provision or in appointments specifically to address an older adult's progress in making a connection with a provider. However, because of time constraints or low staff capacity, an aging services agency may not be able to set up face-to-face appointments for older adults. If EASE-D is being implemented jointly by an aging services agency and a mental health agency, and mental health staff are conducting follow-up with older adults determined to be at risk, it is also less likely that pretreatment care management can be delivered in person. In either of these cases, it is probably best to conduct care management over the telephone.

At times, making follow-up contact with older adults may not be a simple process, whether in person or over the telephone. Programs conducting pretreatment care management in person may find that older adults stop coming regularly to the agency or break scheduled appointments. Similarly, telephonic pretreatment care only works if older adults have access to a phone and are able and willing to have a conversation with pretreatment care managers. If older adults change their phone number, disconnect their phone, have significant hearing loss, or do not return the messages pretreatment care managers leave for them, it may be very difficult to provide adequate follow-up services.

There may be times when older adults request that pretreatment care managers work with their family members, rather than directly with themselves. We have encountered this request most often when older adults are living with and being cared for by their adult children. Working with family members is certainly permissible, particularly if older adults request this service. Family members may also be the ones to request being the point of contact with pretreatment care managers; this, too, is acceptable, but only when older adults agree to such an arrangement. In the event that an older adult has a cognitive impairment severe enough to prevent their capacity to consent to pretreatment care management, pretreatment care managers can work with family members to ensure that their loved one is evaluated by a mental health provider in the community.

There may not be a single ideal approach for every older adult served by the program. If possible, it may be useful for aging service programs to allow for both in person and telephonic care management services.

FREQUENCY AND DURATION OF PRETREATMENT CARE MANAGEMENT

Several factors should be considered when determining the frequency and duration of follow-up, including older adults' motivation to seek help, the concrete and emotional obstacles older adults may face as they seek treatment, the availability of treatment providers in the community, and what outcome is considered desirable by older adults and by program staff.

The ideal situation is one in which older adults are motivated to seek treatment, know where to find accessible services in the community and engage with those services in a relatively short period. However, the ideal situation is not likely to be the one most frequently encountered by older adults and their pretreatment care managers. Older adults may experience difficulties as they seek treatment for depression, ranging from the concrete barriers to more personal challenges.

For example, even highly motivated older adults may not be able to obtain a timely appointment with their doctor for a diagnostic evaluation. Older adults seeking professional mental health services in their neighborhood may face a lack of mental health services or may encounter waiting lists for those services that do exist. They may also struggle with chronic physical illness, including sensory or mobility impairments or the loss of functional capabilities leading to increased difficulty keeping an appointment with a provider. They may lack accessible transportation to a provider's location. Older adults may be particularly reluctant to connect to a provider if they are ambivalent about seeking help for depression, skeptical about the benefits of treatment, or ashamed or embarrassed about having symptoms of depression. They may require a longer period of personal contemplation as well as additional information and support from their pretreatment care manager to determine how best to overcome these barriers.

We have tried several different approaches to determine the most helpful pretreatment care management frequency, and have conducted follow-up on a monthly, biweekly, and weekly basis. After several rounds of trial and error using the various approaches, we have found the most effective frequency of follow-up contact is at least once per week, for a minimum of 4 weeks. When follow-up contact is less frequent than weekly, older adults may have increased difficulty making contact with a provider as a result of being unable to resolve concrete barriers or address ambivalence or other personal difficulties.

However, a 4-week follow-up period is the *minimum* amount of support an at-risk older adult may need to connect to services. Some participants, depending on their particular circumstances, may require as many as 8 weeks or longer of follow-up, as the following example illustrates.

Case Vignette: Mrs. W.

Mrs. W., a Caucasian woman in her early 70s, lived with and provided care for her husband, who had a progressive illness. Mrs. W. was identified as being at risk for depression after completing a depression screening questionnaire. Mrs. W. reported that her symptoms had intensified over time as caring for her husband became more physically and emotionally demanding. Mrs. W. accepted a referral to see her doctor for an evaluation for depression and consented to pretreatment care management services over the phone.

During the initial weeks of follow-up, Mrs. W. reported that she was unable to see her doctor because her husband's needs were so great that even when she remembered to make an appointment, she felt that she could not possibly leave her husband long enough to do so. Her pretreatment care manager discussed possible options with Mrs. W., including having another family member stay with her husband for a few hours during her appointment, and enrolling in the free caregiver's support program offered by her local senior center. It took nearly a month of such conversations before Mrs. W. was able to make an appointment with her doctor and arrange for a family member to stay with her husband. In the 4th week of follow-up, Mrs. W. reported that her appointment would take place within the next 3 weeks.

In all, it took 7 weeks of follow-up before Mrs. W. could see her doctor. By the end of the 7th week, Mrs. W. reported that she had seen her doctor, who confirmed a diagnosis of clinical depression and who provided a prescription for an antidepressant. Mrs. W. also reported that she had begun the process of applying for home care services for her husband and that she was planning on attending a weekly caregiver support group at the senior center as a way of managing the stress of being a family caregiver. During the last contact with her pretreatment care manager, Mrs. W. reported reduced levels of stress as a direct result of taking steps to manage the burdens of caregiving and her depression symptoms.

WHEN TO END PRETREATMENT CARE MANAGEMENT SERVICES

Given the need for flexibility when providing pretreatment care management to at-risk older adults, it may be challenging to determine when to end follow-up services. Although the total period of pretreatment care management is influenced by the established program protocol and adjusted on a case-by-case basis, we find that there are usually three typical outcomes that necessitate the end of pretreatment care management. These are (a) the older adult meets with a qualified provider for an evaluation for depression; (b) the older adult chooses not to meet with a provider and does not have an evaluation; and (c) the older adult does not respond to the pretreatment care manager's outreach attempts. There is also the special case in which older adults get stuck in the process of pretreatment care management, which will be discussed in a later section.

Older Adult Connects With Provider

Because EASE-D is designed to encourage an initial evaluation for depression rather than to ensure a specific clinical result, a case is considered to have a successful outcome as soon as an older adult confirms meeting with a primary care physician or mental health provider for an evaluation. This is true even if the older adult is not diagnosed with depression or if no formal treatment recommendation is given. Although the formal relationship ends once older adults have completed their initial consultations, the pretreatment care manager can continue to be a resource to older adults. For example, older adults can be encouraged to reconnect with their pretreatment care managers if they find themselves in need of additional mental health resources, such as a new referral, or other information about community-based services.

Older Adult Does Not Connect With Provider

There will always be cases in which older adults choose not to connect with a provider after the minimum follow-up period of 4 weeks. Even when pretreatment care managers provide adequate information and support, some older adults will decline an evaluation. There may be several reasons older adults do not follow up with a provider. Some of the most common we have encountered include:

- Older adults deciding that their symptoms are not troublesome enough to seek treatment;
- Older adults determining that their symptoms have improved since the screening took place and do not require treatment;
- Older adults reporting preoccupation with managing physical health care concerns, which take precedence over addressing depression symptoms;
- Older adults reporting preoccupation with family caregiving responsibilities, which take precedence over having an evaluation; and
- Older adults experiencing embarrassment about getting a mental health evaluation that feels too difficult to overcome.

Older adults who decline depression evaluations can still be given information about where to find a provider in the future and can be encouraged to make contact with their pretreatment care manager at a later point, if they wish to have support and guidance as they seek treatment.

Older Adult Does Not Respond to Outreach

Pretreatment care managers should not continue to reach out to older adults beyond the minimum follow-up period of 4 weeks if older adults do not respond to any outreach attempts during that time. If older adults do not participate in pretreatment care management after regular and consistent attempts to engage them, continuing outreach would misallocate staff resources that could otherwise be devoted to following up with participating older adults. If, however, an older adult reaches out to a pretreatment care manager after the case has been closed, his or her case can be reopened and the follow-up process can proceed in the same manner as with any other case.

Older Adult Seems "Stuck" in the Process

Occasionally, pretreatment care managers will work with older adults who seem to be stuck. They will not commit to seeing a provider for an evaluation for depression, but neither will they formally decline doing so. They may report feeling better since their depression screening, now that they have their pretreatment care managers to talk with regularly. Some may even ask to continue to the weekly conversations indefinitely as a form of therapy for their symptoms.

When managing these "stuck" cases, it is useful for pretreatment care managers to clarify the nature of the contact between themselves and the older adults with whom they are working. While validating an older adult's point of view when he or she reports feeling better as a result of having regular follow-up contact, the pretreatment care manager can suggest that he or she might continue to do as well, or even better, once he or she has connected with a mental health professional who could be available to him or her on an ongoing basis to help them address the depression symptoms directly.

Additionally, pretreatment care managers can also explore older adults' ambivalence about seeking an evaluation if it seems to be interfering with an older adult's progress in connecting to a provider. If, after clarifying the pretreatment care manager's role and attempting to address continued ambivalence or stigma, older adults do not wish to meet with a provider, follow-up should end. Not only are staff resources misallocated when pretreatment care management is not being used for its intended purpose, but also the follow-up contact can become an inadvertent barrier to seeking formal treatment services, if continued indefinitely. Tactfully, and with care, pretreatment care managers can explain that their role is to help older adults connect to a qualified provider, and that follow-up will not be available for an extended period if the older adult does not wish to follow up with his or her referral.

When ending follow-up contact, pretreatment care managers should give resource information to older adults, in the event that they wish to find a health care or mental health provider on their own at another time. Resource information may include a list of local area mental health programs, any mental health, or crisis intervention hotline numbers available in the community, as well as a reminder that their doctor is an available resource. Additionally, pretreatment care managers can encourage older adults to contact them directly if they decide they would like assistance in following through with the initial referral for mental health evaluation they received when they were originally screened for depression.

THE ROLES OF PRETREATMENT CARE MANAGERS

When conducting follow-up, pretreatment care managers likely will wear several hats throughout the process. Older adults who participate in EASE-D are unique individuals with their own histories, perspectives, and current life circumstances, all of which will come to bear on the nature and quality of the pretreatment care management process. Pretreatment care managers will serve as supportive listeners, problem solvers, coaches, and, at times, crisis counselors. Each role is described, along with corresponding tips to help staff conduct successful pretreatment care management.

Pretreatment Care Manager as Active and Supportive Listener

Psychosocial and environmental stressors, such as relationship difficulties, lack of social support, the challenges of caregiving, scarce community resources, and financial stress may all contribute to the development or exacerbation of depressive symptoms. During follow-up, older adults are likely to talk to pretreatment care managers about these and any other stressors they experience. Such information is not incidental—it is central to understanding and building on older adults' strengths as they face these challenges.

For many older adults, a pretreatment care manager may be one of the few people with whom they discuss depression symptoms or any other related life difficulties. Competent listening skills are essential for pretreatment care managers to facilitate an older adult's progress toward meeting with a provider for a depression evaluation. Practicing active listening requires more than asking older adults the questions on a data collection tool and documenting the answers. Pretreatment care managers will often need to solicit additional information to understand each older adult's individual situation. By communicating empathetic understanding of an older adult's situation and by asking targeted questions, pretreatment care managers can encourage the development of openness and trust in their working relationship with older adults.

At times, older adults may be so in need of emotional support that they may require significant time to share their personal stories before the pretreatment care manager can ask the standardized follow-up questions. Some older adults may seem more interested in speaking about their various difficulties to their pretreatment care manager than about following through on their referral, and they may not respond directly to the standard follow-up questions when they are asked. In these cases, it is critical for pretreatment care managers to listen not only to what participants say, but also to what they are *not* saying, as well, because the dynamic that reveals itself during follow-up contact can be used by the pretreatment care manager to help an older adult connect to treatment, as this case illustrates.

Case Vignette: Mr. S.

Mr. S., a man in his late 60s, was experiencing multiple psychosocial difficulties in addition to his depression symptoms, including conflict in his primary relationship and the possibility of losing his housing. Mr. S. often needed significant time to discuss each of these problems before he could address his progress meeting with a provider about his depression. His pretreatment care manager took care to listen supportively to Mr. S. and to offer resources for handling his concrete difficulties, including helping him connect to a case manager at the local senior center who could assist with the housing challenges.

In each call, after acknowledging and addressing Mr. S.'s challenges, his pretreatment care manager broached the subject of his progress in connecting with a treatment provider. Mr. S. said he recognized that his depression was getting worse. He also said he felt it prevented him from taking active steps to manage his housing and other difficulties. His pretreatment care manager acknowledged that Mr. S.'s interpersonal and housing problems added increased stress to his life and that this stress could be related to the worsening of Mr. S.'s depression symptoms. The pretreatment care manager also suggested that getting help for his depression might help Mr. S. work toward resolving his other challenges. The pretreatment care manager also asked Mr. S. explicitly how he felt about getting mental health treatment. Mr. S. reported that although he was aware that his depression and living situation were going from bad to worse, he also felt reluctant to see a mental health provider.

At this point, Mr. S. and his pretreatment care manager could discuss his ambivalence openly, and his various concerns about treatment could be addressed through the pretreatment care management process. Eventually, over several more weeks of discussion, Mr. S. chose to have an evaluation from his primary care doctor and, upon receiving a diagnosis of depression, he received a prescription for an antidepressant and a referral for psychotherapy. Mr. S. sought ongoing treatment from the mental health program to which he had been referred, and connected with service providers at the senior center to work toward meeting his concrete needs.

Pretreatment Care Manager as Coach

As much as pretreatment care managers will be a source of emotional support to the older adults with whom they work, they will also be a source of helpful information about accessing mental health resources in the community. For many older adults, accepting a referral for a depression evaluation is the beginning of a potentially confusing journey into the world of mental health services. Many older adults may not understand what exactly to do with their referral, even if the person who screened them for depression gave guidance to meet with their primary care provider or a mental health professional for an evaluation. They may be confused about how to make an appointment for a depression evaluation, or about what to say to a provider once they are in a doctor's or a therapist's office. If older adults want to work with a mental health professional, they may not know how to find local mental health programs and may not know what to expect when they reach out to a mental health professional for help. Older adults may have many questions about the types of treatment available and may have even more questions about the safety and efficacy of treatment.

To speak effectively to older adults' concerns, pretreatment care managers will need to know enough about the community's health care and mental health systems to be able to troubleshoot any difficulties older adults may stumble on as they try to access treatment. They will also need to have access to reliable information about mental health treatment, including psychotropic medications and the types of effective nonmedical treatments for depression, such as individual or group counseling and psychotherapy techniques. Such information will not be a substitute for a medical evaluation or a formal mental health consultation; however, supplying older adults with basic information about mental health interventions and how to access them may be an effective bridge to evaluation and treatment services.

For example, if an older adult encounters a waiting list at a local mental health clinic, and subsequently feels discouraged from seeking any treatment at all, the pretreatment care manager should be able to provide potential alternative resources for treatment, such as another local clinic, so that the older adult does not lose too much momentum. Or, if an older adult is unable to think of what to say to a primary care doctor or to an intake coordinator at a mental health program, a pretreatment care manager can role-play these scenarios or discuss strategies to help the older adult prepare for that initial conversation in a medical office or at a mental health clinic.

One of the most important functions of pretreatment care management is helping older adults negotiate whatever barriers to treatment arise. These barriers may range from concrete issues to those challenges that are more emotional or psychosocial in nature. The pretreatment care manager should explore these barriers to best facilitate their connection to a provider. Described next are some of the most common concrete and psychosocial barriers.

Concrete Barriers

Access to Services. Typical concrete barriers for older adults include those related to accessing service providers. Older adults may be uncertain about where to find a provider in their communities, especially if they do not regularly see a primary care physician. Unfortunately, some communities also lack qualified providers, particularly those that specialize in geriatric mental health. In addition to general barriers related to access, older adults may experience financial barriers that prevent them from accessing treatment. These include a lack of health insurance coverage or having medical insurance that does not cover mental health treatment. Even older adults who do have coverage may still have limited financial resources that make medical or mental health co-payments difficult to afford. If an older adult's budget is very limited and there is not affordable public transportation available, getting to a provider may seem prohibitively expensive, particularly if the older adult does not have family or friends who are able to provide transportation.

Pretreatment care managers can be especially helpful to older adults by providing information about local mental health resources in the community. Although these are usually given immediately following the depression screening, older adults may misplace this information or need help to find additional providers if the original information is not suitable. At times, providing resources can be as simple as suggesting that older adults visit their primary care physician for an evaluation for depression. Otherwise, the pretreatment care manager will have to be knowledgeable enough about community mental health resources to suggest additional possibilities for services. If the community is service-poor, the pretreatment care manager may need to research local resources or establish collaborative relationships with mental health agencies to locate useful options for participants.

Financial Barriers. Financial barriers may be challenging for pretreatment care managers to address directly, though there may be ways in which they can help older adults cope with this difficulty. If agencies implementing EASE-D have the means to provide older adults with short-term financial assistance, it may be possible to mitigate the financial barriers to transportation and provider co-payments, at least for the initial consultation. If older adults lack health coverage altogether or their medical insurance will not cover mental health visits, pretreatment care managers can research the availability of lower cost treatment alternatives, such as mental health clinics with sliding scale fees, clinical trials for which older adults may be eligible, and advising older adults with medical (but not mental health) coverage to speak with their doctors for a consultation.

Unfortunately, it may not be possible to develop an effective strategy for managing financial challenges to service with every single older adult, especially in service-poor areas with few or no free or low-cost treatment alternatives. It will be important for agencies implementing EASE-D to record the incidence of financial barriers to treatment to advise program funders of the need to incorporate financial aid as a program component, as well as to advocate for systemic changes that would permit greater access to low-cost services.

Emotional or Psychosocial Barriers. Other barriers older adults may face are more psychosocial in nature than they are concrete. Some of the more common emotional or psychosocial barriers include general ambivalence about mental health treatment, specific concerns about available treatments for depression, and misconceptions about the relationship between depression and aging.

Pretreatment care managers may find that exploring concrete challenges feels easier than working with an older adult's more personal difficulties. Often, older adults are more forthcoming with their concrete challenges than they are with their emotional reactions when they consider meeting with a mental health provider. However, it is helpful for pretreatment care managers to inquire about older adults' emotional reactions, particularly if older adults do not bring them up on their own. This is especially the case if, despite having managed concrete obstacles to service, older adults have not connected to a provider, because this may be a sign of an emotional barrier interfering with the help-seeking process.

Ambivalence About Mental Health Treatment. Ambivalence about seeking mental health services is common for people of all ages and cultural backgrounds. For many older adults, ambivalence may be exacerbated by multiple factors, including the social stigma associated with mental disorders, the belief that depression is a character weakness, rather than a real and treatable illness, and concerns about the value and safety of treatment, especially with regard to psychotropic medications. Exploring these concerns as they arise is a particularly important function for pretreatment care managers. Doing so enables pretreatment care managers to provide realistic information about the potential benefits, and the potential limitations, of treatment.

Concerns About Psychotropic Medications. Even after participating in mental health education sessions, many older adults may still feel that at best, treatment is not effective, or at worst, may cause them harm. Exploring older adults' concerns about treatment is often particularly relevant when discussing psychotropic medications. In mental health education sessions and during conversations with pretreatment care managers, many older adults report concerns that having an evaluation for depression will result automatically in being given a prescription for an antidepressant, which they will then be compelled to use. Some older adults worry that antidepressants are physically addictive. Others are concerned that psychotropic medication will interact harmfully with the medications they are already taking or will produce such serious side effects that they are not worth using, no matter how severe their depression symptoms may be.

It is critical that pretreatment care managers do not minimize older adults' concerns about psychotropic medications. Pretreatment care managers should develop a basic understanding about antidepressants sufficient to provide some general information about these medications. Most pretreatment care managers in aging service or mental health agencies are not medical professionals and should not give older adults medical advice. Whenever significant questions about medications arise that are beyond their expertise, pretreatment care managers should refer older adults to their physicians. However, some of the basic facts care managers can reasonably provide about antidepressants include the following:

- Antidepressants alleviate depression symptoms such as depressed mood, appetite changes, which cause weight gain or loss, sleeping difficulties, and fatigue, among others;
- Antidepressants do not cause physical addiction;
- Antidepressants may cause physical side effects, some of which may abate over time; however, if side effects are long-lasting or so uncomfortable,

they prevent the older adult from using the medication long enough to relieve depression symptoms, older adults should discuss this with the prescribing physician. Older adults should also review their current medications with their prescribing physicians to ensure safety when adding an antidepressant to their treatment regimen;

- Antidepressants may take time to achieve a positive effect. Although some people may notice their symptoms improving within 3–4 weeks, others may not feel the full therapeutic effects for as long as 6–8 weeks;
- Antidepressants do not work the same way for everyone; sometimes, people may need to try more than one medication to find one that works best for them; and
- It is an older adult's choice whether to use psychotropic medications at all.

Concerns About Mental Health Counseling or Psychotherapy. It is common for many people, including older adults, to feel embarrassed or ashamed about speaking with a mental health professional about their symptoms and life circumstances. For some older adults, doing so may seem like an admission of deep personal failing for having emotional difficulties in the first place. Other older adults may feel that their emotional difficulties are so personal that they should not be disclosed to anyone, including doctors or aging service providers. In addition to feeling embarrassed or ashamed, older adults may also be worried that talking about their problems will do little to solve them, or might even make them worse. They may also be concerned that mental health professionals will not be able to understand their own unique situations.

Pretreatment care managers should also be sensitive to the influences of family and culture, both of which may affect an older adult's feelings about seeking mental health treatment, particularly counseling or psychotherapy. Most often, family support and cultural practices are significant positive resources for at-risk older adults. However, the influence of family and the internalization of cultural beliefs may also foster emotional conflict for older adults who are considering mental health treatment. In many cultures, it is considered inappropriate to reveal personal difficulties except with close family members or, perhaps, trusted friends. Reaching out to a stranger, such as a doctor or a mental health provider, to discuss emotional difficulties or personal problems may feel akin to dishonoring one's family or betraying one's cultural values.

Additionally, conflicts may arise within families about when or why an older adult should seek outside help. Older adults may find themselves at odds with their loved ones if they believe they need help to manage depression, but their family members, who may provide emotional and financial support, personal caregiving, or other necessary assistance, do not.

Family members may not understand the impact of depression on the health and well-being of their older adult loved one and may believe that it is inappropriate to seek outside assistance for personal problems, particularly if those problems are emotional in nature or might involve other family members.

Pretreatment care managers may need to provide particular encouragement about seeking services from a mental health provider, particularly when older adults do not want to speak with their primary care doctor and do not want to use psychotropic medications. They should be familiar with the types of psychotherapeutic treatments and other supportive services available, such as individual and group psychotherapy and peer- or professionally-led support groups. They should also be able to describe the general functions of these mental health services, so that older adults have a realistic understanding of what services exist and how they may be helpful in treating depression. Additionally, pretreatment care managers should have enough knowledge of the available mental health services to be able to refer older adults to programs in or near their communities.

Just as pretreatment care managers should be prepared to address questions related to psychotropic medications, they should also be prepared to address similar types of questions older adults may have about speaking with a mental health professional. Some basic information pretreatment care managers can give to older adults include:

- A description of the types of mental health counseling available, such as individual and group psychotherapy;
- A description of what the older adult can expect from mental health counseling. Mental health counseling involves creating a working relationship between the older adults seeking help for depression and a mental health professional, the goals of which are to help older adults:
  - Understand thoughts and feelings contributing to depression symptoms;
  - Develop skills to solve problems contributing to depression symptoms.

Additionally, pretreatment care managers can help encourage older adults to advocate for themselves as they engage with mental health providers. Pretreatment care managers can:

- Encourage older adults to bring questions about mental health treatment to providers. Questions or concerns about mental health counseling can and should be discussed with the mental health provider; in fact, this is a normal and expected part of treatment;
- Support older adults to seek the most effective mental health providers. If older adults are dissatisfied with the treatment relationship with a

provider, they have the option of finding another (in some service-poor communities, doing so might be easier said than done, but such a suggestion may serve to empower older adults to find services they feel will be the most beneficial). Pretreatment care managers are available to help them find additional providers, if needed; and

▪ Promote older adults' self-determination. It is an older adult's choice whether to engage with a mental health professional at all.

Misconceptions About Depression and Aging

Unfortunately, many people, including older adults themselves, believe that depression is a normal part of aging. This especially may be the case if they are struggling with age-associated life stressors, such as bereavement, chronic physical illness, or functional disabilities. Several older adults with whom we have worked have articulated this belief, even after participating in mental health education workshops about depression. Older adults may ask their pretreatment care managers, "Isn't it normal for me to be depressed at my age?" or "Doesn't it make sense that I'm depressed, because I have so many health problems and I'm as old as I am?"

For these older adults, depression symptoms may seem to be yet another problem they associate with growing older, and as a result, they may not believe that treatment is necessary or useful. Through their multiple follow-up contacts with older adults, pretreatment care managers have an opportunity to reinforce the information provided to older adults in the depression workshop and to underscore the fact that although depression may come on the heels of significant life stressors, it is a real illness that can be treated successfully and does not have to be endured without help.

Care Managers as Crisis Counselors

Conducting Additional Depression Screenings
As older adults feel increasingly comfortable speaking with pretreatment care managers, they may discuss their depression symptoms more openly, especially when asked about them directly. Although some symptoms of depression may remain fairly constant for any given person, it is not uncommon for symptoms, such as depressed mood, hopelessness, or lack of pleasure or interest in activities, to worsen over time, particularly if an older adult is also facing especially difficult life circumstances.

It is important for pretreatment care managers to pay close attention to older adults' disclosures about depression symptoms over time, because they may help indicate when a secondary depression screening may be worthwhile or when to involve emergency intervention services. As with pretreatment care management in general, a secondary depression screening can be conducted in person or over the phone. Pretreatment care managers may broach the issue by acknowledging the older adult's particular difficulties and offering to administer another screening to determine how he or she is feeling at the present time, compared to when the first screening occurred.

A second screening may be especially useful when a significant time has elapsed, such as 4 or more weeks, after the first depression screening and a clinical evaluation has not yet taken place. Another screening may provide an additional opportunity for pretreatment care managers to encourage an older adult to see a provider, particularly if the older adult's symptoms have not improved or have gotten worse. If an older person's symptoms seem to have improved, this can be acknowledged also, and used to further discussion about whether an older adult feels a clinical evaluation is necessary. Additional depression screenings can also help pretreatment care managers to know whether older adults are experiencing suicidal ideation or need emergency services.

Suicide Risk and Emergency Interventions

As discussed in chapter 1 (under "Depression and Suicide"), clinical depression is a major risk factor for suicide, and older adults are the group statistically most likely to complete suicide. As a result, it is especially important that pretreatment care managers remain aware of the potential risk for suicide presented by older adults with depression. Even without the benefit of a formal screening process, it is usually possible to ask an older adult if he or she has been thinking about suicide, and pretreatment care managers should not hesitate to ask. As with other aspects of pretreatment care management, a direct approach is usually the most productive.

Although an older adult with significant symptoms of depression may never seriously consider suicide, the risk of suicidal thinking may increase if depression symptoms are prolonged or become more severe. If an older adult's depression symptoms have remained constant or gotten worse, and if he or she has not yet had a clinical evaluation from a doctor, psychiatrist, or another mental health professional, it is all the more important for pretreatment care managers to be prepared to address this issue.

It is essential for pretreatment care managers to have adequate training on how and when to ask participants about suicidal ideation so that they will be primed to ask about suicide at the right time and will make any necessary interventions. If agencies implementing EASE-D do not already have a suicide protocol in place, which they can adapt for use in this model, it is will be useful for them to link with mental health service providers in the community who can provide technical assistance and training. If an outside mental health agency is collaborating with an aging services program to provide depression screening or pretreatment care management, they should review their own emergency intervention protocol with the host aging services agency to ensure effective coordination between programs in the event of a clinical emergency.

In addition, it is helpful to have a written version of the emergency intervention protocol available for pretreatment care managers to use during their routine follow-up contact with older adults. Like the standardized pretreatment care management protocol document, the suicide risk assessment document can serve both as documentation and as a guide for pretreatment care managers, to ensure that the most helpful questions are asked.

Depending on an older adult's level of suicidal ideation or intent, and the availability of emergency intervention services in the community, several different outcomes may result. The most typical outcomes of suicide risk assessment are:

- Continued referral to their primary care physician or a mental health provider. When older adults do not report high levels of preoccupation with suicidal thinking, have not reported prior suicide attempts, and have not reported any plan or intent for self-harm, they can continue with following up on their referral to a doctor or a mental health professional for an evaluation and/or treatment;
- Referral to a mobile crisis team for evaluation. Mobile crisis teams are comprised of mental health professionals who are able to meet with at-risk older adults in their homes or elsewhere in the community. Cases requiring mobile crisis team intervention are usually those where older adults express strong preoccupation with suicidal thinking (with or without prior history of suicide attempts), have formulated or are contemplating formulating a plan for self-harm, and are unable to contract with a pretreatment care manager for safety until they can be seen by a provider. Mobile crisis team referrals can also be made if older adults have mobility impairments that make getting to a provider difficult, if alcohol or substance abuse or misuse is reported, or if the pretreatment care manager believes the mental status will worsen significantly within the next 24–48 hours; and
- Referral to emergency medical services (EMS; 911). This intervention is necessary if older adults report clear intentions to harm themselves or complete suicide or are experiencing a psychiatric emergency, such as psychosis. It is important to determine whether older adults have formulated a plan for self-harm or suicide, although clear reports of intention for self-harm, even without a fully articulated plan, can be enough justification to alert emergency services.

DEVELOPING DATA COLLECTION INSTRUMENTS

A comprehensive data collection instrument should be able to capture general information about the older adults being served so that programs can report their program information easily. Additionally, the instrument should help pretreatment care managers document enough details about an individual older adult's circumstances to help them manage the complex dynamics involved in each particular case. A standardized data collection tool will help guide pretreatment care managers through their task and will enable them to chart older adults' progress and challenges as they seek treatment. It also encourages consistency in documentation among different pretreatment care managers and helps to provide quality assurance in data collection.

The data collection tool should contain standard questions which pretreatment care management staff will ask each older adult. Data collection instruments should provide ample space to note the dates of follow-up contact, the relevant details of the conversation between the older adult and the pretreatment care manager, as well as any other pertinent information not otherwise captured elsewhere in the standard questions listed in the instrument. Program managers should periodically assess these notes to detect common barriers as well as successes. This will assist managers in making any necessary program modifications.

We use our data collection tool in a hard copy form during follow-up contact with each older adult. We enter the information in a computer database that helps us to note any significant program trends. Data collection tools can be tailored to meet the specific needs of each organization implementing EASE-D, and can be as simple or as detailed as necessary for each program's purposes. Most programs will find it useful to capture most, if not all, of the following:

Demographic Information

Demographics are useful to identify trends among the older adult population being served. This information only needs to be collected at the beginning stages of pretreatment care management, unless an older adult's experiences a significant change in his or her demographics, such as a change household composition, which would need to be noted. Some useful demographics to collect include, but are not limited to, the categories listed here:

- Age
- Gender
- Race and/or ethnicity
- Income status
- Cohabitation status/household composition

Status of Referral

The status of a referral indicates whether older adults have made contact with a qualified provider for evaluation for depression. The status of a referral should be documented during each follow-up contact with older adults. Ideally, the referral status changes over time, as older adults move from not having met with a provider, to making an appointment with a provider for an evaluation, to meeting with the provider face-to-face. The data collection form can include the following questions about the status of a referral:

- Has the older adult made an appointment with a medical or mental health provider for an evaluation for depression (yes or no)?
- If the older adult has not made an appointment, why not? What, if any, barriers are preventing making the appointment?

Collecting information about the barriers older adults encounter can be particularly helpful for the pretreatment care manager. Once these barriers are identified, they can be addressed by providing whatever additional support and information is necessary to help older adults overcome them.

Status of Appointment

The status of an appointment refers to whether older adults keep a scheduled appointment with a medical or mental health provider. This should be documented once older adults report having made an appointment with a provider. The data collection form can include the following questions about the status of an appointment:

- Did the older adult keep the scheduled appointment (yes or no)?
- If the older adult has not kept the appointment, why not? What, if any, barriers prevented keeping the appointment?

As with referral status, collecting information about what prevented older adults from keeping appointments can help pretreatment care managers assist older adults navigate any challenges they are experiencing.

Depression Screening Results

It will be important to track whether the depression screening results were shared with the older adult's provider during the evaluation appointment. Older adults do not necessarily need to bring a copy of the depression screening instrument to the provider to have a productive conversation about depression. However, we have found that when older adults do not bring the instrument to their appointments, the discussion about depression may not take place at all. Alternatively, during the appointment, the impact of depression symptoms may be minimized, especially if a subsequent screening or other evaluation does not take place in the provider's office.

Asking older adults whether they have brought their depression screening instrument to their appointments and whether they discussed their depression symptoms can help pretreatment care managers address previously hidden barriers to treatment, such as the lingering effects of stigma. When older adults do not bring the depression screening instrument or discuss their depression symptoms with their provider, they might report they forgot to do so. Although some older adults may truly forget, others do not discuss their symptoms because they continue to feel embarrassed or ashamed at the prospect of doing so. Discussing how older adults feel about talking with a provider can be a useful way to address any discomfort, both before and after an appointment takes place, but particularly when an older adult visits a provider without having a discussion about depression. The data collection form can include the following questions about whether the depression screening results were shared:

- During the appointment, did the older adult discuss the results of the depression screening with provider (yes or no)?
- If the older adult did not discuss depression with a provider, what prevented him or her from doing so?

Outcome of Appointment With Provider

The results of depression evaluations may vary significantly between providers, and it is helpful to document professional recommendations to identify trends among providers who are working with at-risk older adults. The data collection form can include the following questions about the outcome of an appointment:

- During the appointment, did the provider review the screening instrument, if a copy was provided (yes or no)?
- Did the provider conduct an evaluation for depression, including, but not limited to, taking a medical and mental health history, asking about symptoms, their severity and duration, and related life circumstances (yes or no)?
- What, if any, treatment recommendations did the provider make (these may include, but are not limited to, a referral to a mental health specialist

for psychotherapy or a psychiatric evaluation or a prescription for psychotropic medication, or both)?

■ If the provider did not recommend treatment for depression, why not? Did the provider determine the older adult was not depressed? Did the provider diagnose another disorder responsible for the older adult's symptoms?

Participant Feedback

Documenting older adults' responses to their experience with a provider helps to determine any necessary next steps. The data collection form can include the following questions to solicit feedback from older adults:

■ How did the older adult feel about the provider's response?
■ Does the older adult intend to follow up on any treatment recommendations?
■ What will be the older adult's next steps (e.g., keeping follow-up appointments with doctor, beginning treatment with a psychotherapist, continuing to take antidepressant medications)?

ADDED INCENTIVES TO PRETREATMENT CARE MANAGEMENT SERVICE

As professionals who care about older adults' well-being, we might hope that education about the potential benefits of treatment for depression would be incentive enough for at-risk older adults to seek an initial consultation with a provider. Indeed, some older adults do visit with a primary care physician or a mental health professional shortly after their depression screening. However, for many older adults, having an evaluation for depression involves taking several proactive steps, including sorting through feelings about seeking help, deciding what type of provider to see, making an appointment and traveling to that appointment, once it is made. Although perhaps unspoken, a central question for at-risk older adults is often, "What's in it for me?"

Even when older adults have screened positive for and acknowledge depression symptoms, they may not necessarily feel that there will be any clear benefit from following through with their referral for an evaluation and treatment. As a result, it may be helpful to build incentives in the general program structure, both to bolster motivation for seeking help and to demonstrate concern for older adults at risk. For some older adults, the availability of an incentive may positively influence whether they accept a referral for a mental health evaluation.

Conditional Cash Transfers

In New York City, a pilot project, called Opportunity NYC, uses conditional cash transfers (CCT) to encourage successful outcomes in academics, employment, and health care by offering individuals and families financial incentives to engage in educational and work-related activities and medical services (for more information about Opportunity NYC, visit the Web site http://opportunitynyc.org). With this type of intervention in mind, we decided to include a similar financial incentive to encourage older adults to have an evaluation for depression.

If you plan to incorporate a financial incentive in your program, you will need to determine its monetary value. A financial incentive is meant to be encouraging, not coercive. We believe that a financial incentive should be worth enough to be meaningful to the older adults who receive it but not so high in value that it is impossible to resist. Our incentive took the form of a prepaid gift card worth $25, deliverable to those older adults who kept at least one evaluation appointment with a qualified treatment provider. During the referral process, we informed at-risk older adults that they were eligible to receive the CCT after confirming with their pretreatment care managers that they had an evaluation appointment with the provider of their choice. For many initially ambivalent older adults, the CCT provided a clear and concrete benefit for following through with a referral that was distinct from the potential advantages of treatment. Additionally, for those older adults who had financial difficulties and for whom an extra appointment meant an unanticipated insurance co-payment or extra travel expenses, the CCT provided a welcome means of offsetting the extra costs incurred for that initial visit.

Financial incentives are not a requirement for implementing EASE-D, nor will they always directly encourage the desired result. Even when a financial or other incentive is included, some older adults may not deem it worthwhile enough to offset their ambivalence about seeking help for depression. Additionally, it will not always be possible for agencies to build incentives in the formal structure of the program. However, if possible, agencies implementing EASE-D may want to consider building some sort of incentive into their service model. Particularly for those older adults who are struggling economically, a financial incentive may provide encouragement that may help to overcome barriers to accepting a treatment referral. If a specific cash amount cannot be built in the program, it may be possible to build other types of incentives of lesser monetary value, such as subway, bus, or taxi fare, which could be built into the program to offset some of the financial concerns older adults may have.

A FINAL WORD ABOUT THE BENEFITS OF
PRETREATMENT CARE MANAGEMENT

It has been our good fortune to be the recipients of the positive feelings older adults have had about their contact with their pretreatment care managers and about their experience with EASE-D. It is not uncommon for older adults to tell us at the end of the follow-up period that, had they not participated in the program, they might not ever have received treatment for depression. On multiple occasions, older adults have expressed their satisfaction with the entire program and have reported that although being eligible for a financial gift might have been what influenced them to accept a referral for an evaluation, it was the encouragement and support of their pretreatment care manager, coupled with the benefits of seeing a provider for depression, which made the program truly worthwhile.

CHECKLIST FOR PROVIDING PRETREATMENT
CARE MANAGEMENT

Staffing

- Designate staff to conduct follow-up:
  - Mental health workers   _____
  - Aging services staff   _____
  - Are bilingual staff necessary?   Yes/No

Designing Program Protocol

- Decide how services will be delivered:
  - Over the telephone   _____
  - In person   _____
  - Both, on a case-by-case basis   _____

Frequency and Duration of Follow-Up

- How often will follow-up occur?
  - Weekly   _____
  - 2-week intervals   _____
  - Monthly   _____
  - Other   _____

■ For how long will follow-up occur?
  ■ 4 weeks   _____
  ■ 6 weeks   _____
  ■ 3 months   _____
  ■ Other   _____

Data Collection Instrument

■ Demographic information   _____
■ Referral status   _____
■ Appointment status   _____
■ Discussion of depression with provider   _____
■ Outcome of depression discussion   _____
■ Feedback from older adult participant   _____

Program Incentives

■ Will program use incentives?   Yes/No
■ If yes, what type?
  ■ CCT   _____
    ■ What is value of CCT?   _____
  ■ Transportation   _____
    ■ Carfare   _____
      ■ What is maximum carfare?   _____
    ■ Provide transportation   _____
    ■ Other   _____

REFERENCES

Belnap, B. H., Kuebler, J., Upshur, C., Kerber, K., Mockrin, D. R., Kilbourne, A. M., et al. (2006). Challenges of implementing depression care management in primary care setting. *Administration and Policy in Mental Health Services Research, 33*(1), 65–75.

Bollini, P., Pampallona, S., Kupelnick, B., Tibaldi, G., & Munizza, C. (2006). Improving compliance in depression: A systematic review of narrative reviews. *Journal of Clinical Pharmacy and Therapeutics, 31*(3), 253–260.

Counsell, S. R., Callahan, C. M., Clark, D. O., Tu, W., Buttar, A. B., Stump, T. E., et al. (2007). Geriatric care management for low-income seniors: A randomized control trial. *Journal of the American Medical Association, 298*(22), 2623–2633.

Dobscha, S. K., Corson, K., Hickam, D. H., Perrin, N. A., Kraemer, D. F., & Gerrity, M. S. (2006). Depression support in primary care: A cluster randomized trial. *Annals of Internal Medicine, 145*(7), 477–487.

Nutting, P. A., Gallagher, K., Riley, K., White, S., Dickinson, W. P., Korsen, N., et al. (2008). Care management for depression in primary care practice: Findings from the RESPECT-Depression trial. *Annals of Family Medicine, 6*(1), 30–37.

Simon, G. E., Ludman, E. J., & Operskalski, B. H. (2006). Randomized trial of a telephone care management program for outpatients starting antidepressant treatment. *Psychiatric Services, 57*(10), 1441–1445.

Unützer, J., Katon, W., Callahan, C. M., Williams, J. W., Jr., Hunkeler, E., Harpole, L., et al. (2002). Collaborative care management of late-life depression in the primary care setting: A randomized controlled trial. *Journal of the American Medical Association, 288*(22), 2836–2845.

Zanjani, F., Miller, B., Turiano, N., Ross, J., & Oslin, D. (2008). Effectiveness of telephone-based referral care management, a brief intervention to improve psychiatric treatment engagement. *Psychiatric Services, 59*(7), 776–781.

6

Developing Program Materials for Outreach and Education

To provide effective outreach and mental health education to older adults and their providers, it is important to craft materials that support the goal of providing quality mental health education to older adults and their service providers. This chapter will help you develop different types of program materials, including (a) informative material for aging services staff and other professional stakeholders who may help implement Educating About and Screening Elders for Depression (EASE-D) model, (b) outreach material to recruit older adults to participate in mental health education, and (c) educational and resource materials for older adults and their service providers. At the end of the chapter, we will provide you with a checklist you can use to create effective program materials.

INFORMATIONAL MATERIAL FOR SERVICE PROVIDERS

As part of the process of introducing an aging services program or other organizational stakeholders to the EASE-D model, we convene an initial planning meeting to discuss the program. It is valuable to have informational materials at this first meeting to share with program staff, including a helpful tip sheet highlighting simple actions staff can take to ensure the success of EASE-D. The tip sheet should be informative, but pithy, so that staff can quickly glean the purpose and process of mental health education and depression screening.

Key points we include in this material include information about the project stakeholders, the target population, the goals of the project, and a short description of each workshop topic. The tip sheet quickly provides aging services staff an opportunity to learn about the purpose of the project and more specifically, how we plan to implement EASE-D in their center. If you are a provider of aging services and wish to collaborate with a mental health organization to bring in mental health education and depression screening, a similar tip sheet can be developed to highlight the workshop topics that would be ideal for the mental health organization to provide at your agency. Tip sheets are relatively straightforward documents and should not be difficult to construct. Here are some helpful design consideration guidelines about how to create a useful tip sheet:

- Be brief: Material should be concise and easy to read.
- Focus the message: Answer the questions that staff have up front, such as the following:
  - What is it that you are proposing to do in the center (educate, screen, link to treatment)?
  - What is the purpose of the workshops?
  - How many sessions will there be (single session or series of sessions)?
  - What is the length of time of each session?
  - What should be the minimum and maximum number of participants?
  - What are the dates and times of the sessions?
  - Is there a cost to the program?
  - Is there a cost to the participants?
  - Who runs the sessions and who does the follow-up after screenings?
  - What is it that you expect from stakeholders?
  - Contact information.

The following sample items are an excerpt from a sample tip sheet we have used in our project when meeting with the directors of senior centers that will host our program.

Tips for conducting successful workshops include the following:

- Create designated space for workshop activities, whenever possible (distinct from common areas);
- Advertise workshop in advance (in monthly calendar, on daily announcement board, or during daily or lunchtime announcements at the center);
- Schedule workshop so that it is not in conflict with other activities, such as parties or other classes; and
- For speakers of other languages, do not schedule the workshop at the same time as regular English as a Second Language (ESL) classes, unless it is done in advance.

We usually put this information on one to two pages (usually double sided, for brevity), but we are also sure to review the specifics of the program during the meeting. As helpful as it is to have informational materials at your disposal, they should complement, not replace, an in-depth discussion about program implementation. The combination of thoughtfully designed materials and a meeting to discuss the program ensures that everyone involved has a solid understanding of the goals and the approach that you will take during program implementation.

OUTREACH MATERIAL FOR OLDER ADULTS

The second type of program material that we create consists of outreach material to advertise to older adults. Although senior centers will usually put information about the mental health workshops into their monthly calendar, this is often not enough to ensure good participation. In order to grab elders' attention, we develop catchy flyers that senior centers can post throughout their program space and hand out individually to older adults. We also make sure to translate these flyers into the main languages spoken at the center, to ensure that as many older adults as possible are aware of the workshops.

The content and language used in the flyers to promote mental health workshops is critical, because the way you convey information about the mental health education sessions will either encourage or discourage attendance. For example, how many older adults are likely to attend workshops advertised with the headlines "Come Talk About Depression" or "All You Need to Know About Mental Health Problems"? There is such stigma surrounding mental health that we have found it helpful to advertise in ways that engender receptivity among older adults. Of course, we subscribe to truth in advertising, but do not underestimate the value of creative penmanship!

For example, review the list of mental health education topics that follows. The description of each workshop topic highlights the clinical issue it will address. The second listing, in bold, is a rewording of the workshop title to convey what will be covered without being overly clinical or stigmatizing.

1. Talk About Clinical Depression/**Understanding the Blues**
2. Dementia and Alzheimer's Disease/**Memory Loss**
3. Medication Management Strategies/**Using Medications Safely**
4. Learn About Anxiety Disorders/**Understanding Stress and Anxiety**

As you can see, some of these topics need little in the way of changes. For example, most older adults take medication, so there is little stigma about attending an educational session on medication safety. We have also found this to be the case with memory loss, because many older adults harbor some concerns about their memory and are eager to hear more about this topic.

The two topics that often present the greatest challenges for recruitment are depression and anxiety, because these subjects most clearly relate to mental health. As you can see from the previous examples, we try to find language that will normalize the workshops so that older adults will be comfortable attending the session. As with everything, our titles are not necessarily the "perfect" ways to frame the workshop but, rather, are suggestions to guide your thinking about the use of language. If you are creating outreach materials such as flyers or handouts for older adults, it may also be helpful to discuss the content of these with other program stakeholders, such as mental health providers or other aging service professionals, to brainstorm content ideas and to ensure that language is appropriate. It might also be helpful to get the opinions of elderly stakeholders, such as members of a senior center's senior advisory council, to make sure that the advertising content is clear and nonstigmatizing.

All outreach materials should be easy to read, attention grabbing, and visually engaging. If you are conducting workshops where English is a second language, all material should be translated and reviewed to ensure cultural competence (we will review this concept in more detail in the next section).

Distributing Outreach Materials to Older Adults

In addition to posting outreach materials, aging services staff should speak directly to their older adult members about the program to encourage their participation. The most successful outreach strategy is a combination of eye-catching material and the willingness of staff to talk with their participants about the interesting workshops that will be coming up. It is also helpful to make multiple announcements within the program over time, because some older adults may need to hear about the workshop several times before they will feel comfortable signing up or participating. Repeated announcements also normalize mental health workshops as a routine part of health education and communicate a message to older adults that these are valuable topics to address.

EDUCATIONAL MATERIALS FOR OLDER ADULTS

During workshops, we distribute several pieces of information to participants. These materials reinforce the knowledge gained during the workshop and serve as a resource for older adults following the workshop. The items we give include:

- A one-page summary of the major points covered in the workshop;
- Local mental health resource information (in case they want to reach out for help or want to give this material to friends and/or family); and
- Promotional items that always include the phone number of a local mental health or substance abuse hotline that individuals can call to access mental health services or if they are in crisis.

There are some general considerations that are helpful to keep in mind when developing educational materials for older adults. Because of changes in memory, older adults may learn differently than younger generations. Although not universally the case, as people age, they may experience changes in their ability to read and comprehend educational material. It may take more effort for older adults to process information, understand densely written text with many ideas, and stay focused on new information without distraction (National Institute on Aging, 2008).

In fact, the workshops that attempt to reframe depression or other mental health topics for older adults are actually more challenging to deliver successfully than other types of workshops. Research has documented that cognitive flexibility, or the ability to change long-standing opinions and accept new information, may be less prominent in older adults because of possible memory changes (Byrd, 1985; National Institute on Aging, 2008; Stevens, 2003). For this reason, one needs to contemplate innovative ways to "de-bunk" long held misconceptions about depression in educational materials.

For example, sometimes older adults may only partially remember information. If you highlight in your text that "many people think incorrectly that depression is a normal part of aging," older adults might forget the context in the way you gave the information. Therefore, instead of understanding that depression is not caused by older age, they may only remember the section of the sentence that reads, "depression is a normal part of aging" (which is not exactly the message you want to communicate!).

The National Institute on Aging (2008) has developed a series of recommendations for developing printed materials:

- Write clearly and succinctly: Reduce the number of inferences that must be made from your writing. Omit unnecessary words. Instead of writing, "many people find it helpful to talk to the primary care physician about side effects from their medications," write, "talk with your doctor about any side effects from your medication." Avoid all clinical or other jargon that the older person might not understand.
- Limit the number of key points: Put no more than three to five points per section to reduce the amount of information readers need to remember (this is a particularly helpful strategy to compensate for possible short-term memory issues).
- Limit the action steps you ask your reader to take: It might be difficult for an older adult to retain more than a couple of steps at once (this is especially true for individuals with early stage Alzheimer's). Therefore, limit the suggestions so that the reader can more easily follow these recommendations.
- State information in the positive: This is helpful if you are concerned that older adults might be remembering your information incorrectly. Instead of stating "many people think that it is natural to be depressed as you get older," state, "most older adults are not depressed."

■ Use pictures to illustrate your point: It helps the reader identify with the information if you can incorporate a picture into the text. However, stay away from complex diagrams and charts that could be confusing or require interpretation.

■ Put your key points up front: Put the most crucial information at the beginning of the text to ensure that older adults read it.

■ Develop section headings: If your document is lengthy, it helps to divide it up into sections with clearly identified section headings. This will keep people focused on what they are reading.

■ Repeat, repeat, repeat: Repetition is key to helping older adults remember the essential points in your document.

In addition to these general recommendations, one should consider the following factors when designing any written materials for older adults:

■ The education level and literacy of older adults;
■ The culture and language of your target audience; and
■ Potential vision impairments which will affect the design of the materials.

The Education Level and Literacy of Older Adults

When creating informational material, it is essential to choose language that older adults with a range of reading levels can easily understand (Meyer, Young, Bartlett, 1989; Stevens, 2003). If older adults have to struggle to comprehend the material because they do not understand the particular words or because the overall concepts seem too complex, they will experience frustration, which will undoubtedly prevent learning. Because mental health topics may be uncomfortable for some older adults to discuss, it is even more important to make sure that all information is engaging and easy to read.

There is a tremendous amount of information available about how to develop health literature for individuals with low literacy. In 2003, the National Center for Education Statistics (NCES) sponsored the National Assessment of Adult Literacy, a national survey given to adults age 16 and older. More than 19,000 adults participated in this survey, and after analyzing the data, the NCES concluded that 14% of adults (at the time, 30 million people) lack the skills to perform simple and everyday literacy activities. Most adults read between the eighth and ninth grade level; however, those at the lowest literacy level only read at the fifth grade level.

Health literacy is a concept that has grown in importance as organizations have come to realize its negative impact on a person's health. Health literacy, as defined in *Healthy People 2010*, is "[t]he degree to which individuals have the capacity to obtain, process, and understand basic health information and services needed to make appropriate health decisions" (U.S. Department of Health and Human Services [DHHS], 2000). Those who are most at risk for inadequate or marginal health literacy skills include older adults, immigrant populations, low-income, and minority groups (Berkman et al., 2004; Gazmararian et al., 1999; National Patient Safety Foundation, 2003). Of older adults, 67% have inadequate literacy skills, and 81% of patients age 60 and older at public hospitals cannot read or understand basic materials such as prescription labels (Williams et al., 1995). If you are a provider of aging services, you might think that you know who among your program participants have low literacy skills. However, individuals often hide their literacy challenges quite skillfully because of embarrassment and shame about not being able to read (Parker, 2000).

The National Work Group on Literacy and Health ("Communicating with patients who have limited literacy skills," 1998) recommends writing all health-related material to be readable at a fifth grade level. Even then, this material will still be too difficult for about 25% of the population. Sometimes, providers may be concerned that by creating material at a low-literacy level, they will inadvertently offend those with higher literacy levels. In fact, research has shown this not to be the case. People of all education and literacy levels prefer materials that are easy to read and are not offended by the use of simple language (Davis et al., 1993). Another commonly held misconception is the assumption that keeping the language simple will result in the document seeming childish, but remember, writing for a *fifth grade reading level* is different from writing for *fifth graders*. Specifically with health literacy in mind, remember to:

- Keep the language simple;
- Keep the sentences short and to the point;
- Keep the number of points you want the person to remember to two or three at most; and
- Use the active voice.

Using Language Effectively

It is important to ensure that the text you create is simple and easy to understand. Use plain language that is free of jargon or technical terms (National Institute on Aging, 2008; Parker, 2000). It is best to use common and everyday words. The following exercise highlights how to take words that might be difficult for someone with low literacy to understand and transform them into easy to read language.

Exercise 1. Look at the table of words on the next page (Table 6.1). The words on the left could be complex to an individual with low literacy. Think of a replacement word you might use that would be easier to understand.

TABLE 6.1   Making Language Easier to Understand for Individuals of All Literacy Levels

MORE COMPLEX	PLAIN LANGUAGE SUBSTITUTE
Accompany	
Advise	
Assist	
Commence	
Concur	
Consult	
Purchase	
Utilize	
Primary care provider	
Administer	

Of course, there are ample replacement words you could substitute for the original terms. In Table 6.2, you will find examples of substitutes that we have found to be helpful.

TABLE 6.2   Plain Language Substitute

MORE COMPLEX	PLAIN LANGUAGE SUBSTITUTE
Accompany	Go with
Advise	Tell
Assist	Help
Commence	Start
Concur	Agree
Consult	Ask
Purchase	Buy
Utilize	Use
Primary care provider	Doctor
Administer	Give out

It is also useful to avoid putting too much information in any one document. Most people tend to remember no more than three to five ideas when they read something, so make sure to emphasize the most important points (National Institute on Aging, 2008; Stevens, 2003). If too much content is included in educational material, the reader is likely to come away feeling confused. Material distributed during mental health education should remind the participants of key concepts within the session; the material should not replace attending the workshop. If you have a lot of important material, you might want to consider putting it in a list. If you use a list, always place the most significant items first.

It is also helpful to use examples and to repeat the concepts throughout the materials, because older adults are more likely to remember information when using repetition throughout a document (National Institute on Aging, 2008). For example, you might have noticed that we repeat some of the concepts of health literacy from chapter 3 (see "Health and Mental Health Literacy"), and again use repetition throughout this chapter. At the end of reading this chapter, try to recall the major points about developing materials. They were probably a bit easier to remember by using the technique of repetition.

When putting together educational material:

- Try to avoid technical jargon if possible;
- Use everyday language;
- Keep your sentences short; the average sentence length should be about 15 words;
- Try to keep the style of writing conversational; and
- It is always best to use the active voice and personal pronouns; this is a more engaging style that is more likely to grab the readers' attention.

Exercise 2. Look at the sentences in Table 6.3 and think about how you could make them easier for the reader to understand.

TABLE 6.3 Making Sentences Easier for the Older Adult

MORE COMPLEX	EASIER VERSION
Passive voice: Mental health services are covered by Medicare.	**Use active voice:**
Third person: Participants that experience side effects with their medications should talk to their primary care provider.	**Use first person:**

Were you able to come up with an easier to understand version? Although there are many ways to rewrite these sentences, some examples are given in Table 6.4.

TABLE 6.4 Easier to Read Sentences for the Older Adult

MORE COMPLEX	EASIER VERSION
Passive voice: Mental health services are covered by Medicare.	**Use active voice:** Medicare pays for counseling services.
Third person: Participants that experience side effects with their medications should talk to their primary care provider.	**Use first person:** If you experience side effects from taking any medication, you should talk to your doctor.

How to Tell if a Document Is Easy to Understand

Ensuring that your materials are easy to understand is so important; therefore, we recommend that several individuals review your documents to ensure the concepts in them are clearly articulated. In addition to having your colleagues review the materials, you may be able to use one of the wide varieties of readability tests available to evaluate your documents. These computer-based tools calculate the reading grade level of your materials by evaluating the average length of your sentences and the number of words with multiple syllables. Such tools can be quite helpful. However, even when you use them, we recommend that you ask other program staff to review the documents, because these tools cannot take into consideration whether or not you are using words correctly or in proper context nor can they gauge the meaning of words.

The most common readability tests are the Fry Readability Graph, the Flesch-Kincaid readability tests, and McLaughlin's Simple Measure of Gobbledygook (SMOG) formula. You can check the readability of your document using the Flesch-Kincaid formula and determine the related Flesch reading level by choosing "show readability statistics" under the spelling and grammar options in the toolbar in Microsoft Word. You can easily obtain the other readability formulas by searching for them on the Internet (you can find these Web site addresses at the end of this section).

The two Flesch formulas are related. The Flesch-Kincaid Grade Level reading score ranges from 0–100; the higher the score, the easier the document is to read. In the Flesch Reading Ease test, higher scores also indicate that the material is easier to read. In general, a score between 60 and 70 is acceptable. Table 6.5 gives an interpretation of the score.

TABLE 6.5   Flesch Reading Ease Test

SCORE	READABILITY
90–100	Very easy
80–89	Easy
70–79	Fairly easy
60–69	Standard
50–59	Fairly difficult
30–49	Difficult
0–29	Very confusing

The Flesch-Kincaid score takes the Flesch score and translates it into a reading grade level. It can also mean the number of years of education generally required to understand this text. For example, when we ran statistics on this paragraph, we received a Flesch-Kincaid score of 10, indicating that the text should be understandable by a student in the tenth grade.

As stated earlier, there are many factors involved in a document being easy to understand. Readability tools are only one indication of a document's ease of use; these formulas represent only a small fraction of what you need to consider when creating your materials. Another helpful tip is it to try reading your material aloud to see how it sounds. If it is confusing to you, it will undoubtedly be confusing to the reader.

The Culture and Language of Target Audience of Older Adults

Once you feel comfortable that the language in your document is easy to read and understand, you must ensure that it reflects the culture and language of your target audience. The first step is to make sure to translate all material into the spoken language of the population. Even if an older adult is able to understand a workshop conducted in English, if this is not their language of origin, they might find it difficult to read materials written in English. To ensure readability in the translated version of your text, it is advantageous to arrange for several people who reflect their own culture review this document (Center for Medicare Education Issue, n.d.). For example, in Spanish, words take on different meaning depending on the Spanish-speaking country from which the person doing the translation originally comes. Although written Spanish is often the same throughout Spanish-speaking countries and cultures, there are some variations in how certain words are used, as well as grammatical differences and variations in the translation of idioms (Penny, 2000; Young, 1999).

It is extremely important to know the background of your audience so participants are not unintentionally offended or confused. For example, look at the words listed in Table 6.6. In the left column are the European meanings of the words in Spanish. In the right column are how the words would be interpreted in Latin America.

TABLE 6.6 Varying Translations of Spanish

SPANISH WORD	EUROPEAN MEANING	LATIN AMERICAN MEANING
Coger	To catch	To have sex
Pisar	To step on	To have sex
Coche	Car	Baby stroller
Pinche	Kitchen boy	Someone you are in love with (Chile); stingy (Central America); slang word for "worthless" (Mexico)

In some cases, words will not take on different meanings; however, to avoid confusion, ensure that you are using the correct translation of a word. For example, Table 6.7 shows the translation of certain words from English if the audience were from Spain, and then again if they were from Latin America. Keep in mind, too, that there are also differences even among regions of Spain or countries within Latin America.

TABLE 6.7   Translating English to Spanish Based on Country of Origin

NORTH AMERICAN ENGLISH	SPAIN	LATIN AMERICA
Computer	El ordenador	La computadora
E-mail	Correo electrónico	E-mail
Car	El coche	El carro
Bath	La bañera	La tina

Certain countries have developed their own idioms or words that are unique to their region. For example, words unique to individuals coming from Puerto Rico include:

■ *china*—meaning "orange" in Puerto Rico (ordinarily we hear it as *naranja*)
■ *zafacón*—meaning "trash can" in Puerto Rico (ordinarily we hear it as *basura*)
■ *wikén*—meaning "weekend" in Puerto Rico (ordinarily we hear it as *fín de semana*)

Additionally, there are grammatical differences in different forms of Spanish. The most important difference is the use of the personal pronoun. In Spain, they use *vosotros* to mean "you" (informal address) and only use *ustedes* in a more formal context. In Latin America, they only use *ustedes*, and rarely, if ever, use *vosotros*. These differences also affect the conjugation of words. For example, when translating the sentence, "You (all) have to listen to me" in Spain, the correct form would be "*Vosotros tenéis que escucharme*," whereas in Latin America, the correct form would be, "*Ustedes tienen que eschucharme.*"

Undoubtedly, this discussion has underscored the importance of choosing the right person to translate documents. The translator should not only be bilingual but also should represent the culture of older adults who will be attending your workshop. It is also important that the translator understands the underlying meaning of the text to guarantee accurate translation. Before translating the documents, discuss the English version with the translator to ensure that the intent, tone, and literacy level of the documents match those of the participants to keep the meaning intact. To ensure that older adults will understand the documents, we recommend that older adults from the same culture as the other participants review them. We recommend asking older adults to do this, because there could be generational differences in the meanings of words that only a reviewer who is truly representative of the potential audience can detect. The reviewers should make certain that the meanings of the words are clear, the grammar is correct, and that the entire document is easy to understand.

At times, it is also helpful to go through an exercise of back translation. In this process, one person translates the document into a language other than English and a second person takes the newly translated version and translates it back into English to assess potential changes of the document's meaning in the translation (Rubin & Babbie, 2001). When putting together educational materials, remember that frequently translated documents may be longer than the English version. Having longer documents could influence the printing costs and the overall budget for the project.

Although most people will put together separate documents for each language, there are advantages to having one document with both languages included. By designing the document in this way, bilingual participants can choose between the two languages seamlessly (Young, 1999). If something is confusing in one language, older adults may understand the text more easily by looking at the second language. Additionally, if older adults want to show their materials to their younger family members, having the English translation in the document could be useful, especially if family members are not as versed in the older adult's language of origin.

Design of the Materials

The design of your document is also an important consideration when writing materials for older adults. Many older adults have vision impairments, causing them to have difficulty reading print. There are two main factors to consider when designing documents:

- Contrast
- Font type and spacing

Contrast
You should aim for the highest contrast possible in your document. In general, light letters on a dark background are considered more readable than dark letters on a light background (American Foundation for the

Blind [AFB], 2010; Arditi, 2009). However, some experts believe that black font on a white background is equally as acceptable (Bix, Lockhart, Cardoso, & Selke, 2003; Bradley, Singletone, & Li Wan Po, 1994; Food and Drug Administration, 1999). If you want your document to be noticeable and do not want to use standard white paper, choose a paper color that is light, such as ivory. If you are printing material in color, you should use strong colors, such as reds or yellows. Avoid printing in blues, greens, or purples, and be sure to avoid medium or light color shades. Older adults are often quite sensitive to glare; for this reason, it is best to avoid the use of glossy paper (AFB, 2010; Arditi). When you reproduce materials on a copy machine, use very dark ink.

Font Type and Spacing

Not all fonts are equally legible. Avoid any fonts that are overly decorative because they are difficult to read. Although there are various opinions about which font is the best to use for individuals with vision loss, the AFB recommends using standard Roman or sans serif fonts. Another highly recommended font for individuals with vision loss is Arial. Using bold type is helpful because the thickness of the lettering increases readability. However, you should avoid using italics or putting words in all capitals as the letters in words printed in these ways are more difficult to discern from each other (AFB, 2010).

The type size should be no less than 14 points; any smaller type sizes will deter easy reading and impair comprehension of the document (National Institute on Aging, 2008). Additionally, a font size that is too small may cause eyestrain and headaches. If the older adults in your workshop are likely to have more significant vision loss, such as legal blindness, it is best to have a few large-type (16–18 point) versions of all of the documents (AFB, 2010).

Many older adults with vision loss have difficulty finding the beginning of the next line while reading (AFB, 2010). For this reason, it is best to stay away from single-line spacing; 1.5-line spacing is optimal. Text with letters very close together is especially difficult to read for those with central visual field defects, such as macular degeneration. Where possible, spacing should be wide. Monospaced fonts, rather than proportionally spaced fonts (e.g., Courier and Monaco), seem to be more legible for these readers. Extrawide binding margins are particularly helpful in bound material because they make it easier to hold the volume flat. As with translated documents, it is valuable to ask older adults to review all documents to ensure that the design does not hinder comprehension. Make sure that the older adults find the material easy to read visually, and revise your material based on the comments you receive.

RESOURCES FOR CREATING PRINTED
MATERIALS FOR OLDER ADULTS

For more information about creating printed materials for older adults, refer to this list of resources:

1. *Making Your Printed Health Materials Senior Friendly.*
National Institute on Aging
This 6-page tip sheet offers ideas for how to tailor health information specifically to meet the needs of older adults. You can download and order up to 10 free copies of this brochure at: www.nia.nih.gov/Health-Information/Publications/srfriendly.htm.
2. *Clear and to the Point: Guidelines for Using Plain Language at NIH.*
National Institutes of Health
This 12-page summary provides guidelines and useful examples of how to write in plain language, engage readers, display information, and evaluate materials. It is available at: http://execsec.od.nih.gov/plainlang/guidelines/index.html.
3. *Creating Plain Language Forms for Seniors: A Guide for the Public, Private and Not-for-Profit Sectors* (1998).
National Literacy and Health Program and the Canadian Public Health Association
This 30-page guide, developed with attention to the needs of older adults, offers clear guidelines for creating forms in plain language. The guide includes a section on how to develop easy to understand language to assist clients who need help filling in forms. Included is a glossary of plain words and instructions on how to use the SMOG. It is available at: http://www.cpha.ca/uploads/portals/h-l/pl_forms_seniors_e.pdf.
4. *Clear & Simple: Developing Effective Print Materials for Low-Literate Readers* (1994).
National Institutes of Health and the National Cancer Institute
This guide outlines a process for developing materials with, and for, people with limited-literacy skills. The guide contains five sections. Each section highlights specific considerations for materials development: defining the target audience, conducting audience research, developing a concept for the product, developing content and visuals, and pretesting and revising materials. *Clear & Simple* is concise and easy to use, with key information presented in bulleted lists. It contains many illustrations and offers real-world examples. The 61-page guide includes a list of low-literacy publications and software. A free copy of *Clear & Simple* is available from the National Cancer Institute's Web site: http://www.nci.nih.gov/cancerinformation/clearandsimple.

5. *How to Create and Assess Print Materials.*
   Health Literacy Studies Division of Harvard University
   Harvard University has a health literacy studies division that offers wonderful material on its Web site: http://www.hsph.harvard.edu/healthliteracy/materials.html#two.
6. *The SMOG Readability Calculator* by G. Harry McLaughlin.
   This Java application calculates a SMOG score for any length of text that can be typed or pasted into the calculator. It is available at: http://www.harrymclaughlin.com/SMOG.htm.

RESOURCES WHEN WRITING FOR PEOPLE WITH VISION IMPAIRMENTS

For more information about how to create materials for older adults experiencing vision impairments, the following Web sites offer excellent materials:

■ AFB offers good general reference information at:
www.afb.org/section.asp?SectionID=40&TopicID=200&DocumentID=210.
■ Making Text Legible: Designing for People with Partial Sight.
Available from Lighthouse International at: http://www.lighthouse.org/accessibility/design/accessible-print-design/making-text-legible.

For a more specific reference on creating better color contrast, visit the following Web site:

■ Effective Color Contrast: Designing for People With Partial Sight and Color Deficiencies.
Available from Lighthouse International at www.lighthouse.org/accessibility/effective-color-contrast.

EDUCATIONAL MATERIALS FOR THE PRIMARY CARE PHYSICIAN

In addition to educating and screening older adults, distributing materials within the major healthcare centers in your community is an effective component of a depression screening initiative. In the EASE-D model, at-risk older adults are encouraged to have a clinical evaluation with either their own primary care physician or, if they prefer, a mental health professional. For this reason, it is ideal to reach out to the major healthcare centers in your community to discuss the project and ensure their cooperation before implementing this model. When we first initiated our work, one of our collaborative partners, the New York City Department of Health and Mental Hygiene (DOHMH), developed a wonderful detailing toolkit designed to help physicians identify and treat depression in their elderly patients. DOHMH distributed this toolkit to physicians in areas in proximity to the senior centers with which we were working throughout New York City.

Eliciting the participation of the medical community will require more than simply handing out material, no matter how thorough and engaging the printed material. If possible, these materials should be part of a larger training initiative to help encourage physicians to identify and treat depression among their older patients. Ideally, face-to-face discussions should accompany the distribution of materials. To effect meaningful change, any educational outreach to healthcare providers will need to be an ongoing process (Levav et al., 2005). The information that follows is about the outreach and education program that are offered to physicians as part of EASE-D in New York City.

Engaging Physicians to Treat Depression: Academic Detailing

DOHMH developed the educational materials for healthcare providers used in EASE-D, and these originated from a more comprehensive academic detailing campaign they conducted in New York City. As discussed in chapter 3 (see "Primary Care Physicians"), academic detailing involves sending trained staff to physicians' offices to offer educational resources on a specific therapeutic area, such as depression. Academic detailing, the method used by DOHMH to educate doctors, differs from a similar method, called *industry detailing*, in very significant ways. Industry detailing originated within pharmaceutical companies, which would send out their employees as detailers to market their drugs and help boost sales. Industry detailers used promotional materials to market medications and to encourage their use by physicians, even if they were more expensive or less effective than other available medications. Unlike industry detailing, academic detailing is conducted outside of the self-interests of a corporation. Academic detailers are usually trained healthcare professionals (often nurses or pharmacists) offering more balanced information about medications to help doctors make well-informed treatment decisions, rather than to sell particular medications. Academic detailers provide the most current and state-of-the-art information on the management of a particular illness.

There have been numerous studies confirming the benefit of academic detailing to improve physician performance in various therapeutic areas. The landmark study was done in 1983 by Avorn and Soumerai, in which physicians receiving a detailing campaign (materials sent out through the mail and two follow-up visits by pharmacists) reported a 14% reduction of prescribing overused medications. There are several studies that explore the benefit of detailing with a specific focus on mental health (antidepressants; van Eijk, Avorn, Porsius, & de Boer, 2001; antipsychotics; Ray et al., 1993; Soumerai, 1998). In addition, The Cochrane Collaboration conducted a review in 2007 to see whether academic detailing was effective. They reviewed 69 studies and found that detailing improved prescribing behavior by 5% (O'Brien et al., 2001).

Because of the success of academic detailing, a number of states have introduced academic detailing programs, including Pennsylvania, Vermont, and South Carolina. In several states, legislation has provided increased support for the development and expansion of academic detailing programs. In 2007, both Maine and Vermont passed legislation to support and expand their own detailing programs. In 2008, legislation passed to create academic detailing programs in the District of Columbia, New York, New Hampshire, and Massachusetts. Moreover, noting the value of detailing, the federal government introduced legislation entitled the Independent Drug Education and Outreach Act in April 2009. If passed, this legislation would offer federal grants to develop detailing programs and educational materials for physicians.

The following are examples of the successful programs mentioned previously:

1. Pennsylvania: Independent Drug Information Services (iDiS).
   This program first began in 2005 with an annual budget of $1 million and is sponsored by the Program of Alternative Certification for Educators (PACE) of the Pennsylvania Department of Aging. A group of independent doctors and researchers at Harvard Medical School develop all clinical content. Trained detailers meet individually in doctor's offices and offer information about a range of topics, including pain management, diabetes, mobility, and depression. You can find comprehensive materials available on its Web site at: http://www.RxFacts.org.
2. Vermont: Vermont Academic Detailing Program.
   University of Vermont College of Medicine sponsors this program. It first began in 2004 with a budget of $50,000; the budget doubled in 2008 to $100,000. Each year, a new topic is devoted to the detailing efforts. In 2004, it was heartburn; in 2005, cholesterol; in 2006, hypertension; in 2007, depression; and in 2008, insomnia. Although not as

comprehensive as other Web sites, you can still find some materials on their detailing campaign at: http://www.med.uvm.edu/ahec/TB1+BL. asp?SiteAreaID=290.

3. South Carolina: South Carolina Offering Prescribing Excellence (SCORxE): The South Carolina College of Pharmacy (SCCP) and the South Carolina Department of Health and Human Services (SCDHHS) sponsor this program. Created in 2007, this program provides academic detailing to physicians who serve Medicaid patients with mental health disorders, HIV or AIDS, or cancer. SCDHHS provides $1.98 million to the college to administer this program. You will find general information about their detailing efforts, but are unable to gain access to their specific material on its Web site at http://www.sccp.sc.edu/SCORxE/index.aspx.

In our program in New York City, the academic detailing staff hired by DOHMH distributed a toolkit about depression and met with healthcare professionals to discuss the educational materials and to encourage their use. A comprehensive package of resource materials was included in the toolkit and included clinical tools for healthcare providers, as well as patient education materials that physicians could distribute to their patients.

A great deal of care went into the design of the depression toolkit that physicians received. DOHMH employed a marketing organization to work with them to develop the design concept of all the material. All materials in the toolkit are engaging, easy to read, and repeat the same message. In addition, the educational materials for patients are available in multiple languages (Spanish, Chinese, Korean, and Russian). The face-to-face contact with academic detailing staff, combined with helpful materials for both healthcare providers and their patients, made this campaign successful.

All the materials distributed in the toolkit include the following:

A. Healthcare Provider Resources

1. City Health Information (CHI) booklet on depression
This document gives useful background information about depression and suicide, provides a state-of-the-art screening tool (Patient Health Questionnaire [PHQ]-9), information on medications, and referral information.

2. Depression Pocket Guide
This pocket guide includes instructions about to how to use the PHQ-9 to screen for depression and to assess the efficacy of treatment provided.

3. Research articles on chronic disease and depression
   Articles distributed to physicians included "The Medical Management of Depression" (*The New England Journal of Medicine*, 2005) and "The Vital Link Between Chronic Disease and Depressive Disorders" (DHHS, the Public Health Service, the Centers for Disease Control and Prevention, 2005).

B. Clinical Tools for Healthcare Providers
   1. Adult Preventive Care Flow Sheet
      This document is a handy guideline for comprehensive screenings including smoking, blood pressure, body mass index, colonoscopy, mammography, immunizations, depression, and alcohol use. Two smaller screening tools are included for both depression (PHQ-2) and alcohol abuse (CAGE).
   2. Depression Management Goal Sheet
      A colorful and graphic instrument that can be used with patients therapeutically to help them better manage their depression.
   3. PHQ-2 Stickers
      These colorful stickers, containing key screening questions, help to identify patients at risk of depression and in need of a more complete assessment.
   4. PHQ-9
      This depression screening instrument helps providers identify and treat clinical depression. Copies of the full PHQ-9 were included for use with patients. For more information about the PHQ-9, please refer to chapter 4, "Patient Health Questionnaire (PHQ-9 and the PHQ-2)."
   5. Referral to Mental Health Services
      This document is a colorful handout for physicians to complete on patients that they are referring for mental health services.

In addition to materials for physicians, the toolkit included materials intended for use by the patient, including:

C. Patient Education Materials
   1. Common Symptoms of Depression (Fact Sheet)
      This document is a colorful handout for patients listing the symptoms for depression.
   2. Tips for Handling Depression (Fact Sheet)
      This document is a colorful and graphic instrument that mirrors the "depression management goal" sheet given to providers.
   3. "Depression. It's Treatable. Talk to Your Doctor" Easel
      This document, displayed at the doctor's office, includes the two-question depression screening tool (PHQ-2).

4. "Depression. It's Treatable. Talk to Your Doctor" Palm Card
   This document is a small pocket size handout for patients on depression.
5. "Depression. It's Treatable. Talk to Your Doctor" Poster
   This poster, displayed at doctor's offices, includes a description of the symptoms of depression.

The ultimate goals of the detailing campaign are to encourage physician behavior change and help physicians improve their ability to conduct depression screening, identify depression, and competently prescribe medication for depression. As an added incentive for doctors to read the material, a continuing medical education (CME) credit was obtained by taking and submitting the paper and pencil test found at the end of the CHI.

The detailing campaign for depression cost approximately $150,000 and lasted about 2 months. The individual kits cost about $20 each to reproduce. The detailing campaign undertaken in New York City has a few distinctions from those carried out in other areas. Most campaigns focus solely on medication management issues or concentrate most of their efforts on educating the doctors. Unlike other campaigns, the detailing done in New York City strongly emphasized consumer self-management and included several helpful tools to distribute to patients or for both patients and doctors to use together. Moreover, many of the other campaigns use detailers that are healthcare professionals (either pharmacists or nurses); this campaign used a combination of healthcare workers and individuals who had previously done detailing in the pharmaceutical industry. The campaign employed experienced detailers and used the most effective techniques. Although this detailing campaign has since ended, you can still review the materials online at: http://www.nyc.gov/html/doh/html/csi/csi-depressionkit.shtml.

FINAL TIPS FOR SUCCESS

The outreach and educational materials you create when you put EASE-D into practice will strongly support the goal of providing quality mental health education to older adults and their providers. Take the time to develop materials that will be both engaging and understandable to your intended audience. Make sure that both older adults and content experts review all materials. The content experts, such as mental health educators or practitioners, can confirm that you have highlighted the most critical points in your document. The older adult reviewers will ensure that the documents are easy to read and understand. Additionally, older adults should also review the document to verify the quality of the design and flow.

A checklist of tips that were discussed throughout this chapter follows, to help you develop materials throughout the entire process of your project. You might want to make your own checklist and see how many of the items that are on your list match those on this list.

CHECKLIST FOR DEVELOPING MATERIALS FOR OLDER ADULTS AND THEIR PROVIDERS

Types of Program Materials

- Informational material about EASE-D
  - For aging services providers _____
  - For mental health providers _____
  - For healthcare providers _____
- Outreach material for staff to distribute to older adults
  - Flyers about mental health education sessions _____
  - Other _____
- Educational material for older adults
  - Handouts summarizing key educational concepts _____
  - Handouts with mental health resource information _____
    - Hotline numbers
    - Local mental health providers
    - Other

Content Considerations

- Are critical components included?   Yes/No
- Did a content expert review documents?   Yes/No
- Did someone review the documents for readability?   Yes/No
  - Reviewed by staff   _____
  - Reviewed by older adults   _____
- Is language easy to understand?   Yes/No
- Have documents been translated and back translated?   Yes/No
- Did someone review the documents for cultural competence?   Yes/No
  - Reviewed by staff   _____
  - Reviewed by older adults   _____
- Are sentences short and to the point?   Yes/No
- Are key points limited to no more than 3–5?   Yes/No
- Have you used active voice in writing?   Yes/No
- Have you repeated key concepts within the document?   Yes/No

REFERENCES

American Foundation for the Blind. (2010). *Tips for making print more readable.* Retrieved March 1, 2010, from http://www.afb.org/Section.asp?SectionID=26&TopicID=144& DocumentID=210

Arditi, A. (2009). *Effective color contrast: Designing for people with partial sight and color deficiencies.* Retrieved March 1, 2010, from http://www.lighthouse.org/accessibility/ design/accessible-print-design/effective-color-contrast

Avorn, J., & Soumerai, S. B. (1983). Improving drug-therapy decisions through educational outreach: A randomized controlled trial of academically based "detailing." *New England Journal of Medicine, 308*(24), 1457–1463.

Berkman, N. D., DeWalt, D. A., Pignone, M. P., Sheridan, S. L., Lohr, K. N., Lux, L., et al. (2004). *Literacy and health outcomes. Evidence report/technology assessment no. 87.* (Prepared by RTI International-University of North Carolina Evidence-based Practice Center under Contract No. 290-02-0016, AHRQ Publication No. 04-E007-2, pp. 1–8). Rockville, MD: Agency for Healthcare Research and Quality.

Bix, L., Lockhart, H., Cardoso, F., Selke, S. (2003). The effect of color contrast on message legibility. *Journal of Design Communication.* Retrieved March 1, 2010, from http://scholar.lib.vt.edu/ejournals/JDC/Spring-2003/colorcontrast.html

Bradley, B., Singleton, M., & Li Wan Po, A. (1994). Readability of patient information leaflets on over-the-counter (OTC) medicines. *Journal of Clinical Pharmacy and Therapeutics, 19*(1), 7–15.

Byrd, M. (1985). Age differences in the ability to recall and summarize textual information. *Experimental Aging Research, 11*(2), 87–91.

Center for Medicare Education Issue. (n.d.). Translating materials for non-English speaking audiences [Issue brief]. *Center for Medicare Education, 1*(3), 1–4. Retrieved March 1, 2010, from http://medicine.osu.edu/sitetool/sites/pdfs/ahecpublic/Translating_ Materials_for_NonEnglish.pdf

Communicating with patients who have limited literacy skills. Report of the National Work Group on Literacy and Health. (1998). *Journal of Family Practice, 46*(2), 168–176.

Davis, T.C., Long, S.W., Jackson, R.H., Mayeaux, E. J., George, R. B., Murphy, P.W., et al. (1993). Rapid estimate of adult literacy in medicine: A shortened screening instrument. *Family Medicine, 25*(6), 391–395.

Food and Drug Administration. (1999). Over-the-counter human drugs; Labeling requirements. Food and Drug Administration, HHS. Final rule. (1999). *Federal Register, 64*(51), 13254–13303.

Gazmararian, J. A., Baker, D. W., Williams, M. V., Parker, R. M., Scott, T. L., Green, D. C., et al. (1999). Health literacy among Medicare enrollees in a managed care organization. *The Journal of the American Medical Association, 281*(6), 545–551.

Levav, I., Kohn, R., Montoya, I., Palacio, C., Rozic, P., Solano, I., et al. (2005). Training Latin American primary care physicians in the WPA module on depression: Results of a multicenter trial. *Journal of Psychological Medicine, 35*(1), 35–45.

Meyer, B. J. F., Young, C. J., & Bartlett, B. J. (1989). *Memory improved: Reading and memory enhancement across the life span through strategic text structures.* Hillsdale, NJ: Erlbaum.

National Institute on Aging. (2008). *Making your printed health materials senior friendly.* Retrieved March 1, 2010, from http://www.nia.nih.gov/NR/rdonlyres/ D8994383-6F06-4C07-B560-2A32247D3991/9571/NIA_Health_Materials _TipSheet51308.pdf

National Patient Safety Foundation. (2003). *Eradicating low health literacy: The first public health movement of the 21st century*. Retrieved March 1, 2010, from http://www.npsf.org/askme3/pdfs/white_paper.pdf

O'Brien, M. A. T., Oxman, A. D., Davis, D. A., Haynes, R B., Freemantle, N., & Harvey, E. L. (2001). Influence of educational outreach visits on behavioral change in health professionals (Cochrane Review). *Cochrane Library*, (4). Oxford: Update Software.

Parker, R. (2000). Health literacy: A challenge for American patients and their health care providers. *Health Promotion International, 15*(4), 277–283.

Penny, R. (2000). *Variation and change in Spanish*. New York: Cambridge University Press.

Ray, W. A., Taylor, J. A., Meador, K. G., Lichtenstein, M. J., Griffin, M. R., Fought, R., et al. (1993). Reducing antipsychotic drug use in nursing homes: A controlled trial of provider education. *Archives of Internal Medicine, 153*(6), 713–721.

Rubin, A., & Babbie, E. (2001). *Research methods for social work* (4th ed.). Belmont, CA: Wadsworth.

Soumerai, S. B. (1998). Principles and uses of academic detailing to improve the management of psychiatric disorders. *International Journal of Psychiatry in Medicine, 28*(1), 81–96.

Stevens, B. (2003). How seniors learn. *Issue Brief Center for Medicare Education,4*(9). Retrieved March 1, 2010, from http://www.mathematica-mpr.com/PDFs/howseniors.pdf

U.S. Department of Health and Human Services. (2000). *Healthy People 2010* (2nd ed.). With understanding and improving health and objectives for improving health (2 vols.). Washington, DC: U.S. Government Printing Office.

van Eijk, M. E., Avorn, J., Porsius, A. J., & de Boer, A. (2001). Reducing prescribing of highly anticholinergic antidepressants for elderly people: Randomised trial of group versus individual academic detailing. *British Medical Journal, 322*(7287), 654–657.

Williams, M. V., Parker, R. M., Baker, D. W., Parikh, N. S., Pitkin, K., Coates, W. C. (1995). Inadequate functional health literacy among patients at two public hospitals. *The Journal of American Medical Association, 274*(21), 1677–1682.

Young, S.A. (1999). *Developing, translating, and reviewing Spanish materials: Recommended standards for state and local agencies*. State of North Carolina Department of Health and Human Services Division of Public Health Migrant and Refugee Health Programs. Retrieved March 1, 2010, from http://ncpublichealth.com/pdf_misc/DEVSPAN-web.pdf

7

How to Implement EASE-D
in Your Community

Having a solid understanding of the three main program elements comprising Educating About and Screening Elders for Depression (EASE-D), including mental health education, depression screening, and linkage to treatment, you may be wondering how to implement this model within your own program or network of programs. This chapter will discuss the key components of program implementation, including developing partnerships among stakeholders to deliver all three aspects of the program, meeting the required staffing needs, and managing budgetary considerations. Additionally, this chapter includes guidelines for conducting a programmatic needs assessment and constructing useful tools to evaluate EASE-D.

CREATING COLLABORATIVE PARTNERSHIPS FOR PROGRAM IMPLEMENTATION

Whether it is to promote community investment or to encourage service systems to become more active participants in the program, one critical dimension in EASE-D is partnership and coalition building. As resource rich as any one aging services program might be, it is likely that at a minimum, you will need to identify the mental health resources in your community to involve them in program implementation. It will also help to reach out to the medical centers as well, to encourage the helpful participation of physicians who may evaluate the at-risk older adults identified. An advantage of using the EASE-D model is the opportunity it creates to develop linkages across service systems. Our implementation of the model has been successful because it represents the substantial support of organizations from both aging and mental health.

We have organized our program in collaboration with the following types of agencies:

Government

- The New York City Department for the Aging (DFTA), the largest Area Agency on Aging (AAA) in the United States
- The New York City Department of Health and Mental Hygiene (DOHMH)

Nonprofit

■ The local senior centers that are administered through the New York City DFTA
■ The Mental Health Association of New York City (MHA of NYC)

Each entity has had a pivotal role in the development and ongoing support of this program, operationally or financially. For example, the MHA of NYC runs and operates the program, the DFTA acts as the liaison to the senior centers and directs the program evaluation, the DOHMH orchestrated the detailing campaign for physicians, and the community-based senior centers house the program and encourage attendance of their members. In addition, both DOHMH and DFTA provide financial support for the program.

It is an enormous benefit to establish similar partnerships in your community and working toward coalition building to meet the mental health needs of older adults in the community. General benefits of developing a coalition include:

■ **Resource coordination.** By coordinating resources across service delivery systems or agencies, you will expand your reach in ways that you could not with a single delivery system. Examples of resources include knowledge between programs, staff with varying expertise, publications, and facilities.
■ **Improved collaboration.** Organizations will learn more about members' services and programs. Working together, aging and mental health organizations will develop new opportunities to provide services collaboratively.
■ **Professional development.** Individuals and organizations involved in the coalition will increase their own knowledge of community resources. Increased knowledge will improve the quality of services for individual programs and clients by expanding the base of referrals and the capacity to link older adults to assistance across service systems.
■ **Broader influence.** Coalitions have greater influence over public officials and legislators than individual entities, because they are speaking in a "bigger" voice. Consequently, there is the potential for a greater impact on public policy, public expenditures, and grant opportunities. Coalition-sponsored events and activities, such as public awareness campaigns, can reach greater numbers in the community.
■ **Long-term planning.** As coalitions have more resources available to them; they can undertake more extensive long-term planning, such as a

community needs assessment. Coalitions can identify cross system gaps in service and develop collaborative plans for how to address these needs. (Modified from The National Coalition on Mental Health and Aging, 1994)

Often, regional coalitions evolve out of an identified program need requiring multiple service delivery systems. It can be easier to develop the initial commitment of various agencies when you come together with a specific purpose, such as implementing a single program or intervention. Organizations working together on EASE-D will form a shared vision, which can transform the work of the partnership long after EASE-D is established.

Developing a Coalition

An effective coalition of multidisciplinary partners includes mental health providers, government organizations such as your local AAA or local health and mental hygiene departments, health care providers, aging organizations, and universities and community colleges (The National Coalition on Mental Health and Aging, 1994). Each member of your coalition should have an investment in your program and be able to identify their role in helping EASE-D take shape.

Local mental health programs may be able to assist you by providing workshop presentations and depression screening. These same programs can also serve as a referral source for older adults in need of treatment following a depression screening. There is a built-in incentive for mental health programs to participate in EASE-D, as reimbursement is available through Medicare or Medicaid for the older adults that they may serve in their clinic (third-party reimbursement may also be available, as well). It is also helpful to have health care professionals on the coalition to promote this program with colleagues and older adults. Often, older adults are more comfortable seeking help through their own primary care physician; a doctor who is sensitive and knowledgeable about depression will become your best advocate with their elderly patients in supporting recommendations for treatment. We have found in our work that collaborating with government is advantageous for securing funding, resources and encouraging the political will of all parties. Although not currently an integral part of our program model in New York City, universities can be beneficial in assisting with the creation of program evaluation and tracking materials. Universities can also support the program by lending students for operational support. Additionally, faculty can increase the visibility of your program by documenting your success through submissions to peer-reviewed journals.

STAFFING AND BUDGETARY CONSIDERATIONS

Organizations wanting to put EASE-D into practice will have to consider the staffing and budgetary needs for implementation. Each of the three main elements of EASE-D have implications for staffing and the total budget required to implement the program.

Staffing Considerations

Staffing needs for each mental health education session will vary depending on various factors, including the size of the group, frailty of participants, and diversity of languages spoken. Large workshop attendance, a significant number of frail participants, and a wide range of languages spoken at a given location are all factors that will increase the number of staff you need to run the program.

In general, we designate one bilingual staff person to conduct the mental health workshops and pretreatment care management. It is ideal if this is the same person, as many older adults prefer to receive follow-up from someone they already know, but you can assign these tasks to several different staff members, if needed. The depression screening portion of the educational session generally requires at least two to three staff members to assist the workshop leader, as screenings will need to occur simultaneously for multiple participants. For some workshops, you might find you need up to four staff members present, if the group is very large, or if there are a large number of frail participants or individuals with low literacy or vision impairment. For example, if you were conducting workshops in English and in Spanish at a single location, either you would need to select a single bilingual staff person to run the workshops in both languages and to conduct the pretreatment care management, or you will need additional staff.

In addition to conducting mental health education and depression screening, you will also need staff to assist with the development of all program materials. Administrative support will be helpful to coordinate the scheduling of workshops and photocopying all materials. In general, we assume the actual administration of the program requires approximately three staff (who could be part-time, if necessary). In our program, we conduct workshops in multiple senior centers throughout the five boroughs of New York City; to manage the workload, we have one full-time bilingual staff person to coordinate the program and conduct the majority of the workshops and two to three part-time assistants to help with the depression screening after each workshop.

It is important to consider the level of expertise needed for the staff managing each component of the program. The required skill set will depend on the tasks to be completed in each program element. Beyond considerations of the sheer numbers of participants and their language needs, you should explore the educational background and knowledge base of your staff in your planning process. As you review the staffing needs, keep in mind that to conduct the workshops and the pretreatment care management services, it will be helpful to have staff that are social workers or related disciplines. At the very least, to run a mental health workshop, the workshop leaders and pretreatment care managers should have adequate knowledge of mental health and related health care topics.

However, note that we make a distinction between *education* and *expertise*. You also need to consider the talent and personalities of your staff. You might find that certain staff members (regardless of their educational background) have a gift for speaking in groups, but these same individuals may not be comfortable with the pretreatment care management follow-up with members. Alternately, you might have staff that work well individually with older adults but are not at ease speaking in groups.

For example, at your aging services agency, you might be fortunate to have social workers or nurses on staff able to assist with the depression screening and pretreatment care management. Keep in mind, however, that a person who is a good clinician may not have the expertise necessary to run an engaging mental health workshop with a group of older adults. As you review your staffing needs, you should consider the following:

- Number of available staff who can be designated to work on this program
- Language capabilities of staff: Are bilingual staff available?
- Staff education and expertise: Are staff knowledgeable about mental health available to:
  - Conduct a mental health education session?
  - Conduct depression screenings after the education session?
  - Conduct the pretreatment care management to link older adults to treatment?
- Staff education and expertise: Are the staff available able to:
  - Comfortably address mental health topics with a group of older adults?
  - Manage group process skillfully during educational sessions?

To aid program planning, it may be helpful to review the following list of the different tasks associated with the development of EASE-D. As you review this list, can you identify tasks for which you will need to locate outside staff to execute this program? Alternatively, do you have enough expertise within your program to manage each component? For example, perhaps you have individuals that can assist in back office support and can assist in depression screening, with training. However, perhaps none of your staff has the right personalities or educational training to run a mental health workshop. You should make a list of staff you currently have and staff you would need to run EASE-D (see Table 7.1).

TABLE 7.1   Staffing Needs for Implementation of EASE-D

	NUMBER OF CURRENT STAFF	NUMBER OF STAFF NEEDED
Administrative staff		
Staff to develop workshop content		
Staff to develop materials (outreach and educational)		
Staff to run workshops (can be part-time)		
Staff for screening (can be part-time)		
Staff for pretreatment care management (if not the same as those that run the workshop)		

Budgetary Considerations

Your identified staffing needs will help inform your financial considerations. Obviously, the number of staff needed will affect the funds required to administer the program. The collaborative model of EASE-D can be particularly helpful at addressing budgetary concerns, because it encourages the pooling of personnel and financial resources between agencies.

This list contains budgetary items to consider when implementing EASE-D:

- Staffing;
- Photocopying and producing materials;
- Refreshments;
- Promotional items (giveaways for the workshop participants); and
- Conditional cash transfers (if these or other incentives are being used).

Some of the budgetary items, such as staffing, are obviously necessary to run the program. Others, such as refreshments or promotional items, may be optional. If you work at a senior or community center, you are well aware of the intrinsic benefit of having promotional items and refreshments to recruit participants to events; however, the program can certainly function without them.

Conditional cash transfers or other incentives are also helpful with older adults who require additional encouragement to accept a referral.

As discussed in chapter 5 (see under "Conditional Cash Transfers"), conditional cash transfers compensate older adults for costs such as co-payments for appointments with medical or mental health providers or for transportation. Although these incentives can ease the way for older adults to accept a referral, once in the program and engaged in pretreatment care management, older adults often forget about that aspect of the program. Although these incentives may be helpful, if the budget will not permit them to be included, you can either reduce the amount of money offered or even eliminate them altogether.

Remember, too, that the flexibility of program design can allow for the implementation of a project on a smaller scale, if funds are in short supply. For example, rather than conducting an entire mental health workshop series, organize a single workshop focused on depression, followed by a depression screening. Or, rather than working in a large number of sites over a wide geographic area, concentrate on working within a smaller number of sites or in a particular catchment area, such as a single community or within a single network of senior centers. Starting a pilot project on a smaller scale will reduce the overall costs of implementation and will still provide useful information for agencies that wish to expand EASE-D over time.

Once you have determined the budgetary items you need and the costs associated with accommodating them, you can determine whether you have sufficient funds from within your program to allocate to this initiative or whether you will need to secure funding elsewhere. If, after your program assessment, you determine that you need to locate outside resources, you might find that you can maximize your programming potential by developing a coalition of potential stakeholders.

CONDUCTING A PROGRAMMATIC NEEDS ASSESSMENT

Before implementing EASE-D, you will likely need to conduct a program evaluation to determine how best to put the model into practice. Program evaluation is a commonly used method for systematically developing programs and services (Rossi & Freeman, 1982). One does not have to be a researcher to carry out a useful evaluation. Although not often credited for doing so, administrators use program evaluation to examine all stages in the life of a program, from its initial design, to implementation, and finally to measuring intervention outcomes.

The first step in a program evaluation is conducting a needs assessment and outlining the different components of the program. Another aspect of program evaluation is the creation of a logic model involving program inputs, process, outputs, and outcomes.

Logic Model: Program Inputs, Process, Outputs, and Outcomes

A *logic model* considers the natural flow within the life of the program and is a particularly useful tool for program planning. Through the development of a logic model, one delineates the specific service strategies and outcomes for the program (Kumpfer et al., 1993). Logic models typically convey the relationship among program inputs, process, outputs, and outcomes (Conrad & Randolph, 1999; McLaughlin & Jordan, 1999; Wholey, 1987).

Program inputs consist of required resources for you to implement your program (e.g., funding, staffing, and participants). *Process* refers to how you will implement the program (e.g., methods and interventions used in the program). *Outputs* refer to the units of service (e.g., number of older adults that attended your workshops or number of older adults who tested "positive" to the depression screening tool). Finally, *outcomes* refer to the program's impact on the older adults (e.g., increased knowledge of mental health or increased numbers of older adults who are now in treatment).

What Is a Needs Assessment?

To develop a useful logic model, one should first engage in a programmatic *needs assessment* (Center for Substance Abuse Prevention's Western Center for the Application of Prevention Technologies, 2008). A needs assessment is a way to determine whether there are gaps within a given program or service system (Witkin & Altschuld, 1995). In our case, conducting a needs assessment helps to delineate more clearly the type and number of participants that would most benefit from EASE-D. This type of assessment could entail looking at your individual aging services program, or in the case of an AAA, a network of aging services. It may be advantageous to expand the needs assessment to a community level, especially if you are considering expanding the reach of your program beyond your current members to those individuals in the broader community.

In the following section, we will discuss how to conduct a needs assessment at the program level; however, you can easily apply these concepts to a community needs assessment, just on a larger scale. These days, it is common to need to embark on such an undertaking with limited resources. A community needs assessment is a more complex undertaking than a program needs assessment; unless you have staff with research experience, such a task will necessitate collaboration with a local university or other research institution.

CONDUCTING A NEEDS ASSESSMENT

The first step in a needs assessment is to identify the number of older adults in your program or aging network that are potentially affected by depression, as well as any barriers to obtaining help that they may experience. Additionally, it is helpful to understand how much the older adults in your program already know about mental health and mental disorders, the mental health and health care services that exist in your community, and which topics would be of most interest to them. This information will help you to develop the specific workshops that would be most useful for the older adults you serve. If you are part of a larger network of aging services, this information can assist in targeting efforts.

What Information Should You Collect?

When first undertaking a program assessment, it is helpful to formulate a list of questions you will answer in your analysis (Berkowitz, 1996). All components of the needs assessment will flow from these questions. In other words, what would you want to know before you implement EASE-D?

The following list of questions should help you to get started:

- How much do older adults know about mental health and mental illness?
- How much do older adults know about the mental health services in our community?
- Which mental health topics would be of the greatest interest?
- How many people have depression?
- How many members are already in mental health treatment?
- Have we conducted mental health workshops in the past?
- Have there been difficulties in conducting mental health workshops in the past?
- Do we have any information pertaining to mental health in our members' case files?

With Whom Should We Collect the Information?

Once you have a comprehensive list formulated, you should consider the various sources of the information (Berkowitz, 1996). You might choose to go directly to your membership, talk with staff, or review case records. Examine the preceding list of questions; what would be the best source of information (see Table 7.2)?

As you can see, there are certain questions where you would clearly go to one particular source for the information. Such is the case with the

TABLE 7.2   Sources of Information

QUESTIONS	SOURCE OF INFORMATION
How much do older adults know about mental health and mental illness?	Members
How much do older adults know about the mental health services in our community?	Members
Which mental health topics would be of the greatest interest?	Members
How many people suffer from depression?	Members, staff, client records
How many members are already in mental health treatment?	Members, staff, client records
Have there been difficulties in conducting mental health workshops in the past?	Staff
Have we conducted mental health workshops in the past?	Members, staff, program records
Do we have any information pertaining to mental health in our case files?	Client records

question, "How much do older adults know about mental health and mental illness?" However, some questions will lend themselves to multiple sources of information. To find out how many people have depression, you could obtain answers by asking your membership, asking staff for their impressions, or even examining your case records. You will gain a different perspective depending on the source, or sources, of the information.

When you have multiple sources of information, one could emerge as the most reliable. For example, take the question, "Have we conducted mental health workshops in the past?" Although you could ask the members for this information, it may not be accurate, because members may have forgotten or simply may not have been at the senior center on the day of the event. In this case, talking to staff or looking at programmatic records could be the most helpful. If one source does not emerge as the most reliable, we recommend triangulating your approach. Simply put, use various sources and methods to collect your information, because each will carry with it its own perspective and all will deepen your understanding.

How Should We Collect This Information?

How you collect information will be informed by the source of the information itself. For example, if you wanted to obtain your information from your program staff, the easiest and most expeditious method would be either to talk to them individually or to hold a staff meeting. However, if you are capturing information from a larger network of agencies, or you want to obtain information directly from your members, there are various other options available to you.

A relatively quick and easy way to obtain large amounts of data would be to conduct a survey (Rubin & Babbie, 2001). By asking everyone to complete a short survey, you can collect a large amount of information with minimal effort. You can conduct surveys through a printed questionnaire, over the telephone, by mail, in person, or on the Internet. A self-administered survey is called a *questionnaire*, whereas researchers call surveys administered by staff *interviews*. Those individuals that complete these surveys are known as *respondents*. Depending on the source of information, respondents can be the older adults that attend your senior center, staff in your program, or older adults who reside in the community.

At aging services agencies, staff can distribute self-administered questionnaires for completion on-site or they can mail out the questionnaires to their members. If you are handing out the questionnaires on-site, it is best to have staff available to answer questions. Staff will be helpful to those older adults having difficulty completing the questionnaire because of vision impairment, low literacy, or frailty. It is also a good idea to have extra pens available to hand out to your members to ease the completion of the survey.

Perhaps you are concerned that by simply handing out your survey, you will miss the feedback from members that are infrequently at your center. Or, you might have difficulty finding a time to administer the survey that is not disruptive to your membership. Another option is to mail out your questionnaire to your members and have them send it back to you when it is completed. If this is your chosen option, it is best to include a self-addressed stamped envelope to ensure a better return.

THE PROS AND CONS OF ON-SITE VERSUS MAILED QUESTIONNAIRES

There are advantages and disadvantages for each form of administering the questionnaire and deciding which to use will depend on multiple factors. Handing out your questionnaire for older adults to complete on-site is useful if you are concerned that some of your members may have difficulty completing it on their own. By involving staff to assist, any confusion or questions that arise can be resolved immediately. Staff can also communicate the importance of the survey and potentially increase the number of responses. This is also the fastest method of information collection and good to use if timing is of concern (Rubin & Babbie, 2001). You can pick a time or series of times to administer the survey and collect your responses rapidly. If cost is an issue, conducting a group-administered survey is the least expensive method of data collection (Trochim, 2006). Costs are minimal and include the photocopying of the questionnaires, staff time, and additional pens.

A disadvantage of handing out the questionnaire is that doing so relies on getting information from those individuals that are at your program on the day that you are administering the survey. This can influence your results, because you will never hear from those members who attend your program infrequently and are unlikely to be at the senior center when you are administering the survey. It can also be difficult to ensure that older adults complete the questionnaire on their own. It is common for spouses or partners to complete each other's questionnaire. You might even find group discussions emerging, risking the quality or accuracy of the responses. During these situations, it is best if a staff member can gently reinforce the need to gather responses on an individual basis.

Mailed questionnaires also have advantages and disadvantages. Sending out a mailed questionnaire ensures that your entire membership has an opportunity to respond to the survey. Older adults are able to complete the survey at their own leisure, without their favorite activities disrupted by the administration of the questionnaire. Although the costs and time associated with a mailed survey are more than they would be by simple on-site distribution, it is less expensive than the other methods discussed later (Rubin & Babbie, 2001; Trochim, 2006). The costs of a mailed survey include photocopying, postage, and the inclusion of a self-addressed stamped return envelope. With a large membership, these costs can quickly multiply. You must also allocate more time to complete a mailed survey because of delivery time. Furthermore, because staff are not available to assist with the completion of the questionnaire, this is not a good method to use if you are concerned that your members might have impaired literacy or frailty, which would make it difficult for them to complete the survey on their own (New England States Consortium, 2001). Finally, because you are not overseeing how the questionnaires are answered, it is impossible to ascertain whether the older adults actually completed the questionnaires on their own or whether it was completed by other family members.

USING INTERVIEWS AS PART OF NEEDS ASSESSMENT

Another type of survey is the *interview*. In an interview, staff read questions to the older adults either in person or over the phone and then records older adults' responses. This method allows the greatest control in ensuring that older adults fully understand the questions and offers the greatest response rate (Rubin & Babbie, 2001; Trochim, 2006). However, challenges to this method include time and costs (Frey & Oishi, 1995). This is the most expensive type of survey because it requires staff to individually interview each older adult; this may be unrealistic because of staffing concerns in your program or because you do not have staff that are able to conduct the interview in the older adults' language.

In addition, an interview requires finding a convenient time to speak with respondents, which can be difficult to accomplish during the workday. Interviews generally take longer to administer than a self-administered survey (Frey & Oishi, 1995). A self-administered questionnaire that usually takes about 15 minutes to complete could take 30–45 minutes in an interview. Finally, the quality of the responses you achieve from older adults will depend on the relationship that older adults have with the staff that is administering the interview. This can work to your benefit or detriment when asking personal questions.

It may not be best to conduct an interview when you are asking for personal information, because an older adult may be hesitant to answer questions truthfully, especially when staff who are familiar with the older adult are acting as the interviewers. The anonymity of completing a self-administered questionnaire can result in respondents feeling more comfortable in sharing truthful responses (Hill, Dill, & Davenport, 1988; Klein & Cheuvront, 1990; Werch, 1990).

Conducting an Interview: Tips and Techniques

Interviews can be either structured or unstructured. A structured interview is most common in survey research (Frey & Oishi, 1995; Rubin & Babbie, 2001). The structure of the interview parallels that of a self-administered questionnaire in that there is a specified structure and order to the questions. The guidelines for putting together a structured interview should follow the same principles discussed within questionnaire construction. You certainly want to make every effort to create an interview schedule that is free of jargon and is simple to complete. Fortunately, the interviewer will be able to explain any question that seems ambiguous to the older adult.

An unstructured interview is more of an exploratory process (Rubin & Babbie, 2001). The interviewer, armed with general themes or questions to explore, adapts the specific questions asked as the interview unfolds. The interviewer may ask different questions of each of the respondents but explores the same themes with all respondents. An unstructured interview guide will look very different from a structured guide, more closely resembling what you might find in a focus group. We will discuss focus groups guides later in the chapter (see "Focus Groups," which follows).

Conducting an interview can be extremely beneficial, especially when you are concerned that most of your older adult respondents will be unable to complete a self-administered questionnaire without maximal assistance. However, if you decide to conduct an interview, carefully consider which staff to use as interviewers. A well-intentioned staff person can create bias in an older adult's answers simply by how they ask the questions (even their intonations can guide a respondent's answer). If the interview is conducted in person, unintentional nonverbal cues can also influence responses (Finch, 1984; Ribbens, 1989). It is critical that the interviewer never does anything that would make the older adult uncomfortable answering any of the questions. The older adult's perception of the interviewer should be neutral; he or she should not perceive the interviewer as someone to please. The interviewer's role is to ask the questions in a structured order, provide explanation when the older adult is confused about a specific question, and to write down all answers on the interview guide (Trochim, 2006).

The interviewer must also keep the older adult focused on the task. Often, when an older adult is engaged by a particular question, he or she might veer off course spending time chatting with the interviewer. Questions as simple as, "Who do you live with?" could end up taking an hour to answer if the interviewer is not careful. For example, the older adult could become engrossed in sharing the story of how his or her spouse died, prompting a move to his or her daughter's home, and may engender a conversation about all of the inner dynamics of that family relationship. There is a risk that by the time the older adult has finished this first lengthy story, he or she will be so fatigued that he or she is unable to complete the other 10 questions. This example illustrates the importance of the interviewer gently maintaining focus, while being respectful to the older adult completing the questionnaire. This takes skill and a bit of experience to achieve. Unless you are able to employ seasoned interviewers, it is a good idea to hold a training session with your staff to go over the interview guide and even role-play some situations so they will be better prepared.

FOCUS GROUPS

Another common method of needs assessment is a *focus group*. Focus groups are group discussions centered on a particular theme, or set of themes, and are particularly useful in gathering information in great depth (Lindlof & Taylor, 2002; Thomas, MacMillan, McColl, Hale, & Bond, 1995). In a focus group, a relatively small number of people (10–12 participants are ideal) comes together to have an in-depth discussion, directed by a moderator or facilitator. The moderator skillfully asks questions to promote interactive exchanges among the participants. This methodology differs from surveys, because participants are free to say anything and are not bound to respond only to the questions on a page. These groups often run for about 2 hours, with the facilitator recording the discussion using an audiotape. After the focus group, the moderator should transcribe the audiotape to capture all pertinent information.

In focus groups, it is best to keep the number of questions that are asked to a minimum (no more than six), so there is time for participants to share their thoughts thoroughly. The facilitator should tape record the discussion so as not to miss anything critical. You might also find it helpful to have an additional staff person available to take notes as well, in case the tape recorder stops working, or the recorded voices are not audible. It is also helpful to have refreshments available for the participants as a way of thanking them for their participation and promoting a friendly environment. The focus group generally has three components: the opening, the questions (heart of the focus group), and the ending or wrap-up (Krueger, 1994).

In the opening, you should welcome the participants, explain the purpose of the focus group and most importantly, highlight the group rules. Common focus group rules include (a) everyone will have the opportunity to share their opinions, (b) there are no right or wrong answers, and (c) even the most negative comments are welcome. As you move to the interview questions, ensure that everyone has the opportunity to speak before moving on to the next question. As you end the meeting, it is often helpful to summarize the discussion and the purpose of the focus group and to ask each participant for the most important point that they heard.

Often, people like the focus group method because it is easy to coordinate and because of the generally high quality of the information that is obtained (Chang & Hsu, 2006). However, focus groups also present certain challenges. If you have members that speak multiple languages, you will need to conduct multiple focus groups with moderators that speak those languages, because the use of translators would hinder free-flowing discussion. The facilitator should be someone skilled at promoting an open discussion and adept at managing group process to ensure that everyone is able to talk and no one person monopolizes the conversation. In other words, the quality of information directly corresponds to the facilitator's skill at promoting discussions (Burrows & Kendall, 1997; Krueger, 1994).

Although the transcript of the focus group discussions can be engaging to read and provide unanticipated information, it is exceedingly difficult to analyze textual data (Rabiee, 2004). It is also not an ideal method to use when discussing extremely sensitive topics. Participants in the focus group may not be comfortable sharing personal information in a group situation, especially with people they may know (Krueger & Casey, 2000).

Imagine, for example, how you would feel attending a focus group with your coworkers to talk about the difficulties in your relationship with your significant other!

Table 7.3 highlights the various methods of needs assessment and compares their advantages and disadvantages.

TABLE 7.3   Methodology Used Within Needs Assessment

METHOD	WHEN TO USE	STAFFING	ADVANTAGES	DISADVANTAGES
Survey: Questionnaire (mailed or handed out)	Want to get a large amount of information quickly	None to minimal staff needed	Relatively inexpensive and easy to analyze	Unsure if older adults understood the questions Quantitative data may miss nuances **Mailed survey:** Cannot use where literacy or frailty is an issue or response rate is low
Survey: Interviews (either through the phone or face-to-face)	Want to ensure thorough and accurate responses	Need for staff to conduct interviews	Quality of the information	If multiple languages, must have bilingual staff Time-consuming and costly
Focus groups	Want to fully explore topic in group discussion	Need for facilitator to conduct group	Quality and depth of information	Hard to analyze, facilitator may need to be bilingual

UNDERSTANDING DATA: QUANTITATIVE AND QUALITATIVE

Before reviewing other aspects of survey design, it is helpful to discuss the different types of data that are commonly included in a survey because this affects question construction. Information gathered through surveys are mainly, although not exclusively, quantitative in nature. Quantitative data involves the analysis of numeric information (numbers). Data obtained from surveys are able to describe large amounts of information, generally through the reporting of overall percentages or means. Although the best surveys tend to include some qualitative data, it is usually at a minimum (Rubin & Babbie, 2001). Qualitative data involves the interpretation of data that is textual in nature (words or text).

For example, consider the different ways that you might describe the membership at your center using quantitative and qualitative data (see Table 7.4).

TABLE 7.4   Describing Quantitative and Qualitative Data

QUANTITATIVE DATA	QUALITATIVE DATA
▪ Number attend on a daily basis = 150	▪ Members are fiercely loyal to their center
▪ 80% women, 20% men	
▪ 20% scored at risk of depression on a rating scale	▪ Enjoy bingo and socializing
	▪ Members talk about friends that struggle with extreme sadness

CONSTRUCTING A QUESTIONNAIRE FOR A NEEDS ASSESSMENT

When creating a questionnaire, you should adhere generally to the same principles used to create program materials (for more information, refer to the discussion in chapter 6, under "Educational Materials for Older Adults"). A questionnaire should be easy to read and understand (Borgatti, 1998). As questionnaires are self-administered, they often need minimal staff intervention. In general, the longer and more complex a questionnaire is to complete, the fewer questionnaires that you will receive back (Bogen, 1996). Think about the questionnaires that you have likely completed over the years and then refer to the descriptions of questionnaires that follow. Which one would you be most likely to complete with carefully thought out answers?

- **Questionnaire A.** This questionnaire has poor focus and asks many intrusive questions without a clear reason for doing so. The directions are complicated and the language is difficult to understand. The author has reduced the font size to include more questions and has reduced the amount of white space between the questions, making it difficult to read. Finally, the questionnaire reads like a book and is more than five pages long.
- **Questionnaire B.** This questionnaire clearly explains its purpose. It has subheadings to lead the respondent through the instrument. The author has reduced the number of questions asked. The questions are easy to understand and the questionnaire is easy to read visually. The question-naire is only two pages long.

Clearly, you will obtain better returns from Questionnaire B and the quality of the responses is likely to better, as well. Respondents will undoubtedly take more time to complete a questionnaire that is pleasing to the eye and easy to understand. How can you ensure that the questionnaire you are constructing resembles Questionnaire B and not Questionnaire A? The following list contains some helpful tips for putting together a questionnaire:

- Keep it short, simple, and focused;
- Keep the number of open-ended questions to a minimum;
- Avoid loaded and leading questions; and
- Avoid double-barreled questions.

Keep It Short, Simple, and Focused

There is nothing worse than answering extraneous questions having little to do with the main purpose of the survey. As you design your questionnaire, it is likely that you will need to resist the temptation to include interesting questions having little to do with the main purpose of the assessment. A lengthy and unfocused questionnaire is likely to result in the respondent's resentment, poor quality of responses, and diminished returns (Borgatti, 1998). As you construct the questions for the questionnaire, make sure to keep the language simple that members of all literacy levels will be able to understand. You should never use technical language and make sure that the meaning of the question is clear (Martin, 2006). When you ask older adults to complete the survey while at your program, the time they use to answer your questions will take them away from other activities. If it takes too long, they will likely discard the survey so as not to miss their favorite activity. It is a good idea to review the questionnaire and ensure that each item relates to one of the questions put on your original list at the beginning of the assessment. Be parsimonious in your approach to creating your questionnaire; remember, each additional question will reduce the number of responses that you receive.

Keep the Number of Open-Ended Questions to a Minimum

The two main question types included in surveys are *closed-ended* and *open-ended* questions. In closed-ended questions, the potential answers are limited to a fixed set of responses. The following are all examples of closed-ended questions: yes–no questions, multiple-choice questions, or scaled questions. For example:

1. **What is your gender?**
   ____ Male
   ____ Female

2. Are you currently taking any medication for depression?

____ Yes

____ No

____ Unsure

3. What is your race/ethnicity? (check ALL that apply)

____ Hispanic or Latino

____ Asian

____ White or Caucasian

____ Black or African American

____ Native American or Alaskan Native

____ Native Hawaiian or Pacific Islander

____ Other: Please specify: _____

4. Over the last 2 weeks, how often have you been bothered by any of the following problems (see Table 7.5: PHQ-2)?

TABLE 7.5 Patient Health Questionnaire 2

	NOT AT ALL	SEVERAL DAYS	MORE THAN HALF THE TIME	NEARLY EVERY DAY
Little interest or pleasure in doing usual activities.				
Feeling down, depressed, or hopeless.				

Questions 1 through 4 are all examples of different types of closed-ended questions. In each case, the respondent has a predetermined set of responses. Note that all questions are numbered; this will keep the respondent from missing items as they go through the questionnaire. Notice, too, that in Question 2, we have included an "unsure" option to allow for those respondents who do not know whether they are taking medication for depression. Including an "unsure" or "does not apply" response category is an important strategy. Incorporating these response categories helps respondents answer all of the questions; they are not likely to skip these questions simply because there was not an appropriate category for them to answer. Otherwise, when information is missing on a questionnaire, it will leave you wondering whether they overlooked that question or simply did not know how to respond. Frequently, the "unsure" categories will be meaningful, especially in designing mental health-related programming. For example, knowing the number of older adults who are unsure whether they are taking medication for depression can inform your planning on a medication management workshop.

All response categories should be exhaustive. This is often accomplished by including an "unsure" and an "other" category to ensure that every option is captured. Remember, if you include "other," always ask the respondent to specify their answer; this way, you will be able to appreciate the uniqueness of their response.

Question 3 is a check-all-that-apply question. It is important to include simple directions that allow respondents to select multiple choices from the list. Otherwise, they may think that they need to choose only one option. This could result in your missing critical pieces of information. Finally, you may recognize Question 4 from our discussion on mental health screening tools in chapter 4. This question is actually the first two questions of the PHQ-9. Scaled questions such as these are also common close-ended questions. Analyze scaled questions together as they are less meaningful when examined as separate questions. For example, in Question 4, only those older adults that checked off "several days" or more to either question are at risk for depression. In the case of the PHQ-9, you actually combine all nine questions to determine whether someone is at risk for depression. Unless you are creating a multiple-choice question, all response categories should be mutually exclusive (each option is distinct from the other). To ensure the quality of the information, we need to eliminate all ambiguity.

Closed-Ended Versus Open-Ended Questions

Questionnaires usually contain primarily closed-ended questions; however, it is best to pepper your survey with at least a few open-ended questions. Open-ended questions do not have predetermined categories and instead, the respondent simply writes in their answer. For open-ended questions, it is important to include enough space for older adults to write in their answers. If your members speak and read a language other than English, you will need to translate all the data from the questionnaires. When translating the questionnaire from English to another language, you should adhere to the principles of translation discussed in chapter 6 on developing program materials (see under "Educational Materials for Older Adults").

The following are some examples of open-ended questions:

1. **Where were you born? (e.g., United States, China, Korea, Puerto Rico, Dominican Republic, etc.)**

_____

2. **Are there any other health and wellness topics you would like to hear about in the future?**

_____

_____

Some questions could be either open or closed ended. For example:

1. **How old are you?** _____   **How old are you?**
                                          ___ Younger than 60
                                          ___ 60–64
                                          ___ 65–74
                                          ___ 75 or older
2. **What activities do you participate in at your center?**
   _____   ___ Meals
                                          ___ Educational workshops
                                          ___ Bingo
                                          ___ Arts and crafts
                                          ___ Other: _____

There are advantages and disadvantages to both types of questions. Closed-ended questions are easier to answer, easier to analyze, and take less time for the respondent to complete. However, these types of questions also tend to box people into certain categories (Martin, 2006). Respondents will sometimes check off a category, even if they do not have an opinion. Open-ended questions allow older adults to fully express themselves and communicate the unexpected. Individuals are not restricted to one answer and can give unlimited responses. However, these types of questions also present certain challenges. Although the older adult may like the freedom to write what is on his or her mind, it is tiring to have many open-ended questions, because they require more energy and time to complete (Fowler, 1995). These questions are also more difficult to analyze because you are sifting through a significant amount of text and uncovering common themes to the data (Martin). The quality of the information relies on whether you are able to accurately read and understand the responses. If the older adult's handwriting is difficult to decipher or if the response is confusing, you are likely to lose the ability to use that information.

Avoid Loaded and Leading Questions

Take care to review the wording of all questions to ensure that the responses you obtain will not be biased (Fowler, 1995; Martin, 2006; Schaeffer & Presser, 2003). Questions that are *leading* (phrased in such a way that the respondent can predict the answer that you are looking for) or *loaded* (containing words carrying unintended connotations) can sway the respondents' answers and invalidate the results of your needs assessment. The following is an example of a question that is both leading and loaded:

> The administration is considering eliminating fresh fruit from its lunch menu. Given the nutritional impact that this is likely to have among our participants, do you support this decision? ____Yes   ____No

Avoid Double-Barreled Questions

Questions should contain one idea; do not try to combine multiple questions into one item. This type of question, called *double-barreled*, is difficult to answer. For example, how would you answer the following question, "How satisfied are you with meals and location of your senior center?"

What if you thought the meals at your senior center were wonderful, but you were dissatisfied with the location of the center? It would be better to separate this question into two separate questions, one asking about the meals and the other specifically about the location.

Exercise: Evaluating a Questionnaire

Now that you know more about constructing a useful questionnaire, it is time to practice your skills. Look at Questionnaire A (Table 7.6) and try to identify its problem areas. How might you improve on them?

TABLE 7.6   Troubled Questionnaire A

Exercise 1a. Troubled Questionnaire A on Mental Health
Title: Older adults experiencing mental health problems
1. What is your age?   ____ Younger than 60   ____ 60–65   ____ 65–75
2. Have you had a myocardial infarction? ____   Have you attended any of the following workshops given at your center?   ____ Nutrition   ____ Depression   ____ Medication
3. Participating in senior center activities is considered to help older adults stay healthy, would you attend any health workshops that we offered in the future?   ____ Yes   ____ No
4. What workshops topics would you be interested in attending at your center? Please check all that apply.   ____ Medication   ____ Stress   ____ Memory loss

Were you able to identify the problems with the preceding questionnaire? See the annotated questionnaire that follows (Table 7.7) for the identified problem areas.

TABLE 7.7 Identified Problems With Questionnaire A

Exercise 1b. Identified Problems With Questionnaire A
Title: Older adults experiencing mental health problems   **(Emotionally charged title might prevent some older adults from responding)**
1. What is your age?   ____ younger than 60   ____ 60–65 **(How would you answer if you were 65? Make sure categories do not overlap.)**   ____ 65–75 **(How would you answer if you were older than 75? Needs an older-than-75 option to ensure that the options are exhaustive.)**
2. Have you had a myocardial infarction? _____ **(Technical wording—could be confusing, better to ask if they have had a heart attack.)**   Have you attended any of the following workshops given at your center?   ____ Nutrition ____ Depression ____ Medication **(Make sure to include question numbers so this question will not be over-looked. The list is not exhaustive. What should you select if you have not attended a workshop? Can you check all that apply? What should you select if you have attended more than one type of workshop? If so, you need to let the respondent know that they should check all that apply.)**
3. Participating in senior center activities is considered to help older adults stay healthy, would you attend any health workshops that we offered in the future? **(Leading question, also no option for "no opinion.")**   ____ Yes   ____ No
4. What workshops topics would you be interested in attending at your center? Please check all that apply. **(It would be difficult to have an exhaustive list of all potential workshop topics; this would be better suited as an open-ended question.)**   ____ Medication   ____ Stress   ____ Memory loss

Did you also notice how difficult the questions were to read? The close positioning of the questions and the small font size would certainly have made it difficult for most older adults to read. Remember, if you want your members to spend their valuable time completing your survey, you need to spend the time to create a questionnaire that looks engaging and professional.

Once you have constructed your survey, we recommend piloting the instrument with older adults to ensure that it is easy to understand. It is a good idea to have a short discussion with the older adults who have volunteered to complete the pilot survey to obtain their recommendations for revisions, especially before the survey goes "live."

DATA ANALYSIS: QUESTIONNAIRES AND FOCUS GROUP INTERVIEWS

Once you have conducted your needs assessment and have your surveys returned and your focus group interviews transcribed, what do you do next? If you are fortunate to have staff skilled in analytics, they can take the information and process the results for you. However, most organizations do not have such resources available to them. Another option would be to collaborate with a local university to see if there is a professor or student that could process your information. If this is still not an option, do not worry—there are still simple steps you can take when analyzing your information.

Analyzing Data From Questionnaires

Before you begin to examine your data, you should first go back to that initial list of questions that you constructed when first undertaking the needs assessment. Writing out your questions will help you develop a plan for data analysis, because you can cross-check the actual questions with the items on the questionnaire that answer those questions.

What questions did you want to have answered? For example, your list might look like this:

- What is the profile of older adults that attend my senior center? (Questions 10–12)
- How many older adults have attended mental health workshops at my center in the past year? (Question 6)
- How many older adults seem to have some form of depression? (Questions 1–9)
- Do I see a difference in the percentage of older adults that are at risk for depression when I look at my multiple senior center programs? (Program site by Questions 1–9)

In the preceding example, to answer the first question, you would look at Questions 10, 11, and 12. These are likely your demographic questions, which would describe the individuals who answered your survey (age, gender, race/ethnicity). Question 6 on your survey will answer the second question on your list. The third question is a bit more complex, because we know that the depression questions are summed together in an index, involving Questions 1 through 9. The final question would be of interest if you have multiple centers, or perhaps are within an AAA, and are contemplating where to focus your energies in EASE-D. Here you would want to make sure that you clearly identify which senior center the person completing your survey attended; then you would assess whether the risk for depression differed by program. This can be a more sophisticated analysis, using various types of statistical techniques. However, you can also simply examine the data for trends. Remember, your aim is not to conduct a rigorous study or publish your reports in a peer-reviewed journal but rather to assist in program planning of EASE-D.

Once you have your questionnaires completed, the easiest way to examine them would be to use a computer software program. Putting the information in a spreadsheet package, such as Microsoft Excel, or using an online survey package, such as Survey Monkey, will expedite the process. If you are using a spreadsheet, the columns should represent the questions and the rows the individual responses. The spreadsheet should look something like the example in Table 7.8.

TABLE 7.8   Spreadsheet of Data

RESPONDENT	PROGRAM SITE	AGE	GENDER	ATTENDED WORKSHOP DEPRESSION	ATTENDED WORKSHOP MEDICATION	ATTENDED WORKSHOP OTHER	OTHER WORKSHOP SPECIFIC
1	Center A	65	Female	Yes	No	No	
2	Center B	63	Male	No	No	Yes	Nutrition
3	Center A		Female	No	No	No	

The preceding example places each data element in a separate column and each respondent in his or her own row. In reviewing this example, you can conclude that Respondent 1 attends Senior Center A and is a 65-year-old woman who has only attended a depression workshop, whereas Respondent 2 attends Senior Center B and is a 63-year-old man who has attended an "other" workshop, which is specified in a text field as nutrition. What can you tell about Respondent number 3? Although we do not know her age, we do know that she attends Senior Center A and has never attended a workshop at her senior center.

One common mistake that people new to research or needs analysis often make is to place multiple-choice questions in one column on a spreadsheet. Although on the questionnaire, the following examples seem to be one question, there are actually more questions hidden beneath than what is readily apparent. For example:

1. Have you attended any of the following workshops at your senior center in the past year? Check all that apply.
   ___ Depression/emotional wellness
   ___ Medication management
   ___ Other (please specify: _____)

Or
2. Race/ethnicity: Check all that apply.
   ___ White/Caucasian
   ___ Black/African American
   ___ Hispanic
   ___ Asian/Pacific Islander
   ___ Other (please specify: _____)

Question 1 requires four columns, one for each option and one for the open-ended response. How many columns do you think that Question 2 would require? Although this can be confusing, because this is a multiple-choice item, you will need six columns. Remember to include a column for the open-ended text field. In general, the instruction, "check all that apply," will necessitate one column per possible response on your spreadsheet. It is helpful to place all open-ended items in the body of the spreadsheet, although this type of information is analyzed using a different method.

Analyzing Data From Focus Group Interviews

Analyzing information gathered through a focus group is a very different process than with data from questionnaires. The information is textual in nature, so instead of reporting percentages or other numbers, you are revealing common themes lurking beneath the text (Krueger & Casey, 2000). Your first step in analyzing focus group data is to transcribe the audiotapes verbatim (word for word). For ease of analysis, it is best to single space all individual comments and double space between speaker's comments. Although there are various methods you can take when interpreting the information, the following list gives you a suggestion for one possible method:

1. Review all transcripts to get a general idea of potential themes. Pay particular attention to whether several participants within the same focus group made similar comments and whether participants from different focus groups (if you are doing more than one) made similar comments.
2. You should list potential themes by question. Start your list with general, broad-based categories. Do not worry if some of the quotes do not seem to fit anywhere. If they do not seem to either respond to the particular question asked or the goal of the focus group, just put them aside for now. You do not have to use everything said in the focus group.

3. Now begins the "arts and crafts" component of the analysis. Take large paper and write out the broad-based themes. Cut and paste each quote that captures the essence of those themes and place them on the corresponding page.
4. Within each category, begin looking for comments that share similar thoughts and group them into subcategories. Categorize the subcategories and give them an identifier given that describes the particular domain.
5. Finally, review all categories and ask yourself, was anything confirmed through the themes, anything refuted, anything surprising?

Exercise: Evaluating a Questionnaire

Look at the focus group responses that follow (see Table 7.9). In the following exercise, try to identify how you might categorize the quotes. Do you see any subcategories? What did you learn?

TABLE 7.9   Focus Group Transcript of Question 1

Comment 1: Participant J. "I don't think that older adults are interested in attending classes; they really come to the center to socialize and have a good meal."

Comment 2: Participant H. "Yes, I agree. At my center, the men really just want to play pool. They don't want to sit for class."

Comment 3: Participant L. "I don't think that is the issue. I think that people get concerned that if their friends see them in a class on depression, they will assume that they are crazy."

Comment 4: Participant J. "Definitely! I am concerned about what people think. I don't want people to think I have a problem."

Comment 5: Participant B. "I think it has to do with when the classes are held. People like to do many different activities and often the classes are at the same time as our sewing class."

Comment 6: Participant L. "I remember a dear friend suffered from depression, it was such a difficult thing."

Comment 7: Participant A. "I don't think you will find any barriers. Members love attending all workshops."

Comment 8: Participant C. "I agree. At my center, members flock to any workshop having to do with health issues."

Question 1: What are the potential barriers to holding an educational workshop on depression in your senior center?

Now that you have seen the focus group responses, review the following general categories and subcategories (see Table 7.10). Do you see anything emerging from this short illustration?

TABLE 7.10 General Categories That Emerge From Question 1

RANGE OF ACTIVITIES	CONCERNED ABOUT WHAT OTHERS THINK	NO ISSUE
Comment 1: Participant J. "I don't think that older adults are interested in attending classes; they really come to the center to socialize and have a good meal." **Subcategory: No interest classes** **Comment 2: Participant H.** "At my center, the men really just want to play pool. They don't want to sit for class." **Subcategory: No interest classes** **Comment 5: Participant B.** "I think it has to do with when the classes are held. People like to do many different activities and often the classes are at the same time as our sewing class." **Subcategory: Timing of classes**	**Comment 3: Participant L.** "I think that people get concerned that if their friends see them in a class on depression, they will assume that they are crazy." **Comment 4: Participant J.** "I am concerned about what people think. I don't want people to think I have a problem."	**Comment 7. Participant A.** "I don't think you will find any barriers. Members love attending all workshops." **Comment 8. Participant C.** "At my center, members flock to any workshop having to do with health issues."

General Categories

As you probably noticed through the preceding exercise, there is definitely an art to analyzing focus group information. You might find that how we categorized the comments are different from how you might have interpreted the same information. Notice how we have identified a participant with each comment. In this way, we can tell that Participant J thought members are not interested in taking classes but was also concerned about what others might think if they attended such a workshop. In the case of the first broad category, two different subcategories seemed to emerge (lack of interest in classes and the timing of classes). We also took out statements that did not contribute to the meaning of the quotes, such as "I agree" or "Definitely."

DEVELOPING PROGRAM EVALUATION TOOLS

As we have previously stated, the first step in implementing EASE-D should be to conduct a simple needs assessment of your membership base. This could be with your one program or with multiple programs. Once you have a good sense of the needs of your membership, the types of workshops that would carry the most appeal, which programs you will target (if you have more than one) and have developed your logic model, the next step is to look at the other components of the program model to ensure that all pieces are in place before undertaking this initiative.

Pretests and Posttests to Evaluate Mental Health Education

EASE-D lends itself to using various useful evaluation tools in the operation of the program, weaving themselves into the fabric of the program design. One such tool is a *pretest* and *posttest questionnaire* that we give out during each workshop. The purpose of the pretest questionnaire is to determine how much older adults know about the mental health topic prior to the mental health education session; the purpose of the posttest questionnaire is to determine whether older adults have changed their understanding of the mental health topic after participating in the session. If the mental health education has been successful, you will see a significant increase in older adults' knowledge after participating in the session.

We administer the pretest and posttest as a single workshop packet to each older adult who participates in education sessions. The questionnaires are anonymous to allow for an honest appraisal of the program. However, we always make staff available to assist an older adult that may have difficulty completing the survey based on frailty, vision loss, or cognitive impairment. Although you must allocate additional time within each session for the completion of these surveys, we have found that the information captured has been invaluable to the development of the program. The information that we incorporate into each pretest and posttest includes:

- Demographic information on workshop participants;
- Section to capture new health or mental health needs;
- Knowledge-based questions on the workshop topic;
- Satisfaction based questions; and
- New workshop ideas.

Demographic Items

The pretest always include demographic items (age, gender, race/ethnicity, etc.) to better identify the types of individuals that are attending our workshops. Demographic information can help us ascertain if categories of older adults are not attending our workshops; if so, we know we will need to improve our outreach strategies. For example, by asking for race/ethnicity, we can ensure that our workshop participants represent the various racial and ethnic groups that attend the senior center.

New Health or Mental Health Needs

We always include questions that capture other potential needs of the membership. For example, although our programmatic focus is to identify those older adults who may be at risk for depression, we have also asked questions about other concerns, such as anxiety, drinking behavior, and medication management. The answers we collect from these questions have enabled us to construct additional workshops for our mental health education series, such as a workshop on anxiety and a workshop on the safe use of medications.

Knowledge-Based Questions

It is helpful to include knowledge-based questions to ensure that older adults understand the mental health information discussed during each workshop. We tailor the knowledge-based questions to the learning goals of each workshop. The knowledge-based questions for a depression workshop will relate to the information given in the workshop about depression. The knowledge-based questions for a workshop about anxiety will relate to the information given in that particular workshop.

We include approximately five or six knowledge-based questions for each workshop; each question highlights a different learning concept. We include exactly the same knowledge-based questions on both the pretest and the posttest to determine the knowledge gain resulting from workshop attendance. All participants answer true–false questions, with an additional "I don't know" option included. If, after reviewing the pretest and posttests, we find older adults are having difficulty understanding a concept, we will alter the delivery of our information to make the concepts easier to understand.

Satisfaction-Based Questions and Soliciting New Ideas for Workshops

Satisfaction questions are included at the conclusion of the posttest to ensure that the workshop leader was easy to understand and that the session was interesting and enjoyable. We also ask older adults to write down which aspects of the workshop were the most helpful, as well as ideas for future workshops. The feedback to these questions allows us to continually refine our approach as mental health educators.

PROGRAM EVALUATION: OUTPUTS AND OUTCOMES

We capture both outputs and outcomes through the evaluation tools. Outputs that we examine include (a) the number of older adults attending workshops, (b) the number screening for depression, and (c) the number testing positive to the depression screening tool. Program outcomes we evaluate include (a) older adults' increased knowledge of mental health, (b) their satisfaction with program, and (c) the number who have a mental health assessment with their either primary care provider or mental health professional.

The information we collect from the pretests and posttests and the depression screening instruments remains confidential for program evaluation purposes; the information we use does not have any personal identifiers. We only retain personal information for those older adults who receive pretreatment care management services. We maintain all materials for those older adults accepting a mental health referral in a separate file from the rest of the program information. As discussed in chapter 5 (see "Developing Data Collection Instruments"), pretreatment care managers record all interactions with the older adults on a standardized data collection tool and also conduct and document a final interview describing the result of the appointment with a medical or mental health provider. We examine this information to document the number of older adults that connect with a qualified care provider for clinical evaluation and treatment, because this is a critical outcome of our program.

All of the information gathered during program implementation contributes to the ongoing support of the program. Analyzing program data allows us to improve current workshops and to develop and test new workshop ideas. Additionally, gathering information about important program outcomes has enabled us to secure continued funding for EASE-D in our community, because we are able to document the program's successes.

IMPLEMENTING EASE-D IN YOUR COMMUNITY

Throughout this chapter, we have outlined the various components to consider as you develop EASE-D in your setting and community. We have discussed the value of conducting a needs analysis and developing a logic model in the initial stages of this undertaking. We have also discussed the importance of taking into account both staffing and budgetary needs. In addition, we have highlighted the use of developing tools for program evaluation. Each of these steps is instrumental to enriching your program and in obtaining its continued financial support. Finally, woven into the fabric of EASE-D is the benefit of establishing partnerships and coalitions. The partnerships that you will likely establish in the development of EASE-D will award you the opportunity to lay the groundwork for a coalition of organizations, enriching your community with mental health programming and, in turn, educating others to the extensive benefits of aging programs.

CHECKLIST FOR IMPLEMENTING EASE-D

Staffing Needs

- Administrative oversight _____
- Program coordination _____
- Mental health educators _____
- Depression screening staff _____
- Pretreatment care managers _____

Funding Needs

- Staff _____
- Materials development _____
  (workshop content, outreach/educational resources) _____
- Refreshments _____
- Promotional items _____
- Conditional cash transfers or other incentives _____

Logic Model and Needs Assessment

- Outputs _____
- Outcomes _____
- Needs Assessment: Method
  - Self-administered questionnaires _____
  - Interviews administered by staff _____
  - Individual interviews _____
  - Focus group interviews _____
- Data analysis
  - Survey data (quantitative analysis) _____
  - Focus group interviews (qualitative analysis) _____

Program Evaluation

- Pretests and posttests _____

Potential Collaborative Partners

- Aging services providers   _____
  - Community centers   _____
  - Senior centers   _____
  - Network of aging services   _____
- Mental health providers   _____
- Local government agencies   _____
  - Health or mental health departments   _____
  - Area agency on aging   _____
- Institutes of higher learning or research
  - Universities   _____
  - Colleges or community colleges   _____

REFERENCES

Berkowitz, S. (1996). Understanding and developing needs assessments. In R. Reviere, S. Berkowitz, C. C. Carter, & C. G. Ferguson (Eds.), *Needs assessment: A creative and practical guide for social scientists* (pp. 15–51). Washington, DC: Taylor & Francis.

Bogen, K. (1996). *The effect of questionnaire length on response rates: A review of the literature*. U.S. Bureau of the Census, Retrieved March 2, 2010, from http://www.census.gov/srd/papers/pdf/kb9601.pdf

Borgatti, S. (1998). *Principles of questionnaire construction*. Retrieved March 2, 2010, from http://www.analytictech.com/mb313/principl.htm

Burrows, D., & Kendall, S. (1997). Focus groups: What are they and how can they be used in nursing and health care research? *Social Sciences in Health, 3*(4), 244–253.

Center for Substance Abuse Prevention's Western Center for the Application of Prevention Technologies. (2008). *Using a logic model for evaluation planning*. Retrieved March 2, 2010, from http://captus.samhsa.gov/western /resources /bp/step7/eval2.cfm

Chang, M. Y., & Hsu, L. L. (2006). Qualitative research: An introduction to focus group methodology and its application. *The Journal of Nursing, 53*(2), 67–72.

Conrad, K. J., & Randolph, F. L. (1999). Creating and using logic models: Four perspectives. *Alcoholism Treatment Quarterly, 17*(1–2), 17–32.

Finch, J. (1984) "It's great to have someone to talk to": The ethics and politics of interviewing women. In C. Bell & H. Roberts (Eds.), *Social researching: Politics, problems, practice* (pp. 70–87). London, UK: Routledge and Kegan Paul.

Fowler, F. J., Jr. (1995). *Improving survey questions: Design and evaluation*. Thousand Oaks, CA: Sage Publications, Inc.

Frey, J. H., & Oishi, S. M. (1995). *How to conduct interviews by telephone and in person*. Thousand Oaks, CA: Sage Publications, Inc.

Hill, P. C., Dill, C. A., & Davenport, E. C. (1988). A reexamination of the bogus pipeline. *Educational and Psychological Measurement, 48*(3), 587–601.

Klein, K., & Cheuvront, B. (1990). The subject-experimenter contract: A reexamination of subject pool contamination. *Teaching of Psychology, 17*, 166–169.

Krueger, R. A. (1994). *Focus groups: A practical guide for applied research*. Thousand Oaks, CA: Sage Publications, Inc.

Krueger, R. A, & Casey, M. A. (2000). *Focus groups: A practical guide for applied research* (3rd ed.). Thousand Oaks, CA: Sage Publications, Inc.

Kumpfer, K. L., Shur, G. H., Ross, J. G., Bunnell, K. K., Librett, J. J., & Millward, A. R. (1993). *Measurements in prevention*. Rockville, MD: U.S. Department of Health and Human Services, Public Health Service, Substance Abuse and Mental Health Services Administration, Center for Substance Abuse Prevention.

Lindlof, T. R., & Taylor, B. C. (2002). *Qualitative communication research methods* (2nd ed.). Thousand Oaks, CA: Sage Publications, Inc.

Martin, S. (2006). *Survey questionnaire construction*. Washington, DC: U.S. Census Bureau.

McLaughlin, J. A., & Jordan, G. B. (1999). Logic models: A tool for telling your program's performance story. *Evaluation and Program Planning, 22*(1), 65–72.

The National Coalition on Mental Health and Aging. (1994). *Building state and community mental health and aging coalitions: A "how -to" guide*. Retrieved March 2, 2010, from http://www.empowermentzone.com/coalesce.txt

New England States Consortium. (2001). *Designing effective survey methods for frail elders symposium proceedings*. Retrieved March 2, 2010, from http://www.gmu.edu/departments/chpre/research/MMIP/TApapers/TApaper11.pdf

Rabiee, F. (2004). Focus group interview and data analysis. *The Proceedings of the Nutrition Society, 63*(4), 655–660.

Ribbens, J. (1989). Interviewing—An "unnatural situation"? *Women's Studies International Forum, 12*(6), 579–592.

Rossi, P. H., & Freeman, H. E. (1982). *Evaluation: A systematic approach* (2nd ed.). Beverly Hills, CA: Sage Publications, Inc.

Rubin, A., & Babbie, E. (2001). *Research methods for social work* (4th ed.). Belmont, CA: Wadsworth.

Schaeffer, N. C., & Presser, S. (2003). The science of asking questions. *Annual Review of Sociology, 29*, 65–88.

Thomas, L., MacMillan, J., McColl, E., Hale, C., & Bond, S. (1995). Comparison of focus group and individual interview methodology in examining patient satisfaction with nursing care. *Social Sciences in Health, 1*, 206–219.

Trochim, W. M. (2006). *The research methods knowledge base* (2nd ed.). Retrieved March 2, 2010, from http://www.socialresearchmethods.net/kb/

Werch, C. E. (1990). Two procedures to reduce response bias in reports of alcohol consumption. *Journal of Studies on Alcohol, 51*(4), 327–330.

Wholey, J. S. (1987). Evaluability assessment: Developing program theory. In L. Bickman (Ed.), *Using program theory in evaluation* (pp. 34–56). New Directions for Program Evaluation, no. 33. San Francisco, CA: Jossey-Bass.

Witkin, B. R., & Altschuld, J. W. (1995). *Planning and conducting needs assessments: A practical guide*. Thousand Oaks, CA: Sage Publications, Inc.

8

The Benefits and Challenges of Program Implementation

Like any intervention, Educating About and Screening Elders for Depression (EASE-D) will have its share of benefits to offer and challenges which should be identified as part of the ongoing planning process. The chief benefits, early identification of older adults with depression who are at risk for depression and successful linkage for treatment, are likely to be enough of an incentive for aging service agencies to undertake using EASE-D, either alone or in partnership with mental health organizations; however, the challenges exist at all stages of implementation and require management to help ensure successful program outcomes.

This chapter will review both the common advantages as well as the most common programmatic difficulties in implementing EASE-D and will review how you might address these problems to ensure successful programmatic outcomes.

THE BENEFITS OF EASE-D

The benefits of providing mental health education and offering depression screenings within community-based aging service programs are many. The chief benefits of EASE-D can be divided into two types, those that benefit the individual older adults at risk for depression and those that benefit organizations implementing the program. For older adults, they include raising awareness of depression and its available treatments, reducing the stigma associated with depression, identifying depression when it is present, and increasing the opportunity for older adults at risk for depression to follow through with referrals for mental health services.

There are also significant benefits for aging service agencies. Programs implementing EASE-D will be able to build collaborative working relationships across both the aging and mental health service sectors. The partnerships they create with other organizations will allow them to broaden their base for referrals within the mental health service system and may create the foundation for other innovative projects to address mental health among older adults. Mental health agencies, too, will benefit from collaboration on implementing EASE-D with aging service providers, because they will be able to cross-refer older adults they are serving to aging service programs.

Aging service programs may find that by addressing mental health needs, they can help at-risk older adult members remain actively engaged in senior center programming and reduce the risk of attrition because of unrecognized and untreated depression. Additionally, they will have established within their programs a flexible model of education for older adults, which can be adapted to address several mental health and health concerns. Aging service programs will be better able to meet the mental health needs of their members, and in the process, will increase their capacity to focus on health and wellness promotion and maintenance in general.

The Benefits for Older Adults

Raising Awareness of Depression and Its Treatment

Older adults who receive mental health education significantly increase their awareness about the impact of clinical depression. Concrete information about risk factors, symptoms, and available treatments helps older adults understand the context in which depression arises and helps them to know when and where to reach out for treatment for themselves or for a loved one. Education about physical and emotional self-care provides useful information to at-risk older adults about positive actions they can take to support themselves as they connect to treatment.

As we have seen, it is not uncommon for older adults to be able to identify the symptoms of depression, but to attribute them to something other than the disorder itself. Depression may be seen as a personal character defect, rather than as a treatable illness. Additionally, older adults may ascribe depression to chronic illness, bereavement, or financial stress, and not recognize it as a problem separate and apart from these other difficulties. As these other problems can be common in later life, and may indeed contribute to the development or exacerbation of depression symptoms, some older adults may see depression as an inevitable consequence of aging, which cannot be alleviated within the context of such stressors.

Educating older adults about depression not only increases their awareness about it, but also provides an opportunity to disentangle symptoms of one disorder from another and can serve as a gauge to determine what mental health or wellness topics should be addressed in future workshop sessions. An initial workshop about depression invites older adults to ask questions about other mental or behavioral disorders, such as anxiety, substance abuse, or dementia.

The goal of mental health education is not only to provide information but also to encourage older adults to take part in a depression screening.

Mental health workshops become critical components of the early identification process, because they enable older adults to reflect on and discuss their own thoughts, beliefs, and experiences before a depression screening questionnaire is ever administered. Providing information interactively, in a familiar environment, such as a senior center or other community organization, may help ease older adults' concerns about completing a depression screening questionnaire and speaking to someone about any symptoms he or she may be experiencing.

Reducing Stigma

For many older adults, stigma is a genuine barrier that must be addressed before the identification of depression and connection to treatment can begin. Despite the considerable advances in mental health treatment and increased public visibility and awareness of mental disorders, stigma remains a significant issue and should not be underestimated. Older adults reporting symptoms of depression may not only feel embarrassed about talking to others about depression, but may also feel deeply ashamed of themselves and on behalf of their families, as well. Embarrassment and shame can be significant personal barriers to seeking help for depression, regardless of the effectiveness or availability of treatment.

Concerns about reporting depression may go well beyond fears of social judgment or personal embarrassment. Before and during depression screenings, older adults commonly raise concerns that going to a professional for help will result in being forced to take medication against their will or, perhaps, even being involuntarily committed to a hospital psychiatric unit or nursing home. Often, workshop leaders and those conducting individual depression screenings will need to explain repeatedly the role of the mental health providers and essential aspects of treatment before an older adult is willing to take part in a screening for depression or to consider seeking help.

Implementing EASE-D in aging service programs addresses the stigma associated with mental disorders in an environment that is usually perceived as safe and familiar. Literally, "being where the client is" immediately addresses stigma by not requiring older adults to make any special effort to seek out information about mental health. Mental health workshops can be offered in the same manner that other health-related classes are given, such as sessions on nutrition or diabetes management. Additionally, they can be marketed internally as "health promotion" workshops that have a particular focus on emotional well-being.

Identification of At-Risk Older Adults

The most obvious benefit of screening older adults for depression is identifying those older adults who may be at risk and helping them connect to treatment services. Depression screenings provide an opportunity for older adults to engage in a supportive discussion of their emotional well-being without their having to seek specialty mental health services on their own. Depression screenings can serve as an early intervention, helping to identify those older adults for whom depression is a relatively recent occurrence. They can also identify older adults who may have histories of chronic or episodic depression who are experiencing a resurgence of symptoms, but have not yet connected with treatment resources. Depression screenings can also help older adults address any challenges they have with mental health treatment they may already be undertaking.

For example, during depression screenings, older adults who have experienced recurrent episodes of depression will remark that they are aware of being depressed, and that completing the questionnaire simply confirms what they already know. Some may report that they are currently in treatment but do not believe they are receiving adequate services or support and do not feel there is much they can do about it. The conversation with the person conducting the depression screening can help older adults obtain more appropriate services, as the following vignette illustrates:

Case Vignette: Ms. S.

Ms. S., a woman in her early 70s, attended a workshop about depression at her local senior center. During the workshop, Ms. S. was outspoken and lively and reported a prior history of depression that occurred as a young adult and again during her midlife years. Throughout the workshop, Ms. S. repeatedly discussed the benefits of treatment she had received and encouraged fellow participants to "do something about depression" if they were affected by it.

After the workshop, Ms. S. participated in a screening and was found to have significant depression symptoms, despite receiving treatment at an outpatient mental health clinic. She reported that she wanted to encourage the others, so she deliberately told her story to seem as if depression was no longer an issue for her. Ms. S. reported that she was taking the same antidepressant for years, and that although she did not feel the medication was working the way it should be and had discussed this with her psychiatrist during the last several visits, she felt the doctor was not responsive to her concerns. Ms. S. also reported having a counseling session with a social worker once a month at a local mental health clinic. Despite asking for more frequent counseling sessions, Ms. S. was not able to get additional appointments for psychotherapy with her therapist. Ms. S. stated that she was dissatisfied with her treatment but did not know what to do about it.

The person administering the depression screening explored the possibility of Ms. S. seeking services elsewhere if she felt she was not receiving adequate treatment. Ms. S. reported that it had not occurred to her to find other services—she figured she would just have to accept whatever treatment she got. Ms. S. took a referral from the screener and received pretreatment care management over the next month, during which time Ms. S. connected with another mental health clinic that was able to provide her with a reevaluation of her antidepressant medication as well as an increased number of sessions with a new therapist.

Facilitating the Connection to Treatment

Barriers to connecting with a primary care physician or mental health professional may be significant, even for older adults who seem highly motivated to seek evaluation for depression following their screening. As described in chapter 5 (see "Concrete Barriers"), common concrete barriers include physical illness, being the primary caregiver for a loved one, mobility impairment, transportation difficulties, not having a primary care physician, a shortage of mental health providers in a particular community, and lack of insurance coverage. Additional attitudinal barriers may be present as well, including ambivalence about treatment, the effects of stigma, and a continued perception that depression is a natural function of the aging process and that nothing can be done to alleviate it.

A critical aspect of the EASE-D model is the provision of supportive pretreatment care management to every older adult who accepts a referral and consents to follow-up services. Although generally a short-term service, pretreatment care management is often the key to helping older adults make the necessary connection to a qualified professional for a clinical evaluation and treatment recommendation. Through the provision of regular follow-up contact, older adults are supported, encouraged, and given useful information to help them navigate the challenges unique to their experience of connecting with a provider for services.

Although pretreatment care management may not solve all of the complications older adults may face, it can do much to troubleshoot these difficulties to assist older adults in their efforts to connect to services. One of the strongest benefits of this program component is its ability to continue with the psychoeducation begun in the mental health workshops, as well as to help older adults manage feelings of ambivalence or shame associated with seeking help for depression. The following example illustrates the usefulness of the contact with pretreatment care managers:

Case Vignette: Ms. M.

Ms. M., a woman in her mid-80s, lived alone and had limited contact with her family. She had several physical illnesses, including cardiovascular disease, diabetes, and arthritis. Except for a daily visit to her local senior center, Ms. M. did not leave her apartment unless it was absolutely necessary. Ms. M. had a high score on the depression screening questionnaire; she accepted a referral to visit with her primary care physician and agreed to receive follow-up contact from a pretreatment care manager.

During the initial weeks of follow-up, Ms. M. made no effort to meet with her doctor or any other helping professional about her depression. She reported that she was not motivated to speak with her doctor because she was skeptical that anything could be done to help her, because she saw her depression as being caused by her age. In conversations with the pretreatment care manager, she repeatedly asked, "I'm old, and I'm sick. Isn't depression natural at my age and condition? What can be done to help me, anyway?"

Over several weeks, her pretreatment care manager provided Ms. M. with psychoeducation about depression, including the relationship between chronic physical illness, stress, and depression symptoms. After several weeks of discussion, Ms. M. agreed to make an appointment to discuss depression with her doctor, who confirmed a diagnosis of clinical depression. The doctor provided a referral to a local mental health treatment program and a prescription for an antidepressant medication. During her last follow-up conversation with her pretreatment care manager, Ms. M. reported that initially, she felt she had to "just deal with" the problem of depression and did not fully understand that treatment was an option until she saw her doctor, and it was only after she had a consultation that she realized that help was available to her.

A secondary benefit of pretreatment care management is the opportunity it provides to collect useful data for subsequent program development. Using a standardized data collection tool allows program staff to collect whatever information is necessary to understand the individual and systemic challenges older adults experience as they seek services. This information is invaluable when creating future refinements in the program as it progresses, or advocating for systems change on a local level and beyond. Programs implementing EASE-D can analyze collected data to look for particular patterns in older adults' responses to follow-up, the responses of primary care physicians and mental health providers to those older adults who present for evaluations, and patterns of service use, all of which are critically important when designing and implementing mental health services for older adults.

Linkage to Treatment Services

Another important benefit of the mental health education and screening program is its ability to help at-risk older adults connect to evaluation and treatment services. For some older adults, an evaluation will mean a determination that depression is not present or is not clinically significant enough to warrant intervention, or that there is an underlying medical problem causing symptoms that needs to be addressed. For others, however, the initial connection with a provider will mark the beginning of treatment for clinical depression, whether psychosocial, pharmacologic, or both. Effective treatment, leading to significant symptom reduction or remission, will help older adults maintain occupational and social functioning, including participation in community-based programming and other forms of civic engagement. For many older adults, depression treatment will be critical in ensuring that older adults live their lives with as much satisfaction and fulfillment as possible.

The Benefits for Organizations

Creating Collaborative Relationships Among Service Providers

Often, providers in aging service and mental health agencies work in relative isolation, providing specialized services without a system of collaboration to ensure a full range of assistance to older adults. Aging service programs may informally identify mental health needs among their members but may not have adequate resources on-site to address them. Alternatively, mental health providers may be treating older adults with mental health needs but may not have enough knowledge of their local aging service system to provide connections to helpful community resources or entitlements.

No single agency or service system can be expected to meet all of their consumers' needs. However, through collaborative partnerships, providers of aging services and mental health agencies can build an increasingly comprehensive approach to working with older adults affected by depression. Such interagency cooperation can be essential for implementing EASE-D, because it is unlikely that either mental health providers or aging service programs have enough financial or staffing resources to administer such programs entirely on their own. Through collaboration, aging services providers can capitalize on available personnel and financial resources to support older adults who have mental disorders. Not only will older adults benefit, but the respective part-nering agencies will also, through cross-training in aging services and mental health. Providers of aging services can particularly benefit from the training mental health professionals can offer about how to identify older adults at risk for depression or other mental health concerns. Mental health providers can benefit from being able to serve older adults referred from aging service agencies within their own treatment programs, increasing their revenue. At the same time, increased knowledge of community-based aging services pro-grams can help mental health professionals develop a source of referrals for older adults in need of socialization or case management services specific to age-related benefits or entitlements.

When successfully implemented, EASE-D can lead to enhanced part-nerships in other initiatives geared toward improving the quality of life for older adults. For example, in New York City, because of the successful collaboration on EASE-D between the Department for the Aging and the Mental Health Association of New York City, our respective agencies were able to work together on two other projects focused on meeting the mental health needs of older adults. Increased collaboration between aging service and mental health service providers may help both compete more effec-tively for foundation and government grants, as well.

Flexibility of Program Model

EASE-D is flexible enough to be tailored to address multiple topics, includ-ing mental disorders other than depression. The workshop format, empha-sizing interactive knowledge building and the development of peer-to-peer learning, lends itself to adaptation. Other common conditions affecting mental health, such as anxiety, substance abuse, or dementia, can also be addressed. Workshops can be developed with a structure similar to the one used to educate about depression, and it is likely that the same person-nel who provided the depression workshop will also have the expertise to address the other mental disorders that may affect older adults. Workshops can occur on a stand-alone basis or be part of a series of mental health and health-related workshops. Programs implementing EASE-D may begin with a single workshop focused on depression and then build a series of mental health-related workshops, which may allow greater numbers of at-risk older adults to be identified and referred for evaluation and treatment.

Workshops can also be arranged as part of a larger educational series focusing on health-related subjects, as well as one concentrating on mental health topics. A dual health and mental health focus may be particularly use-ful in addressing the stigma associated with mental illnesses, because a focus on health conditions can provide a context for understanding related mental health problems. Additionally, developing workshops that have an explicit focus on physical health may encourage the attendance of older adults who otherwise might be reluctant to attend a mental health workshop. For example, a workshop on diabetes management can include information about the frequent co-occurrence of diabetes and depression symptoms and can highlight the telltale signs of depression of which older adults should be aware. At the same time, a depression workshop can also include information about physical health problems that can increase the risk of developing depression.

Placing the initial educational focus on physical health problems not only provides a forum for older adults to discuss concerns about their health, but also helps underscore the message that many mental disorders, like physical illnesses, can be treated. This message persists on an individual basis during the provision of depression screening following mental health education. The next vignette illustrates the ways in which these co-occurring issues can be discussed in a manner that addresses mental health in the context of physical health.

Case Vignette: Ms. D.

Ms. D., a woman in her mid-60s, attended a workshop about health conditions and depression and was found to be at risk after completing the depression screening questionnaire. When her symptoms were explored, Ms. D. remarked that she had persistently depressed mood for more than 3 years and could not recall ever having felt significantly depressed at any other time in her life.

When the screener asked Ms. D. if she thought anything happened 3 years ago to trigger her depressed mood, Ms. D. stated that she was diagnosed with diabetes 3 years before and had been struggling to manage the illness ever since. The screener then asked Ms. D. if she had ever reported her emotional symptoms to her doctor, to which Ms. D. replied, "It never occurred to me to mention it to my doctor, and she's never asked me about it before. Do you think that's something I should do?"

At this point, the screener reviewed with Ms. D. the information that had been covered in the workshop, explaining to Ms. D. that depression and diabetes often co-occur, and that, often, untreated depression can make it more difficult to manage diabetes, and that uncontrolled diabetes may contribute to making her depression symptoms worse. After further discussion, Ms. D. accepted a referral to discuss depression with her doctor and consented to pretreatment care management. During follow-up contact, Ms. D. reported receiving a diagnosis of clinical depression, a prescription for an antidepressant to address her depression symptoms, and a second referral to see a mental health professional for counseling.

Addressing Unmet Mental Health Needs as a Benefit for Service Provision

It is clear that there is a benefit for older adults at risk for depression when they are screened and make a successful link to evaluation and treatment services. However, there is also a benefit for aging services programs when they are able to connect their members to needed mental health treatment. Often, programs struggle to serve older adults with unaddressed mental health needs. Older adults who receive treatment and support for depression not only alleviate their symptoms but also may improve their capacity to function more effectively and to work more productively with their providers in aging services.

For example, an older adult with depression may be more difficult to engage in a senior center's activities. They may have increased apathy and lack the desire to participate in recreational or social pursuits; as a result, they may drop out of programming altogether, resulting in lowered service levels for the program and increased social isolation for the older adult. Older adults with depression may have decreased energy and capacity to concentrate and have more difficulty following through with other types of service provision, as well. They may not keep appointments with case managers or other program staff, even when staff are trying to connect older adults with necessary services or entitlements. If they do meet with service providers, they may have increased difficulty following through with the necessary steps to securing services or other benefits. Difficulties with engagement and lack of follow through, if not understood as potential by-products of depression, may lead to frustration and dissatisfaction on the part of service providers and older adults alike. By addressing older adults' mental health through the provision of EASE-D, providers may be better able to understand and meet the needs of their members more effectively.

Redefining Aging Services: Health and Wellness Promotion as a Core Function

In the last decade or more, aging service programs, particularly senior centers, have been called on to redefine their role in the community and to offer an increasingly wide range of services to their members. In 2000, the Older Americans Act incorporated amendments which enumerated the goals of "multipurpose" senior centers. These goals include a mandate for senior centers to become established providers of "health and wellness programs," which aim to promote good health and well-being among older adults (Pardasani, Sporre, & Thompson, 2009). Many senior centers and other aging services programs are heeding this call to redefine themselves and, whenever possible, devoting space and resources to exercise classes, fitness equipment and nutrition services.

Although mental health may not be an initial area of service expansion for aging services programs, it should not remain neglected. Mental health is critical to general health maintenance and successful aging. As we have seen, untreated depression wreaks havoc on the health and well-being of older adults, causing an array of difficult somatic symptoms, worsening other health outcomes, increasing disability, and overutilization of the health care system. Offering mental health education helps aging service programs contribute to older adults' ability to empower themselves with knowledge about depression and resources for treatment. Providing on-site depression screening allows aging service programs to offer their members a nonstigmatizing way to address depression without requiring them to seek specialty screening services outside of the aging services system. Conducting pretreatment care management provides aging services programs an effective strategy to support older adults in their efforts to secure treatment. By implementing EASE-D and incorporating mental health interventions into their repertoires, aging service programs will find themselves on the forefront of the paradigm shift toward health and wellness maintenance.

TROUBLESHOOTING CHALLENGES IN IMPLEMENTING EASE-D

The benefits of implementing EASE-D are significant for both older adults and their service providers. EASE-D can become the basis of regular and sustained efforts between aging service and mental health providers to identify older adults at risk for depression and connect them to treatment. However, as with any intervention, the benefits of EASE-D may also be accompanied by several challenges that will need to be navigated throughout program implementation. Providers of aging services will find that some of these challenges are beyond their immediate control. Some of these problems include a lack of mental health resources in a given community or the lack of effective responses to at-risk older adults from a particular health or mental health provider. There are other potential impediments, however, that programs implementing EASE-D can address effectively, such as technical difficulties about using depression screening instruments to identify at-risk older adults, coordination challenges between agencies, and finding adequate resources for staffing the program. Although many of these challenges are addressed in earlier chapters, some of the more significant are highlighted in the following sections.

Lack of Specialized Mental Health Treatment Services for Older Adults

Despite the impending demographic changes which will occur with the aging of the baby boom generation, both the medical and the mental health service systems have not yet developed an adequate response to address the mental health needs of older adults. As a result, the identification of depression during a screening may be the beginning of what could be an older adult's frustrating journey to obtain adequate treatment and support. Older adults may have limited access to mental health providers, particularly those who have expertise in treating mental disorders occurring in late life. If older adults have mobility impairments and their communities do not provide viable transportation options, access to existing treatment programs is further compromised. Older adults may also struggle with accessing good mental health treatment if their primary care physician does not have the necessary training to diagnose and treat depression effectively, does not have the expertise to provide helpful referrals to mental health specialists, or does not have the time or inclination to adequately monitor older adult patient's treatment adherence and progress.

Whenever possible, it is desirable to refer older adults to programs that have particular expertise in geriatric mental health. However, in many communities, such programs do not exist. Although successful models integrating health care and mental health services have been created, such as Improving Mood-Promoting Access to Collaborative Treatment (IMPACT; discussed in chapter 2, see "Which Model Is Right for My Organization?"), these have not yet been universally implemented. The lack of specialized programming for older adults with mental health needs is an issue with which communities are going to grapple for a number of more years to come.

Additionally, older adults who are able to access some kind of mental health treatment may feel out of place in the conventional mental health settings available to them. As one older adult we worked with stated, "I don't feel right sitting in my depression support group with all of these younger women. They're talking about issues which have nothing to do with me, and I feel like they can't relate to my problems, either." Additionally, programs may work with older adults whose primary language is other than English, making it difficult, if not impossible, to find linguistically and culturally appropriate services in some communities.

Providers of aging services will not be able to address, single handedly, these large and systemic challenges to serving older adults with mental health needs. Despite these complexities, however, we believe it is worthwhile to educate older adults about depression and advise them of the treatment options that exist in their communities. The health care community increasingly recognizes the need for including mental health interventions, such as depression screening and clinical care management, into their standard practice. Mental health providers, too, are increasingly aware that older adults will comprise a greater proportion of the population they serve and will require clinical interventions appropriate to their needs. Referring an at-risk older adult to their primary care physician or to a mental health provider may not immediately yield the desired results, but with the assistance of pretreatment care management, older adults can be supported through the process of finding another, more suitable provider, and will be better equipped to advocate for themselves as they seek appropriate treatment options.

Unsatisfactory Responses of Primary Care Physicians

Many older adults feel more comfortable having an evaluation for depression from their primary care physician, rather than seeking a consultation from a mental health professional. In addition to the familiarity older adults have with their regular doctors, many find it less stigmatizing to have a medical appointment rather than an appointment with a mental health specialist, such as a psychiatrist. Some primary care physicians are well attuned to the signs of clinical depression and respond effectively to older patients seeking evaluation for depression. At times, however, older adults seeking evaluation and treatment services from their primary care physicians face several barriers, including difficulty getting a timely appointment, lack of appropriate evaluation for depression and suicide risk, inadequate recommendations for treatment, or insufficient treatment monitoring.

Additionally, there are still some primary care physicians who believe that depression is simply a condition of older age, rather than an illness to be taken seriously and treated. In our follow-up with older adults, we have heard reports of doctors making statements to their patients such as, "You're 80 years old, and you're managing a chronic illness. It's only natural that you're depressed." When receiving this sort of message, some older adults may feel discouraged about seeking out further assistance and give up, resigning themselves to the idea that being depressed is their new "normal." Other older adults may feel frustrated by the lack of response from their physicians, feel they have wasted their time making an appointment, and may not know where else to turn for help.

If possible, it may be helpful for agencies implementing EASE-D to reach out to local health care providers to advise them that older adults at risk for depression may present themselves for clinical evaluations after a depression screening. This will help prepare doctors to expect to have conversations with their older adult patients about depression. In addition to preparing local health care providers, this type of outreach can help agencies gain some understanding about which practitioners may be more receptive to discussing depression with older adults. In areas which are too geographically large or too densely populated with health care providers for agencies to conduct significant personal outreach, a letter explaining EASE-D may be a useful way to advise health care providers about the program.

Although programs implementing EASE-D cannot control the reactions of physicians or other providers, pretreatment care management can help to mitigate less than helpful responses. The support older adults get from their pretreatment care managers may help counter the negative responses from their doctors about depression, and encourage them to continue making the effort to obtain treatment. Additionally, pretreatment care managers will be able to work directly with the older adult to help connect them to other mental health treatment services where they exist in the local community.

Difficulties in the Screening Process

Conducting a depression screening is not simply a matter of asking older adults to complete a simple questionnaire. There are multiple variables to consider before embarking on the process, and these include managing the potential challenges of administering a screening tool, ensuring participant confidentiality, and programmatic time constraints.

Administering Depression Screening Instruments

There may be several difficulties administering depression screening instruments in aging service settings, some of which may be unique to individual older adults being screened and some of which may be because of the depression screening instrument itself. For example, completing the screening instrument may be difficult for older adults who have low literacy or visual impairments. These problems can be ameliorated by having staff read the questions on the instrument aloud and recording older adults' answers directly on the instrument. If reading aloud is necessary, it may be helpful to relocate to a quiet area in the room or elsewhere in the center to ensure that older adults can hear what is being read to them and can respond in privacy.

Language may also be a consideration when administering the screening instrument. It is not uncommon for older adults to have verbal fluency in English but not be able to read English well enough to complete a screening instrument on their own. Although the staff person conducting the screening might be able to translate the instrument for an older adult, this on-the-spot translation may inadvertently lead to errors in administering the instrument. A more helpful approach is to bring different translations of the same instrument to workshops. This eliminates the need for translation and, if the instrument has to be read aloud, the depression screener's attention can be on helping older adults understand and answer the questions, rather than focusing on finding an appropriate translation for the questions.

As discussed in chapter 4 (see "What Are Important Factors to Consider When Choosing a Screening Tool?"), there are several factors to consider when selecting a depression screening instrument. Once you select an instrument, however, it will be helpful for program staff to note any particular challenges that arise during actual screenings. Some difficulties, such as language barriers or low literacy, can be anticipated and managed. For difficulties that seem to be particular to the instrument itself, however, it will be helpful to devise strategies to mitigate any structural problems with administering the instrument. For example, if older adults seem to have difficulty understanding a particular instruction or question on a depression screening instrument, having a standardized way of explaining the misunderstood text can help the screening process flow more smoothly.

However, depression screening instruments should never be revised. Rewriting items on a depression screening instrument may inadvertently change the meaning of each item, resulting in an inaccurate screening outcome. It is better to take the extra time required to explain the instrument in greater detail, provide an impromptu translation, or otherwise address problems with the screening instrument than to attempt to re-create a tested and validated screening tool. If a particular instrument proves to be too difficult to use with a given population, there are several other instruments available for use, and one or more of these may prove more suitable.

Privacy and Confidentiality

A common difficulty during program implementation is ensuring privacy and confidentiality during the depression screenings. In New York City, where space is often limited, we encounter many senior and community centers that do not have facilities adequate to conduct screenings in a completely private setting. Usually, the workshops and the depression screenings have to take place in the very same room, often a dining room or large activity rooms in which most center events take place. Some older adults are interested enough in being screened that the lack of total privacy does not hamper their engagement in the process. For other older adults, there is a legitimate concern that they might be overhead by their peers or by the staff members of their local center.

Every effort should be made to preserve as much privacy as possible during depression screenings. There are often a few options program staff can take, which, although not ideal, may help to mitigate the lack of private office space in which to do screenings. One option may be to borrow any available office space that program staff can find within the center. This may not be possible if there is only one administrative office housing multiple staff during the workday. However, it may be possible on occasion to reserve office space in advance or even to borrow it for a short time without prior arrangement if the need arises. If there is no available office space, there may be another space, such as a computer lab or arts and crafts room, which is not in use that can be used to provide a private space for screening.

Other potential options include meeting with older adults in hallways with little traffic or even temporarily going outside of the center to conduct the depression screening if space is at a minimum and privacy is a concern. If going outside is not an option, and no other office or activity room space exists, it is still usually possible to designate space for screening in certain areas of the main room where the workshop was given and to make sure that only individuals being screened are in that area of the room at any given time. If there is not a formally designated area, there may be isolated corners of the room that participants and screeners can use on an impromptu basis. Although using isolated corners of the room does not provide complete privacy during screenings, there is often enough physical space between participants that concerns about privacy can be mitigated, if not completely eliminated.

Occasionally, screeners may be working with an older adult who is too physically frail to move easily to another room, or to another section of the same room, and the screening may need to take place right where they are sitting. Another frequent occurrence is the reluctance of some older adults to move to another space for the screening for fear of calling unwanted attention to themselves. This concern can be so strong that in some cases, an older adult would prefer to forego a depression screening rather than move to another, more private location. If an older adult cannot be persuaded to move to a more secluded location, it is usually best to honor his or her request to remain in place. In these instances, it is helpful to ask other nearby older adults if they would be willing to move to another location, especially if they have already been screened and are merely chatting with friends or engaging in nonscreening-related activities.

Lack of Coordination Between Collaborating Agencies

When a single aging service or mental health agency is managing all aspects of the program, collaboration is largely an internal matter among staff members. However, aging service providers and mental health agencies working in partnership to administer EASE-D may encounter challenges to effective collaboration. Many of the aging service agencies implementing EASE-D will be community-based organizations, such as senior and community centers, many of which have limited space available for outside programming and very full calendars of events. As a result, some of the most likely coordination difficulties include finding a mutually available date and time for the program to take place and finding adequate space in which to conduct the workshop and screenings.

One way to mitigate collaboration challenges is to meet with everyone involved in the workshop to discuss program implementation and provide an opportunity for sharing of practical and technical information. We have found it helpful to schedule a training session about geriatric mental health for aging service agency staff prior to the workshop with older adults. Advanced training underscores the potential benefits of mental health education and depression screening to their program's members and cements the needed partnership between mental health and aging services. In addition, it also ensures that staff from mental health agencies understands the operations of the aging service provider, so that the workshop for older adults can fit as seamlessly as possible into the general operations of the senior or community center.

However, even with seemingly adequate coordination, difficulties may still emerge during the implementation of the program. One of the most significant difficulties we have encountered is the stigma associated with mental disorders. Most references to stigma in this book refer to that which is experienced by individual older adults as a barrier to treatment; however, stigma may also be an organizational barrier to program implementation. Although aging service providers are usually extremely supportive of the project and willing to work closely with mental health agency staff to assist in implementation, program staff might not share the same enthusiasm, resulting in unexpected coordination difficulties, such as lack of adequate advertisement of the workshops and lack of outreach to older adults to encourage participation.

Unexpressed discomfort with the subject of mental health may manifest during program implementation. For example, we experienced surprising difficulty implementing the project in a particular senior center that had a seemingly very cooperative and supportive staff. After a planning meeting, a training session about depression among older adults, a discussion about how to market the workshop to senior center members, and confirming the mental health workshop with staff several days in advance of the planned date, we arrived at the senior center to find the workshop had not been advertised in the monthly calendar of events nor did it appear as an activity on that day's schedule. To add to these difficulties, the senior center had scheduled another competing event, an exercise class, at the very same time as our workshop. Not surprisingly, none of the older adult members of the center were aware of the workshop, and it proved impossible for us to recruit any older adults to participate on the spot.

When we followed up with the senior center's staff to determine what happened, they reported their previously unvoiced concern that none of the older adults would come to the workshop if it were advertised because it would feel too stigmatizing for them. The staff's honesty about their concerns provided an additional opportunity to discuss the importance of advertising the workshop as a way of normalizing mental health education to older adults. We also explained that the purpose of the workshop was, in part, to address the issue of stigma and to help older adults know more about depression and its treatment to reduce any embarrassment they might feel about seeking help for their mental health needs. The workshop and depression screening were rescheduled, advertised throughout the center, and ended up being a successful event. Through this experience, we learned the importance of honest exploration with the staff about their concerns about mental health, encouraging older adult participation, and other aspects of implementing EASE-D.

Lack of Program Personnel

Finding adequate personnel for mental health education and depression screenings can be a challenge, particularly if the communities being served are culturally and linguistically diverse. As discussed in earlier chapters, we recommend staffing each workshop with one workshop presenter and a minimum of two to four additional staff to provide screening services. If EASE-D is implemented as a partnership between two or more agencies, it may be possible to form a team of presenters and screeners from each participating agency.

If the program is going to serve older adults whose primary language is not English, staffing may become more of a difficult to manage, even with interagency collaboration. Although it is possible that an organization will have enough bilingual and bicultural staff already available, it is very likely that programs will have to develop a strategy to manage outreach and education to speakers of languages other than English. Depression screenings are best conducted in the same language as the workshops, which requires that screening instruments be translated in advance of the screening, to avoid the potential inconsistencies arising from an immediate or impromptu translation. Often, the most difficult staffing problem is finding enough bilingual staff with the requisite skills necessary to conduct a depression screening in older adults' primary languages.

Collaborating agencies may wish to partner with additional institutions, such as universities or colleges, as a way of locating additional bilingual depression screeners or workshop presenters. For example, bilingual graduate students in social work, counseling, psychology, public health, or related disciplines may also be available for internships within collaborating agencies and participation in EASE-D can provide a valuable learning experience for students.

There may be certain populations within a community, however, which cannot adequately be covered by existing staff or students in any of the collaborating agencies. If programs wish to reach out to these populations, they should plan to hire qualified consultants who can be brought into the program. Another possibility may be to recruit and train bilingual and bicultural older adults as volunteers or paid consultants to help with program implementation.

Difficulties With Pretreatment Care Management

Difficulty Contacting Older Adults

As discussed in chapter 5 (see "Older Adult Does Not Respond to Outreach"), one difficulty with pretreatment care management is being unable to make contact with older adults following the screening and referral process. There are several reasons for being unable to make contact. At times, older adults may give incorrect contact information. Although the correct contact information may sometimes be obtained from the aging service provider organization in which EASE-D is being implemented, even their information may be out of date or otherwise unavailable. The correct information may be obtained at a later date directly from older adults themselves, if they attend subsequent workshops, but there is not a way to guarantee that older adults will be seen again.

At other times, older adults' phones may become disconnected, making it impossible for pretreatment care managers to contact them. In these cases, it is helpful to send an outreach letter to older adults asking them to make follow-up contact with their pretreatment care manager, but these letters cannot guarantee a response. Finally, there are some cases where pretreatment care managers attempt follow-up contact for weeks, leaving numerous messages at the older adults' home and at the senior center, all of which go unanswered. In these unfortunate instances, support cannot be provided to older adults and it is impossible to know the outcome of having given the referral.

Lack of Bilingual Pretreatment Care Managers

Another potential impediment to pretreatment care management is not having bilingual staff available to follow up with older adults who have taken referrals. Although previously discussed as a potential obstacle to conducting workshops or depression screenings, the ability to follow up with older adults in their preferred languages is also critical to ensuring success. During the planning phase, it will be important for programs to ensure that the staff who are able to conduct the mental health education and depression screening components are also available for pretreatment care management. If pretreatment care management cannot be provided in the language older adults speak, it is probably worth reconsidering reaching out to older adults speaking those particular languages until enough personnel can be secured to provide all of the components of EASE-D.

Older Adults Getting Stuck in the Process

In addition to these concrete difficulties, there can be dynamic or interpersonal issues that become important during pretreatment care management. For many older adults, the weekly follow-up they receive is a welcome point of connection, which may feel difficult to give up once they have made a connection to a qualified provider for evaluation. In our experience, older adults sometimes express sadness that their ongoing contact with pretreatment care managers must end, and many want to know if they can extend the follow-up beyond the point of connection to a provider, even if they are beginning treatment.

Some older adults feel such a strong connection to their pretreatment care managers that they may put off seeking outside consultation because the weekly contacts feel therapeutic and seem to obviate the need for additional services. It is not uncommon for pretreatment care managers to hear such comments as "I feel better since you started talking with me. Why should I go see anyone else when I'm already comfortable talking to you?" Although not all older adults will feel a need to have continued follow-up, and many will use it to help them make a connection to an outside provider, pretreatment care managers should be prepared to manage this dynamic appropriately, particularly if it seems that an older adult is reluctant to follow up on their referral in favor of continuing to speak with their pretreatment care managers.

As discussed in chapter 5 (see "Older Adult Seems 'Stuck' in the Process"), it is helpful for pretreatment care managers to remind the older adult occasionally and sensitively that follow-up is not a permanent service and will end once the older adult has had an evaluation for depression. If an older adult seems reluctant to speak with a health care or mental health provider because he or she would prefer to speak with his or her pretreatment care manager, it is useful to clarify the pretreatment care management role and to gently explore with the older adult any other factors which might be making it difficult for him or her to connect to an outside provider. It is also important to acknowledge the older adult's positive feelings about the follow-up contact, while also explaining the importance of getting an evaluation for depression to ensure that he or she has all of the tools possible to maintain positive improvements in mood.

FINAL WORDS ABOUT EASE-D

Despite the challenges entailed in implementing a program of mental health education, depression screening, and pretreatment care management, EASE-D provides a useful method to engage older adults about their own mental health. This type of program is a cost-effective way to provide mental health services to older adults who otherwise might not seek information about depression or treatment on their own.

Conducting mental health education within aging services programs introduces the topic of depression to older adults within a comfortable and familiar environment, similar to other types of health education programs offered in the same settings. The flexible and portable workshop format can be adapted to include other mental health topics in addition to depression and can be offered in multiple languages to diverse groups of older adults. An additional benefit of mental health educational workshops is the opportunity they provide for older adults to learn from each other, as well as from a workshop leader, in a lively and interactive format.

On-site depression screenings provide an opportunity for at-risk older adults to be identified without requiring them to seek screening services from an outside provider. Pretreatment care management supports older adults throughout the process of connecting to a qualified provider for mental health evaluation and treatment services and serves as a bridge between aging service and health care or mental health providers. EASE-D helps aging service and mental health providers form collaborative partnerships that allow both types of organizations to better serve older adults with mental health needs, helping to ensure their continued health, well-being, and fulfillment.

REFERENCE

Pardasani, M., Sporre, K., & Thompson, P. (2009). *New models taskforce: Final report.* Washington, DC: National Institute of Senior Centers, National Council on Aging. Retrieved March 1, 2009, from http://www.ncoa.org/

Index

Note: Page numbers followed by *c* indicate cases, *f* indicate figures, and *t* indicate tables.

Reliability, as measure in screening tools, 84

Repetition, technique of, 147

Research findings, learning environment preference, 56

Resource kits, depression treatment, 30

Resources, educational materials, 153–154

Respondents, defined, 173

Retardation, 87

Roman font, recommended for vision loss, 152

Ross, Jennifer, 111

S

Sans serif fonts, recommended for vision loss, 152

Scale for Suicide Ideation (SSI), 99

Scale for Suicide Ideation-Worst (SSI-W), 99

SCCP. *See* South Carolina College of Pharmacy

SCDHHS. *See* South Carolina Department of Health and Human Services

SCORxE. *See* South Carolina Offering Prescribing Excellence

Screening, Healthy IDEAS principle, 38

Screening for Mental Health, Inc., game developer, 55

Self-empowerment, principle of, 35, 39

Self-esteem, poor, 5

Self-management, 38

Senior advisory council, 142

Senior center advisory council, 59

Senior center directors, 58

Senior center program coordinators, 69

Senior center programming, 48

Senior centers, 1, 48, 55, 68, 111, 113, 164

   goals, 206–207

Sensitivity, as measure in screening tools, 83

Sensory or mobility impairment, 10

Sheik and Yesavage, 89

Signage, as guide to workshop site, 63

Simple Measure of Gobbledygook (SMOG) formula, readability tests, 148

Skills building trainings, 70, 71

Sleeping difficulties, as symptom of major depression, 3, 5

SMOG Readability Calculator, The, McLaughlin, 154

SMOG. *See* Simple Measure of Gobbledygook

Social and physical activation. *See* Behavior activation

Social isolation, 11

Social role functioning, loss of, 11

Social status, loss of, 11

Social workers, 111

Socioeconomic risk factors, late-life depressive disorders, 12

Somatic symptoms, 15

SOQ. Suicide Opinion Questionnaire

Soumerai, Stephen, 156

South Carolina College of Pharmacy (SCCP), 157

South Carolina Department of Health and Human Services (SCDHHS), 157

South Carolina Offering Prescribing Excellence (SCORxE), 157

Spanish translations

   grammatical differences, 150–151

   variations in, 149–150

Specificity, as measure in screening tools, 83–84

Spitzer, Robert, 91

SPLS. *See* Suicide Lethality Scale

Spokane Mental Health, nonprofit mental health organization, 71

Spokane model, mental health education model, 71

SSI. *See* Scale for Suicide Ideation

Vital Link Between Chronic Disease
and Depressive Disorders, The
(DHHS), 158
Vitamin deficiencies, 83

W

Washington State Aging and Disability
Services Administration, 36
Web Sites to Locate Information on
Evidence-Based Programs, 47*t*
Weight loss or gain, as symptom of
major depression, 3
Williams, Janet, 91
Workshops
depression, 56
development of multisession series,
59–60

flexible and portable format, 217
focus on health and mental health,
204–205, 205–206*c*
materials distribution, 142
medication management, 181
presenter and screeners, 214
scheduling, 166
single session vs multisession, 58–59
storytelling, 57
topics, 59

Y

Yesavage, Jerome, 89

Z

Zanjani, Faika, 111

CPSIA information can be obtained at www.ICGtesting.com
Printed in the USA
LVOW04s1606240914

405675LV00018B/965/P

9 780826 171023